MW00873072

The Trekker's Guide

By J.W. Braun

Published by Dragon Wing Express
Copyright © 2019

Cover photo courtesy of Dan Johnson
All *Star Trek* images used in accordance with Fair Use

First Edition: April 2019

ISBN: 9781095369647

For Nick & Nicole, two of DS9's biggest fans

Table of Contents

Foreword

Star Trek: Deep Space Nine has often been seen as second-wave *Trek's* awkward middle child, caught between the beloved *The Next Generation* and UPN's flagship series, *Voyager*. The truth is, not only was *DS9 Trek's* middle child, it was a show that grew during a transitional time of television, helping to usher in the modern serialized format so many of today's television shows have adopted, taking individual episodes, in large part written on-the-fly, and somehow weaving them together to create a greater story.

The first season of *Deep Space Nine* took the traditional *Star Trek* format: stand-alone episodes focusing on one or another character's background. While early episodes did showcase some of the first season weirdness of most *Trek* shows, *DS9's* writers and actors proved early on that they could also deliver top-notch drama in the form of episodes like "Duet." (Although not a fan favorite, I also quite liked "Dramatis Personae," which took the simmering first-season character tensions and turned them up to eleven.) But perhaps even more consequential to the long-term storytelling, that first season ended with "In the Hands of the Prophets," which stood on its own, but also set up the second season's opening three-parter. This would become a familiar pattern, with the final episode of each season setting up a longer next-season arc, giving *DS9* a larger canvas to paint on, with sweeping changes to the Bajoran, Cardassian, and Klingon societies happening on and off-screen, giving the illusion of an epic tale with the space station serving as a focal point.

Yet, while the show didn't skimp on the intrigue and violence of war, *DS9's* storytelling was often at its most brilliant when dealing with the quieter but equally intense moments before, after, and in between. For example, while the fifth season's "In the Cards" is a somewhat farcical quest to get a baseball card, it is also a portrait of a station exhausted and on the brink of war. The sixth season's "Behind the Lines" includes an exciting plot to destroy a key enemy sensor array...told from Sisko's point of view *after* he has given command of the Defiant to Dax, so that he may take a necessary, if personally difficult, position as war strategist. Later in the sixth season, "The Sound of Her Voice" gives the characters a chance to talk honestly about their experience of war with a mysterious far-off voice, so needed when they have lost the ability to talk to each other about it. In between, one of *DS9's* most monumental episodes, "In the Pale Moonlight," tells the story of a very moral man and a choice which may turn the tide of the war, but at what cost? It's these sorts of stories that capture just a glimpse of what the grinding costs of war can do.

Of course, not all of *DS9's* "very special episodes" hit the jackpot. "Melora," for instance, is not terribly offensive in its portrayal of a capable but gravity-bound ensign, but it isn't a particularly compelling story, either. And while in some ways "Rejoined" actually works better now—since same-sex relationships on television are fairly common, the plot can almost stand on its own—it still retains a muddled message and that whiff of ratings bait.

1

But impressively often, when *DS9* took a mighty swing at an idea, it succeeded. (And I'm not talking about the seventh season's "Take Me Out to the Holosuite," although I do like that episode quite a bit—not least because you just know there are Vulcans who act like that.) On the heels of the fourth season's big Klingon story and the addition of Worf came "The Visitor," a more intimate, transformative story of the relationship between Ben Sisko and his son, Jake. While Jake often had a smaller role than most regulars on *Trek* shows, this story illustrates their singular bond. The next season gave us "Trials and Tribble-ations," and what can you say about an episode written explicitly at Paramount's request to celebrate the thirtieth anniversary of Classic *Trek*? It manages to retrofit a story within a story seamlessly while both honoring and having some fun with the classic "The Trouble with Tribbles." (And as a time travel fan, I always appreciate some good time travel meta-humor.) The season after that gave us "Far Beyond the Stars," which is both a sobering reflection on racism and a love-letter to pulp-era science fiction authors, immersive and deeply felt. The portrayal of the pulp magazine office is as romantic—if not terribly accurate—as the racism is horrifying—and far too accurate, even today. Some episodes of television transcend their shows, and, to some extent, the medium itself. This is one of them.

But beyond these pinnacles, one of the more impressive things I have found rewatching *DS9* through the decades is how well the writers understood the recurring cycles of history. Every time I rewatch, I am struck by episodes that feel as if they've been written in response to contemporary events. In the third season's two-part "Past Tense," the government has begun putting inconvenient people in "sanctuaries" where they have no real hope or prospects. In the two-part "Homefront" and "Paradise Lost," the specter of shape-shifters infiltrating society creates a panic about terrorism. Meanwhile, religious leader Kai Wynn uses her position to try to manipulate her way to increased power while Dukat bobs along the surface of every upheaval to Cardassian society, grabbing onto a new leadership role with every change, unable to be dislodged despite his evident crimes against both Bajor and Cardassia.

And yet, even as *DS9* tackles such weighty issues, it also has a lot of fun. Q shows up, the holodeck breaks (once), there are time travel mishaps of all sorts, characters fall in and out of love, and you can set your watch to something terrible happening to O'Brien. But in spite of the sometimes darker, often more complicated setting, Starfleet's ideals remain in place, even if the characters have to negotiate just what that means among aliens with different moral values, or in a time of war. Somehow, the enduring hope that makes *Star Trek* what it is, carries on.

—*Nicole Lowery, April 2019*

Introduction: About this Book

As the spinoff of a spinoff, *Star Trek: Deep Space Nine* has always struggled to gain the respect of an audience at large. Happily, never before have the episodes been so assessable, with the days of fans having to catch the weekly show or having to rent *Star Trek* videos no longer necessary to enjoy the adventures. Today's technology allows even non-*Star Trek* fans to instantly watch just about any episode of any *Star Trek* series, thanks to the internet and streaming services. And yet, even big fans can be forgiven if they have difficulty sorting out the hundreds of hours of *Star Trek* available—save for a quick check online which may also yield spoilers and misinformation.

That's where this series of books, with this being the third volume, comes into play. Throughout this edition, every episode of *Deep Space Nine* is graded, reviewed, and analyzed...and all without giving away plot points and surprises that make *Star Trek* worth watching. If knowledge of one episode is important to enjoy another or if there's a prequel or sequel, the review includes that information as well. (In addition, if the heading for an episode includes a number in parentheses, that indicates it's part of a multi-episode storyline.)

These books are *not* a substitute for watching *Star Trek*. After all, what is? It's been said that a dozen people watching the same episode or movie will have twelve different experiences, and many *Star Trek* fans have a strong personal bond to specific episodes for their own special reasons. But what I will do with this book is share and explain my thoughts and opinions, not to supersede the reader's own thoughts and viewing experiences, but to enhance them with another perspective.

And just who am I, anyway?

I'm J.W. Braun, a guy from Wisconsin. I was born in 1975 and grew up with a family that loved science fiction and fantasy, becoming a *Star Trek* fan in the 1980s after discovering, in succession, *Star Trek: The Animated Series*, the *Star Trek* movies, and *Star Trek: The Next Generation*.

Today, I'm an unabashed fanboy who spends too much time analyzing entertainment and seeking out the people who make things like *Star Trek* possible so I can share what I learn with others. As I review the work, I try to be honest and fair. I can ask no more of you as you read this book!

Me and René Auberjonois

Grading the Episodes

At the top of the reviews, you'll see grades for the episodes. I use the standard American letter grade scale you may remember from school because it's easy to understand. But to spell it out (pardon the pun), here's a guide.

A: Excellent (nearly perfect)
B: Very good (exceeds expectations)
C: Average (par for the course)
D: Poor (below standard)
F: Failure (ugh)

Each review will also include vital information about the episode, including a plot description, the original air date, and the writing and director credits.

Terminology

As you read through the reviews, you'll probably notice that I casually throw out certain terms that not everyone is familiar with. As such, I've included this quick glossary for reference.

Bottle episode: a ship-based episode that only uses existing sets to free up money for effects or another episode. The term was coined by the cast and crew of *TOS*, who compared these episodes to a ship in a bottle.

CGI: an abbreviation for computer generate imagery, effects created by computer after shooting has completed.

Cinematography: the art of recording motion. This includes everything from lighting and framing to the choice of lenses and colors (or lack thereof). It's sort of the kinetic version of painting works of art.

Comedic runner: a humorous subplot that recurs throughout an episode or film.

MacGuffin: something that is only included in the story to serve as a motivator for the protagonists and antagonists.

Plot or storytelling device: something contrived to create a story.

Show/episode: words I do not use interchangeably. I use "show" to refer to a TV series as a whole (such as *Deep Space Nine*) and "episode" to refer to a single installment of a show (such as "Emissary"). Thus, I use the term "bottle episode" rather than "bottle show," even if the latter is more fashionable.

Story credit, teleplay credit or written by credit: writing acknowledgements based on the genesis of the episode. Story credit goes to those who come up with the story idea, teleplay credit goes to those who actually write the scripts the director and actors use, and "written by" is used to acknowledge someone who does both.

Teaser: an opening sequence that attempts to hook the viewer before the theme song and opening credits play.

Technobabble: futuristic shop talk (made up technical jargon).

TOS: *The Original Series*, the classic *Star Trek* show with Captain Kirk (1966–1969)
TAS: *Star Trek: The Animated Series* (1973–1974)
TNG: *Star Trek: The Next Generation* (1987–1994)
DS9: *Star Trek: Deep Space Nine* (1993–1999)
VOY: *Star Trek: Voyager* (1995–2001)
ENT: *Star Trek: Enterprise* (2001–2005)
DSC: Star Trek: Discovery (2017–present)

Trope: a commonly recurring element or storytelling device. Some of them happen so often in popular entertainment, they've got titles. One of my favorites that factors into *DS9* is "the Gilligan Cut" where somebody determinedly says something will never happen before a cut to it happening. It should be noted that inventing or even borrowing a trope isn't necessarily a bad thing. If it works, it works.

And with all that in mind, let's engage, warp factor three!

Season One

Production Order
(with air date order in parentheses)

1. "Emissary" (1st)
2. "Past Prologue" (2nd)
3. "A Man Alone" (3rd)
4. "Babel" (4th)
5. "Captive Pursuit" (5th)
6. "Q-Less" (6th)
7. "Dax" (7th)
8. "The Passenger" (8th)
9. "Move Along Home" (9th)
10. "The Nagus" (10th)
11. "Vortex" (11th)
12. "Battle Lines" (12th)
13. "The Storyteller" (13th)
14. "Progress" (14th)
15. "If Wishes Were Horses" (15th)
16: "The Forsaken" (16th)
17: "Dramatis Personae" (17th)
18. "Duet" (18th)
19. "In the Hands of the Prophets" (19th)

The First Season Cast

Commander Sisko: Avery Brooks
Major Kira: Nana Visitor
Odo: René Auberjonois
Chief O'Brien: Colm Meaney
Dax: Terry Farrell
Dr. Bashir: Siddig El Fadil
Jake Sisko: Cirroc Lofton
Quark: Armin Shimerman

Notable Guest Stars

Patrick Stewart
Max Grodénchik
Aron Eisenberg
John Noah Hertzler
Rosalind Chao
Marc Alaimo
Camille Saviola
Andrew Robinson
Gwynyth Walsh
Barbara March
John de Lancie
Wallace Shawn
Brian Keith
Majel Barrett
Harris Yulin
Louise Fletcher

"Emissary": A

(Pilot) Commander Benjamin Sisko takes command of the Bajoran space station Deep Space Nine, recently abandoned by the Cardassian Empire.

Air date: January 3, 1993
Teleplay by Michael Piller
Story by Rick Berman & Michael Piller
Directed by David Carson
TV rating: 18.8

"Ironic. One who does not wish to be among us is to be the Emissary." —Kai Opaka

DS9's pilot plays out like a *Star Trek* TV movie that simultaneously satisfies while leaving viewers ready for more.

Even if "Emissary" wasn't jumpstarting a new series, it would be a cool little *Star Trek* sidebar with a fun story that uses familiar characters and established parts of the *Star Trek* universe in supporting roles while putting forth a new story featuring original characters, with Commander Sisko at the forefront. In this way, it shows us another path the *Star Trek* franchise could have chosen. Instead of multiple *Star Trek* shows airing at the same time, Paramount could have had one starship crew doing feature films, another crew doing television episodes, and one space station crew, such as the gang at *DS9*, doing a TV movie two or three times a year. Of course, considering the success of the *DS9* series, most fans are probably happy this scenario didn't come to pass. Fortunately, "Emissary" also works perfectly well as a television pilot too, establishing the characters and fleshing out backstories that lay a groundwork for more great episodes to come.

The pilot itself focuses on Sisko, who is mentally wounded and beginning a healing process. After a visit to the Enterprise featuring a guest appearance by Patrick Stewart, we get into the plot proper about a wormhole and its nonlinear alien occupants. Both more political and mystical than the usual fare from *TOS* and *TNG*, the *DS9* pilot sets a mood from the get-go that would later be sculpted into a tone of its own. Meanwhile, the idea of a nonlinear existence, with past moments still in play as we move forward, is a comforting message for Trekkers, implying that the great moments of *Star Trek's* past and present will always be with us—something that's even more relevant in today's age where we can easily rewatch favorite episodes and movies at a moment's notice.

Would *DS9* improve in the future? Of course. But as a strong, confident pilot, "Emissary" delivers the goods. It was nominated for Emmy awards for art direction, sound mixing, and visual effects, winning for the latter.

Did you know? When "Emissary" debuted, it scored higher ratings than any syndicated series premier before it and ranked number one in its timeslot in New York, Los Angeles, Boston, San Francisco, and Washington D.C.

"Past Prologue": C

A member of the Bajoran underground seeks asylum on Deep Space Nine, attracting the attention of Major Kira, not to mention the Cardassians and Klingons.

Air date: January 10, 1993
Written by Kathryn Powers
Directed by Winrich Kolbe
TV rating: 13.4

"In one move and non-violently, we accomplish everything both of us has ever wanted for Bajor." —Tahna

Taking its title from a quote from William Shakespeare's *The Tempest* ("what's past is prologue"), this Kira episode tests the major's loyalty with a predictable story. Even this early in the series, it's easy to figure out where the story is going and what the inevitable outcome will be long before the climax begins to unfold.

Jeffrey Nordling plays his Bajoran freedom fighter so broadly, he comes across as simply unlikeable. Fortunately, there's a B story with a better guest star. Dr. Bashir makes a new friend, and his name is Garak. This "plain, simple tailor" is played by Andrew Robinson, who hams up the subtext, and despite a high profile appearance from the Duras sisters from *TNG*, he steals the show.

Did you know? Admiral Rollman is played by guest star Susan Bay. This cousin of director Michael Bay has been married twice, first to John Schuck, who appears as a Klingon ambassador in *Star Trek IV: The Voyage Home* and *Star Trek VI: The Undiscovered* Country, and second to Leonard Nimoy. She returns in Season Two's "Whispers."

"A Man Alone": C

When a Bajoran terrorist is murdered, the evidence points to Odo as the culprit.

Air date: January 17, 1993
Teleplay by Michael Piller
Story by Gerald Sanford & Michael Piller
Directed by Paul Lynch
TV rating: 13.0

"It's a pretty neat package. His calendar shows he was planning to meet with me at the time of the murder. No one except a shape-shifter could get into the holosuite. And since I'd obviously be called there after the body was discovered, traces of my DNA wind up at the scene of the crime." —Odo

The first Odo episode is a forgettable murder-mystery that begins defining the shape-shifter's loner character. With an A story that focuses on the murder investigation, "Man" develops into a sci-fi *CSI* tale that wouldn't be out of place on *TNG* or even *TOS*. Unfortunately, the whodunnit answer, while creative, leads to a murder charge that contradicts what we're told in *TNG's* "Up the Long Ladder." But then again, maybe Deep Space Nine has different rules, and who really remembers "Up the Long Ladder" anyway?

The pedestrian B story shows the beginning of Jake and Nog's friendship and turns Keiko into a school teacher. While nothing special, it does include a prophetic warning about what Keiko is getting into that pays off in the season finale.

Did you know? The scene in which Jake and Nog first meet, which was Aron Eisenberg's audition scene, was written for the pilot but moved to this episode.

"Babel": D

An old, forgotten booby trap releases an aphasia virus.

Air date: January 24, 1993
Teleplay by Michael McGreevey & Naren Shankar
Story by Sally Caves & Ira Steven Behr
Directed by Paul Lynch
TV rating: 11.6

"Left, become better, control, entire hope." —Jake

If the concept for this budget-saving episode seems like a discarded *TNG* story, that's because it is. In fact, the idea of an aphasia disease on board the Enterprise-D was discussed on and off throughout most of *TNG*'s run. Unfortunately, the ensemble episode comes across as the second-rate filler episode it is—albeit with some cute moments from O'Brien, Quark, and Odo that make it watchable. ("Anything else I can do for you?") Unfortunately, the babble of "Babel" becomes tedious quickly, and the resolution of the crisis is rushed.

It would have been better if the aphasic people could actually communicate with each other, allowing the episode to slide into an A/B story format with the two segregated groups each working separately to solve the problem.

Did you know? Sally Caves, the pen name of Sarah Higley, is the writer who created *TNG*'s Reginald Barclay.

"Captive Pursuit": D+

A reptilian alien, pursued by others of his kind, must stop for repairs at Deep Space Nine, where he befriends Chief O'Brien.

Air date: January 31, 1993
Teleplay by Jill Sherman Donner & Michael Piller
Story by Jill Sherman Donner
Directed by Corey Allen
TV rating: 12.9

"You're saying that this whole thing is a hunt, and Tosk is the prey?" —Sisko

Inspired by *The Most Dangerous Game* by Richard Connell, this character-driven O'Brien piece is an attempt to show off the differences between *DS9* and *TNG*. After all, it's hard to imagine *TNG* having such an informal first contact, complete with Dabo girls, and ending it with one of the regulars disobeying Captain Picard. As a "first contact with the Gamma Quadrant" episode, it's underwhelming, despite a nice effort from guest star Scott MacDonald as "Tosk". The story begins slowly, and the real plot doesn't kick in until halfway into the episode. When it does, it lacks the danger, excitement, and finality of Connell's tale. And yet Tosk himself is a curious and sympathetic character, making the hunt almost worth watching.

Did you know? "Captive Pursuit" won an Emmy for make-up.

"Q-Less": D

Vash arrives on Deep Space Nine, fresh from exploring the Gamma Quadrant with Q.

Air date: February 7, 1993
Teleplay by Robert Hewitt Wolfe
Story by Hannah Louise Shearer
Directed by Paul Lynch
TV rating: 12.8

"It's over, Q. I want you out of my life. You are arrogant, you are overbearing, and you think you know everything." —Vash

With any spinoff series, there's a temptation to bring in characters the audience already knows, both because they require less exposition and because they might bring attention to the new series. Unfortunately, this sort of crossover isn't without its hazards: when the guest stars are used in a way where they overstep their supporting roles and become more central to the story than the regulars, there's a problem—especially for a series that is still attempting to establish itself.

   DS9's pilot serves as a blueprint for how to avoid this trap. "Q-Less," on the other hand, falls right into it. Vash brings a MacGuffin to the station, and, in a follow-up to *TNG's* "Qpid," Q chases her around while the *DS9* regulars step into the background.

   As a Vash episode, it's alright. Jennifer Hetrick knows the character and is a dependable actress capable of carrying a story with little plot movement. As a Q episode, it's not so good. As John de Lancie himself once said, "Q is best used when he deals with large philosophical issues, and skirt-chasing just isn't one of them." As a *DS9* episode, it's watchable, moving at a nice clip, but ultimately unfulfilling—which is probably why Vash and Q would never appear on the show again.

Did you know? This is Hetrick's last *Star Trek* appearance. The actress would go on to guest star on *The X-Files, Beverly Hills 90210, Buffy the Vampire Slayer, General Hospital*, though more people are probably familiar with her appearances in commercials for Tylenol, Edward Jones, Crestor, and Prolia.

15

"Dax": B

New evidence reopens a thirty-year-old murder case, and Dax is the prime suspect.

Air date: February 14, 1993
Teleplay by D.C. Fontana & Peter Allan Fields
Story by Peter Allan Fields
Directed by David Carson
TV rating: 12.1

"The fugitive Dax is charged with treason and the murder of my father."
—Tandro

Star Trek returns to a courtroom setting to explore—and reinvent— the Trill species, raising complex legal and ethical questions in the process.

Similar to how "The Measure of a Man" puts a spotlight on Data but is really a Picard episode, "Dax" focuses on Dax but is really a Sisko episode. Brooks, the featured actor for the first time since the pilot (also directed by David Carson), again proves worthy of being the leading man in the series, giving Commander Sisko a righteous vitality that surpasses even that seen in Picard and Kirk. Meanwhile, the late Anne Haney is his equal, guest starring as the elderly, no-nonsense judge.

The B story, a mystery that begins as a tangent before eventually folding back into the A story, gives Odo some interesting scenes and allows the writers to conveniently duck the difficult questions the episode offers. That said, viewers still learn plenty about the Trill, which is really the whole point of it all.

Did you know? This is the last *Star Trek* script with contributions from D.C. Fontana, one of the franchise's original writers.

"The Passenger": C

An alien criminal, attempting to prolong his life, hides his consciousness inside the mind of another.

Air date: February 21, 1993
Teleplay by Morgan Gendel, Robert Hewitt Wolfe & Michael Piller
Story by Morgan Gendel
Directed by Paul Lynch
TV rating: 11.6

"Like a stowaway on a ship, the pilot's at the helm, but someone else is along for the ride." —Dax

From the writer of *TNG's* "Inner Light" comes this lesser story, a paint-by-numbers sci-fi criminal hunt. While the addition of a new Federation security leader, well played by James Lashly, adds some welcome complexity to the story, viewers are likely to be a step ahead of the mystery throughout the episode. And it's asking a lot of Siddig El Fadil, still trying find his stride as Dr. Bashir, to play another character—which he does terribly here. Yet for all its faults, the episode is an acceptable hour of television, thanks to a story that's deep enough to sustain interest and a script that gives most of the regulars something to do.

Did you know? Writer Morgan Gendel spent a day writing a song for Quark to sing while he's serving people drinks. "I thought it was hysterical," he later said. "But I also thought if I turned it in, they were going to laugh me out of the room."

"Move Along Home": F

Gamma Quadrant aliens visit Deep Space Nine and force Commander Sisko to play hopscotch.

Air date: March 14, 1993
Teleplay by Frederick Rappaport, Lisa Rich & Jeanne Carrigan-Fauci
Story by Michael Piller
Directed by David Carson
TV rating: 11.4

"Double their peril. Double your winnings." —Falow

Considered by some the worst episode of the season, this offbeat gaming episode attempts to summon the spirit of Lewis Carol but plays out more like a live action role-playing convention. (At least Picard doesn't show up to declare, "When one is in the penalty box, tears are permitted.")

The overall problem stems from the marriage of two concepts put forth in the pilot. On the one hand, the premise of the show is that Deep Space Nine is an intergalactic bus station, and its inhabitants—in contrast with the characters from the other *Star Trek* shows—don't fly around the universe seeking adventure, instead letting adventure come to them. On the other hand, Sisko and company have just discovered a shortcut to a new place to explore. It's a really bizarre decision to put these two ideas together, and the writers' solution so far has been to find ways for the inhabitants of the Gamma Quadrant to find their way to the space station. But that's sort of like the Europeans discovering America and having the next step be the Native Americans invading Europe. Fortunately the producers and writers of *DS9*, being rather intelligent, eventually noticed this issue and began to make changes to allow for better use of the wormhole. But that's in the future.

To be fair, this episode has other problems. Most fans can forgive the show for the first meeting with Gamma Quadrant aliens in "Captive Pursuit" being unconventional and underwhelming. But when the second meeting is even more unconventional and consists of aliens forcing Sisko and his friends to play games, alarm bells start sounding. While it's true that many *Star Trek* fans have likely attended gaming conventions, not too many want to watch the sci-fi equivalent. And it doesn't help that the Wadi not only have a silly name but are downright annoying too.

"Move Along Home" nonetheless was nominated for an Emmy for hairstyling.

Did you know? Terry Farrell's work on this episode prevented her from appearing in *TNG's* "Birthright, Part I," much to the actress's disappointment.

"The Nagus": B

When Quark is unexpectedly chosen to be the next ruler of the Ferengi Empire, he becomes a target for murder.

Air date: March 21, 1993
Teleplay by Ira Steven Behr
Story by David Livingston
Directed by David Livingston
TV rating: 10.7

"My mind's made up. I've already chosen my successor. A leader whose vision, imagination, and avarice will oversee Ferengi ventures in the Gamma Quadrant. The new Grand Nagus: Quark!" —Zek

Every once in a while an episode of *Star Trek* comes along that so perfectly defines an alien species, its effects reverberate forever into the future of the franchise. Sure, "Amok Time" didn't invent the Vulcans, but who can think of these logical beings without this episodes creation of the Vulcan hand salute and the accompanying phrase, "Live long and prosper"? The Borg are introduced in *TNG's* Season Two, but it's Season Three's "The Best of Both Worlds" that establishes their creeds of "You will be assimilated" and "Resistance if futile."

With "The Nagus," a Quark episode that's an homage to *The Godfather* (1972), the Ferengi are so completely and successfully defined, the elements of Ferengi culture it invents—from the Grand Nagus to the Rules of Acquisition—not only appear countless times throughout the remaining six and a half seasons of *DS9*, they spill into *TNG*, *VOY*, and even *ENT*. With an A story by Ira Steven Behr and a B story by supervising producer David Livingston, who also directs the episode, the two halves come together nicely to give Season One a memorable farce.

And what a cast! What Celia Lovsky is to "Amok Time," Wallace Shawn is to "The Nagus." (And if that doesn't sum up the differences between the Vulcan and the Ferengi, I don't know what does.) Just as Lovsky, an established star, forever elevates Spock and the Vulcan race with her performance, Shawn does so for Quark and the Ferengi. Meanwhile, the development of Jake and Nog's friendship over the objections of their parents serves as a nice counterpoint.

Did you know? As supervising producer and *DS9's* money watchdog, David Livingston had to explain to many writers and directors that their hope for dozens of background actors in one scene was too expensive, and they'd have to make do with four or five. For "The Nagus," however, Livingston cuts the director a break, allowing a gaggle of Ferengi to appear at once.

19

"Vortex": C

A criminal offers to take Odo to the other side of the wormhole to meet other shape-shifters.

Air date: April 18, 1993
Written by Sam Rolfe
Directed by Winrich Kolbe
TV rating: 9.7

"We are both aliens here, the only ones of our kind. Each of us is alone, isolated, shut out. Others like us only exist in the Gamma Quadrant." —Croden

It's no secret that *DS9* is a Space Western wannabe. It has a frontier atmosphere complete with a bar and a sheriff. The latter, of course, is Odo, and the producers of *DS9* figured that if they were going to have an Odo episode at this stage in the game, specifically one based on the 1953 movie *The Naked Spur*, they might as well get an old Western writer, specifically the one who wrote *The Naked Spur*.

Based on a story that's as old as the hills, where the good guy has to take the bad guy from point A to B and they get to know each other along the way, "Vortex" serves as Sam Rolfe's swan song, as he died a few months after the episode first aired. And while Rolfe's script doesn't reinvent the wheel, it has plenty of heart and offers an opportunity for René Auberjonois to lay the foundation for Odo's character—an honorable sheriff who is nonetheless a lonely man and a creature with a desire to discover the secrets of his origin.

Guest star Cliff DeYoung is fine as Croden, yet another Gamma Quadrant resident who accidentally ends up on Deep Space Nine. Auberjonois himself is fine as well, though he'd improve his take on Odo in future seasons. But there's a reason this sort of story has endured over the years. It works.

Did you know? Sam Rolfe gives Odo's people a name that sticks: the Changelings.

20

"Battle Lines": D

Kai Opaka and several Deep Space Nine officers are trapped on a hostile planet.

Air date: April 25, 1993
Teleplay by Richard Danus & Evan Carlos Somers
Story by Hilary J. Bader
Directed by David Carson
TV rating: 9.9

"Seems we're in the middle of a pretty ugly war." —Sisko

The apparent love child of *TOS* episodes "The Galileo Seven" and "The Day of the Dove," this plodding installment has plenty of action but little meaning. "Battle Lines" explores the pointlessness of war, with Sisko, Bashir, Kira, and Kai Opaka in the A story. The problem is that despite plenty of action, there's really only about twenty minutes of story to spread throughout the episode, and the result is a slow and tedious pacing. More specifically, the fundamental problem seems to be that from a structure standpoint, the shuttlecraft story would be better off as a B story, yet the nature of the plot and the importance of its consequences demand the spotlight of an A story.

To help fill out the episode, O'Brien and Dax's attempt to locate Sisko and company is interspersed. Their part of the episode, a cat and mouse game with an almost sentient planet full of satellites, is an intriguing idea, but it's not given much time and comes to a predictable end, ultimately tying into a conclusion that's abrupt and depressing, doing little to pay off the episode's events.

Did you know? This is the first episode to define the United Federation of Planets. Sisko says, "The Federation is made up of over a hundred planets who have allied themselves for mutual scientific, cultural and defensive benefits. The mission that my people and I are on is to explore the galaxy."

21

"The Storyteller": D

When O'Brien is unexpectedly chosen to be the next spiritual leader of a Bajoran village, he becomes a target for murder.

Air date: May 2, 1993
Teleplay by Kurt Michael Bensmiller & Ira Steven Behr
Story by Kurt Michael Bensmiller
Directed by David Livingston
TV rating: 9.3

"Don't worry, Chief, I have faith in you." —Bashir

Another discarded *TNG* plot makes up an A story here. It's a silly but inoffensive little tale that begins the O'Brien and Bashir relationship with a whimsical charm. It's almost as if the writers were shuffling through pairings and accidently struck pay dirt.

The B story, featuring Padme...er, ah, Varis, the troubled young girl weighed down by the responsibility of leading her people, is reminiscent of *TNG's* "The Dauphin" and is just a filler concept for a filler episode. It does, however, make a nice statement about negotiations: that they're not dilemmas but opportunities. This seems to be forgotten in today's world where compromise is perceived as caving in.

Did you know? Kay E. Kuter, who plays O'Brien's storytelling predecessor, appears in *TNG's* Season Four episode "The Nth Degree" as a giant floating alien head.

"Progress": C

While overseeing an evacuation, Kira must convince a stubborn, old farmer to leave.

Air date: May 9, 1993
Written by Peter Allan Fields
Directed by Les Landau
TV rating: 9.2

"Nerys, this is still my home." —Mullibok

"A remote moon on the brink of destruction, a rebel leader refusing to surrender, and the Federation faces a mutiny within its own ranks."

That's the narration from the original preview for this episode, which is pretty accurate except the moon isn't on the brink of destruction, Mullibok isn't a rebel leader, and Kira isn't in the Federation.

Kira is tossed into the old "cantankerous old coot who stubbornly refuses to cooperate, and we admire him for it" story, with Brian Keith suitably gnarled and grumpy as said old coot. Keith and Nana Visitor are actually fantastic together, and their scenes tend to click. The B story, with Jake and Nog stumbling their way into fortune, adds levity. (The same concept would later serve as the A story for Season Five's "In the Cards.") That said, everything is so vanilla, "Progress" lacks the significance and depth the other episodes of this sort, such as *TNG's* "Preemptive Strike," manage to create.

Did you know? Brian Keith appeared in his first film, *Pied Piper Malone*, in 1924 at age two. He appeared in his final film, *Rough Riders*, in 1997 at age 75. He died June, 24, 1997 of a self-inflicted gunshot wound.

"If Wishes Were Horses": D–

The inhabitants of Deep Space Nine are mystified when their fantasies turn into reality.

Air date: May 16, 1993
Teleplay by Nell McCue Crawford, William Crawford & Michael Piller
Story by Nell McCue Crawford & William L. Crawford
Directed by Robert Legato
TV rating: 9.0

"It seems we have a small mystery on our hands." —Sisko

With a spatial anomaly threatening the station, a holodeck malfunction, an alien species playing with the show's regulars, and one of the regulars playing a double role, this episode, like an homage to Trek's most banal ideas, includes just about every *Star Trek* trope known to man woven together into one snoozer.

What wants to be an off-the-wall episode gives us some danger and some laughs, yet somehow manages to be more pedestrian than a Vulcan jaywalker. The root of the problem lies in an unimaginative take on imaginative elements, with the writers seemingly hoping the fanciful facets will spontaneously coalesce into a fanciful story. This doesn't happen, and "Wishes" ends up being one of Season One's most forgettable episodes as a result.

Did you know? "If wishes were horses, beggars would ride" is an 18th century proverb derived from an older proverb, "If wishes were thrushes, beggars would eat birds."

24

"The Forsaken": B–

Lwaxana Troi visits Deep Space Nine and falls for Odo.

Air date: May 23, 1993
Teleplay by Don Carlos Dunaway & Michael Piller
Story by Jim Trombetta
Directed by Les Landau
TV rating: 9.7

"All the men I've known have needed to be shaped and molded and manipulated. Finally, I've met a man who knows how to do it himself." —Lwaxana Troi

In the old days of television, whenever a show needed to save money, the writers would simply have some characters get stuck in an elevator and let the dialogue carry the episode. *Star Trek* sometimes does a similar thing, but usually the characters are trapped on a planet or held in a brig instead. This episode, however, does the trope straight, featuring Odo and Lwaxana Troi literally trapped in a turbolift and forced to bond. René Auberjonois and Majel Barrett are great together, and the writing is sharp, taking what begins as a lighthearted farce in an unexpected direction and allowing both actors to shine.

Meanwhile, Chief O'Brien deals with a new personality in the station's computer in a B story that doesn't really go anywhere but has a cute ending, and Bashir hosts three ambassadors in a barely there C story that would be more interesting if it was given some time to develop. (In fact, in Season Six's "Statistical Probabilities" the same basic concept is turned into something more substantial.)

Did you know? Here are some shows that have employed the "stuck in an elevator" trope along with the names of the characters that become trapped.

The Dick Van Dyke Show "4 1/2" (1964) Rob and Laura
All in the Family "The Elevator Story" (1972) Archie and some strangers
WKRP in Cincinnati "Fire" (1982) Herb and Jennifer
Magnum P.I. "Paper War" (1986) Magnum and his adversary
The Facts of Life "Concentration" (1986) Blair and her sister
Night Court "Earthquake" (1986) Dan and Roz
Alf "Alf's Special Christmas" (1987) Alf and a pregnant woman
Punky Brewster "Wimped Out" (1988) Punky and Cherie
Doogie Howser, M.D. "C'est la Vinnie" (1990) Vinnie and his French teacher
Star Trek: TNG "Disaster" (1991) Picard and some children
Saved by the Bell "Earthquake" (1992) Zach, Tori, and Mrs. Belding
The Fresh Prince of Bel-Air "The Baby Comes Out" (1993) Will and Phil
Seventh Heaven "Paper or Plastic" (2005) Matt and Lucy
NCIS "Power Down" (2009) Ziva and McGee

"Dramatis Personae": C

The crew becomes infected by the telepathic imprint of a destructive culture, forcing Sisko to build a clock while others begin to plot against him.

Air date: May 30, 1993
Written by Joe Menosky
Directed by Cliff Bole
TV rating: 9.0

"I want you to arrest them: Kira and every Bajoran officer on this station. I want the names of every sympathizer." —Sisko

With a title that's Latin for "the masks of drama," "Dramatis Personae" uses a *TNG*-like plot device to touch on obsessive compulsive behavior and give us a look at what a mutiny on Deep Space Nine might be like. To keep the episode from becoming tedious, the writers wisely give everyone something to do, allowing the drama to move from character to character and not get stuck on one issue like a broken record. The momentum does slow down in the middle as Odo begins to put together the puzzle pieces and discover what's really going on, and the climax is a simple paint-by-numbers *Star Trek* device, but it's clear the actors are having fun doing something different, and the episode has its moments as a result.

ENT's Season Two episode "Singularity" redoes the same basic idea.

Did you know? The clock that Sisko builds in this episode can be seen in the background of his office in many episodes to come.

"Duet": A

While trying to uncover the identity of a suspected Cardassian war criminal, Major Kira makes a shocking discovery

Air date: June 13, 1993
Teleplay by Peter Allan Fields
Story by Lisa Rich & Jeanne Carrigan-Fauci
Directed by James L. Conway
TV rating: 8.9

"I know all your secrets now." —Kira

Still in the red due to its expensive pilot, *DS9* gives us an alternative to an elevator episode: a brig episode. For this concept, we have a prisoner in jail, and the regulars interact with him over the course of the hour. (See also *TNG's* "I Borg"). Without fancy effects, the razzle dazzle of the Gamma Quadrant, or a B story, this sort of idea requires top notch writing and compelling performances to keep the viewer interested. Thankfully, "Duet" has both.

The episode itself, featuring Major Kira, is a mystery which, much like a Garak episode, has lies that are as interesting as the truth. Eventually we discover that the real issue we've been exploring is not the predictable Nazi-like fallout story it seems to be but is instead a bolder, more personal character study that packs an emotional wallop. Nana Visitor is great as usual, but Harris Yulin takes it to another level as the "war criminal". As the two develop their chemistry together, they somehow turn a Season One budget saver into one of *DS9's* most memorable gems and one that was cited by *Cinefantastique* magazine as *DS9's* greatest episode.

Did you know? Nana Visitor loved how Peter Allan Fields wrote for Kira, but in the early years of the show, he was such an infrequent visitor to the set, she didn't know him personally. On one hot day, he did stop by, but not before buying a Coke from a vending machine on the way. Between takes, he approached Visitor to introduce himself. Thinking he was a stagehand offering her the drink, she said "Thank you!" and took it and walked away. Afterward, René Auberjonois, who *did* recognize Fields, approached the writer and offered some advice. "You should visit us more often," he said. "And by the way, I prefer Diet Coke."

"In the Hands of the Prophets": B

Keiko's science lessons cause a religious uprising among the Bajoran community that threatens to destroy the Federation-Bajoran alliance. (Season finale)

Air date: June 20, 1993
Written by Robert Hewitt Wolfe
Directed by David Livingston
TV rating: 8.8

"You are opening the children's minds to blasphemy, and I cannot permit it to continue." —Vedek Winn

This "church versus the school" story with Keiko as the protagonist has a lot of fun with its concept, but it's evident from the beginning that the church is in the wrong. That means the success of the episode doesn't hinge on how effective the debate is, but rather the effectiveness of the antagonist's performance. Enter Louise Fletcher, the Oscar winning actress who wears a hat reminiscent of the Sydney Opera House while portraying Vedek Winn, perhaps the smarmiest character in *Star Trek* history. With no scary make-up, no growling, and no weapon more dangerous than her tongue, she's deliciously evil and steals the show.

The B story about Chief O'Brien investigating a death aboard the station makes good use of a seed planted in the previous episode and eventually ties into the A story, demonstrating that when a religious extremist argues for social change, the real motive is usually hidden beneath the surface.

Did you know? Louise Fletcher won the Academy Award for Best Actress in a Leading Role in 1975 for her performance as Nurse Mildred Ratched in *One Flew Over the Cuckoo's Nest.*

The First Season in Review

Not long after Gene Roddenberry passed away in 1991, Brandon Tartikoff, the new head of Paramount Pictures, called Rick Berman, the executive producer of *TNG*, with a request: he wanted another *Star Trek* series. Berman, though busy with *TNG*, wasn't caught unprepared. Even before Roddenberry was gone, Berman and his right-hand man, writer Michael Piller, had started toying with concepts for a new show. Taking a suggestion from Tartikoff, they began to mold those ideas around the premise of a man and his son living in a frontier town. But after initially considering a planet as the main setting, they instead opted for a space station to limit the necessity of location shooting. And with that, *Deep Space Nine* was born.

The two creators, of course, would need a team of collaborators to help them bring the station to life. Fortunately, they had a deep pool of talent they were already familiar with. After helping Berman and Piller create the look and feel of *TNG*, supervising producer David Livingston, make-up supervisor Michael Westmore, and costume designer Robert Blackman were all willing to increase their hours and work on both *TNG* and *DS9* simultaneously. They were joined by illustrators Rick Sternbach and Michael Okuda , as well as composers Dennis McCarthy and Jay Chattaway, who were willing to do the same. Meanwhile, visual effects experts Rob Legato and Gary Hutzle and *TNG's* director of photography, Marvin Rush, would all make the move to *DS9*. And though *TNG's* production designer, Richard James, declined an offer to switch, opting to stick with the Enterprise, his predecessor, Herman Zimmerman, who had overseen the original design of *TNG's* sets, was happy to return to the *Star Trek* fold and serve as production designer for the new show.

Having a setting alone, however, was not enough. Berman and Piller needed a writing staff to oversee its stories. Fortunately, again thanks to *TNG*, they were in a position to know many who had already succeeded in the *Star Trek* universe. Ira Steven Behr, who had written "Captain's Holiday," joined as supervising producer, and Peter Allan Fields, who had written "Half a Life," came on board as co-producer. Together, they were tasked with working with the outside writers. Joining them as story editor was a young upstart who impressed everyone with his script for "A Fistful of Datas," Robert Hewitt Wolfe.

Casting the show would prove more problematic. After inviting *TNG* guest stars Colm Meaney, Rosalind Chao, and Michelle Forbes to become regulars on the new show, hoping their characters, Chief O'Brien, Keiko O'Brien, and Ensign Ro, would serve as a bridge for *Star Trek* fans, the producers had to settle for just one and a half out of three. Meaney accepted, but Chao, who was pregnant and preparing to do a film, only gave a partial commitment, and Forbes, who didn't want to reprise her character at all, declined altogether, dealing a big blow to Berman and Piller, who had chosen to set the series in orbit of Ro's home planet. Another female role was proposed for Dutch actress Famke Jenssen, who had guest starred in *TNG's* "The Perfect Mate" with a unique make-up design consisting of spots. When she declined, the producers instead cast Terry Farrell in the part...but kept the spots. The male parts were less of a hassle, with Avery Brooks landing the lead, having beaten out several dozen other actors, including Siddig El Fadil.

Whatever the case, *DS9* begins with arguably the strongest pilot in *Star Trek* history, before the money the episode costs forces the show to muddle through the rest of the season on a shoestring budget. To make up for this, the producers bring in several *TNG* alumni, with the Duras sisters, Vash, Q, and Lwaxana Troi all popping in. But this proves to be a losing formula, with the series working better when it brings in guest stars to play new characters, such as Gul Dukat, Garak, and Vedek Winn. Meanwhile, as the writers and regulars attempt to develop the personalities of the Deep Space Nine inhabitants, no one gives them more trouble than Dax, originally conceived as a wise old owl, as in "A Man Alone" where she's "living on a higher plane" and eschewing romance. Behind the scenes, there's nothing more frustrating than the Bajoran noses, designed for occasional use on *TNG*, which restrict facial movements and require constant regluing until they're redesigned later in the season to accommodate a show that features the Bajorans on a weekly basis.

Yet despite these struggles, the first year gives us several standout episodes, such as "Emissary," "Dax," "In the Hands of the Prophets," and the acclaimed "Duet," an impressive haul for a season that didn't begin until January. On the other hand, "Babel," "Move Along Home," and "If Wishes Were Horses" somehow exist as well, demonstrating the need for improvement. (Unfortunately for the show, all its early growing pains were put on display while *TNG* was enjoying one of its best seasons.)

Regardless, *DS9* proved to be a ratings hit, and accolades would eventually follow, with Season One winning three Emmys: one for make-up, one for special effects, and one for the theme song.

Happily, as Sisko might say, the best is still to come.

Season Two

Production Order
(with air date order in parentheses)

1. "The Homecoming" (1st)
2. "The Circle" (2nd)
3. "The Siege" (3rd)
4. "Invasive Procedures" (4th)
5. "Cardassians" (5th)
6. "Melora" (6th)
7. "Rules of Acquisition" (7th)
8. "Necessary Evil" (8th)
9. "Second Sight" (9th)
10. "Sanctuary" (10th)
11. "Rivals" (11th)
12. "The Alternate" (12th)
13. "Armageddon Game" (13th)
14. "Whispers" (14th)
15. "Paradise" (15th)
16: "Shadowplay" (16th)
17: "Playing God" (17th)
18. "Profit and Loss" (18th)
19. "Blood Oath" (19th)
20: "The Maquis, Part I" (20th)
21. "The Maquis, Part II" (21st)
22. "The Wire" (22nd)
23: "Crossover" (23rd)
24. "The Collaborator" (24th)
25. "Tribunal" (25th)
26: "The Jem'Hadar" (26th)

The Second Season Cast

Commander Sisko: Avery Brooks
Major Kira: Nana Visitor
Odo: René Auberjonois
Chief O'Brien: Colm Meaney
Dax: Terry Farrell
Dr. Bashir: Siddig El Fadil
Jake Sisko: Cirroc Lofton
Quark: Armin Shimerman

Notable Guest Stars

Rosalind Chao
Philip Anglim
Louise Fletcher
Max Grodénchik
Aron Eisenberg
Tim Russ
Andrew Robinson
Marc Alaimo
Wallace Shawn
James Sloyan
Kenneth Tobey
Noley Thornton
Richard Poe
John Colicos
Michael Ansara
William Campbell
Bernie Casey
Paul Dooley
Fritz Weaver
Alan Oppenheimer
Molly Hagan

"The Homecoming" (1): B-

Kira rescues a famed Bajoran resistance fighter only to discover he's not what she expected.

Air date: September 26, 1993
Teleplay by Ira Steven Behr
Story by Jeri Taylor & Ira Steven Behr
Directed by Winrich Kolbe
TV rating: 9.7

"This morning I was a slave. Tonight I am a hero." —Li Nalas

DS9 does its own version of *The Man Who Shot Liberty Valance* with a legendary Bajoran serving as the focal point. The whole idea here is that this larger than life figure can't live up to his hype, and that pretty much describes guest star Richard Beymer in the role, making the episode more interesting when he's not present. Fortunately, he is absent for much of the episode, and the ensemble piece moves along at a nice clip with just enough bits throughout, including some location shooting at Soledad Canyon, to keep things interesting.

Did you know? Frank Langella's performances as Minister Jaro in the first three episodes of Season Two are uncredited per the actor's request.

33

"The Circle" (2): A

A terrorist group known as "The Circle" attempts to seize power and expel the Federation.

Air date: October 3, 1993
Written by Peter Allan Fields
Directed by Corey Allen
TV rating: 9.0

"The Circle is for real, Major. They've been armed for a coup and I'm not at all convinced that the military's going to back the provisional government."
—Sisko

In a way, the middle installment of *Trek's* first three-parter, now known as "The Circle Trilogy," serves as *DS9's* second pilot, echoing the first and stirring up enough political intrigue to give many future episodes ideas to explore.

With a confidence that belies a young series, "The Circle" gets going with one of *Trek's* all-time great comedic scenes and then spends the rest of the episode throwing a bit of everything at the viewer, including drama, action, great sets, beautiful locations, and amazing guest stars. Louise Fletcher returns as Vedek Winn, and Philip Anglim reprises Vedek Bareil, with both sharing some fantastic scenes with Nana Visitor. Unfortunately, the episode doesn't really find anything for Richard Beymer to do as Li Nalas, turning the character into a superfluous add-on, but with all the other elements to juggle, it's understandable. "The Circle," nonetheless, gives *DS9* a tone of its own and serves as the template for all Bajoran political thrillers to come.

Did you know? The master shot for a scene set in Kira's quarters, featuring seven characters, was shot in one continuous take, though close-ups and reverse angles were used when the episode was edited together.

34

"The Siege" (3): B–

Sisko and his crew attempt to stop The Circle from taking over Deep Space Nine.

Air date: October 10, 1993
Written by Michael Piller
Directed by Winrich Kolbe
TV rating: 9.0

"Let me reemphasize that you are to take every necessary step to keep Li Nalas alive. Dead, he's a martyr. Alive, he seals our victory." —Jaro

This concluding chapter of "The Circle Trilogy" begins with a fast paced, intriguing story before slowing down about halfway through and throwing in some padding to enable the episode to fill out its mandated duration. Unlike the first two parts, this one shines the spotlight on the regulars and showcases the indisputable fact that the actors are becoming quite comfortable with their parts. It's also evident that the show itself is increasingly stepping away from *TNG* to carve out its own niche in the *Star Trek* universe.

But as an episode by itself, "The Siege" doesn't reach the heights of its prequel, "The Circle," though as a piece of *DS9* history, it's a solid offering with some nifty special effects, and it ties everything up in a satisfactory way.

Did you know? *DS9's* next three-parter would begin with Season Six's finale, "Tears of the Prophets."

"Invasive Procedures": C–

An unjoined Trill holds the Deep Space Nine crew hostage and steals the Dax symbiont.

Air date: October 17, 1993
Teleplay by John Whelpley & Robert Hewitt Wolfe
Story by John Whelpley
Directed by Les Landau
TV rating: 9.3

"The symbiont, Benjamin. He's come to steal my symbiont." —Dax

With the Trill species consisting of a host carrying a symbiont inside, the writers can take the concept and choose from many different directions to go. For this one, the driving force behind the plot is an antagonist's wish to become something more than mediocre. Unfortunately, the episode doesn't seem to share the same ambition. The story has an interesting premise, but it coasts on it in such a "connect the dots" way, it's easy to guess what was said at the writers' meetings. "How about we have someone try to steal Dax's symbiont?" "Okay, he'll have to take over the station to do that. How do we make it plausible?" "How will he get Bashir to cooperate, and how do we make it personal and develop the relationships?" The episode answers these questions just fine and doesn't do anything wrong—although I do have to wonder just how weak-willed Dax is when the trill does nothing to stop its new host from carrying out his plan—but the story lacks the dash of creativity it needs to give it a spark of excitement. In fact, an internal struggle between Dax and the trill's new host would have been a welcome addition. As it is, the episode is sort of like *Die Hard*, but with a wussy villain and a lot of talking instead of action. (Okay, so it's not really much like *Die Hard* after all.)

DS9 returns to the issues of Trill-joining in Season Three's "Equilibrium."

Did you know? In this episode, Tim Russ, who would go on to play Tuvok on *VOY*, plays a Klingon mercenary.

"Cardassians": C

An orphaned Cardassian boy who was raised by Bajorans sparks a bitter custody battle.

Air date: October 24, 1993
Teleplay by James Crocker
Story by Gene Wolande & John Wright
Directed by Cliff Bole
TV rating: 9.1

"I have no intention of allowing a Bajoran court to rule on the custody of my son." —Pa'dar

Touching on some of the same themes as *TNG's* Season Four episode "Suddenly Human," "Cardassians" is about another hard-luck custody battle—but it's notable for bringing back Andrew Robinson in a B story, built around the continuing relationship between Bashir and Garak. The pairing is gold, with their scenes as engaging as the first time around in "Past Prologue."

The Cardassian boy himself gets the A story, with 25-year-old Vidal Peterson playing the 12-year-old kid with a mixture of anger and frustration any boy would have in his situation. Peterson, who previously appeared in *TNG's* "Unification II," gives the adults something nice to play off of, but because of the heavy subject matter, some of the scenes are slow and awkward, and it takes the plot a while to get moving. It might have helped had the show cast a younger child as the Cardassian boy to allow the character to be less sulky and more innocent. The downside would be that his relationships with the adults would be less complex, but the episode never really takes the time to explore these anyway. As it is, the story is at its best when the focus is on Garak and Gul Dukat, with the latter especially excellent as the episode's heavy, even if his evil plan turns out to be more convoluted than that of a *Scooby Doo* villain.

Did you know? Originally, Marc Alaimo's best friend was cast as Gul Dukat, but after shooting commenced on *DS9's* pilot, the producers wanted a stronger performance and brought in Alaimo as a replacement, though he wasn't told who he was replacing. Alaimo went on to appear in 33 episodes of the series.

"Melora": D–

Bashir falls in love with an alien who must use a wheelchair to move about in DS9's gravity.

Air date: October 31, 1993
Teleplay by Evan C. Somers, Steven Baum, Michael Piller & James Crocker
Story by Evan Carlos Somers
Directed by Winrich Kolbe
TV rating: 9.7

"Try sitting in the chair, Commander. No one can understand until they sit in the chair. I have been in one chair or another since I left my homeworld." —Melora

Conceived as a *DS9* regular but confined to one episode due to anti-gravity budget issues, the titular character of this episode would probably have never made it into another episode anyway because the "bitter, overly sensitive disabled person who learns to accept help" is a worn out character trope that nobody but television writers have any interest in seeing. Tweaking the character and giving her the B story would be a better way to introduce her, but the writers so desperately want a Bashir love story, we're stuck with their relationship as the main course. Unfortunately, it comes across as stilted and silly, with El Fadil phoning in his performance, though the episode improves once Bashir is able to break down Melora's guard.

The B story belongs to Quark, who is threatened by a man he double-crossed years ago. It's obtrusive, existing only to give the episode a sense of danger, but at least it's quick and doesn't include Melora and Bashir...for the most part.

Did you know? As an intern for *DS9*, Evan Carlos Somers was familiar with the show's desire to have a character that, like himself, uses a wheelchair and conceived this episode. His script was rewritten by Steven Baum, and Baum's work was subsequently rewritten by Michael Piller and James Crocker.

"Rules of Acquisition": C

When Grand Nagus Zek assigns Quark and a new associate to open negotiations with a planet in the Gamma Quadrant, Quark discovers a secret.

Air date: November 7, 1993
Teleplay by Ira Steven Behr
Story by Hilary Bader
Directed by David Livingston
TV rating: 8.8

"Pel, it's time. We don't want to keep the Dosi waiting. Hurry!" —Quark

If you think *Star Trek* is above the old Shakespearean cross-dressing confusion plot, you probably haven't seen enough *DS9*. Here the show pulls it out for the first time in another Ferengi farce directed by David Livingston, with "Rules" bringing back Wallace Shawn as the Grand Nagus and introducing Hélène Udy as Pel while paying homage to *Yentl*. Like "The Nagus," "Rules" makes no attempt to be subtle or unpredictable, but inside these limitations, it's an acceptable romp, and in the long run it proves to be a landmark episode for two reasons: first, it introduces a new element to Dax's character. She understands the Ferengi and knows how to have fun with them. Future writers would not only embrace this idea but elaborate on it, allowing this spirit to spill over into the Klingon culture as well. Second, we learn that there's a big thing in the Gamma Quadrant called the Dominion, which is vaguely defined as an important power. Both ideas are minor parts of the story, and the irony is that they happen in what is, overall, a forgettable episode, but they would eventually color in the corners of the series overall.

Meanwhile, *DS9* would improve upon the plot here in the Season Three episode "Family Business" by making the story more personal to both Quark and Rom. In the meantime, "Rules" would go on to be nominated for an Emmy for make-up.

Did you know? Hilary Bader originally pitched this story to *TNG,* suggesting Pel become involved with Commander Riker.

"Necessary Evil": A

Quark is injured in an attack that Odo suspects is related to a murder committed five years prior.

Air date: November 14, 1993
Written by Peter Allan Fields
Directed by James L. Conway
TV rating: 9.2

"In this job, there is no unfinished business. The assault on Quark reopens a five-year-old murder case that I've never, not for a moment, closed." —Odo

A good film noir story? Others episodes may try. This one succeeds. Beginning like a Quark episode, our favorite Ferengi is quickly moved out of the picture to allow this one to become the Odo-show. And while it might resemble *The Maltese Falcon* or *Columbo* stylistically, with Odo's voiceovers and whodunnit investigations providing the episode with its drama, the story structure, intertwining the past and present, is virtually identical to a series yet to come: ABC's *Lost* (2004-2010). But whatever "Necessary Evil's" roots or visionary precedents, the episode stands out as one of *Star Trek's* most intriguing, intense, and ambitious stories, thanks to a complex script, breathtaking cinematography, and superb performances. By bringing *DS9's* history alive through Odo's flashbacks, the episode instantly adds layers to the series, giving the show depth it previously lacked. And what's especially wonderful is that it happens so early in *DS9's* run, it helps serve as a launching pad for more great stories, such as Season Five's "Things Past," while the quality of the episode itself raises the bar for all future episodes to come.

Did you know? Writer/producer Peter Allan Fields, who previously wrote for *Columbo*, pays homage to his old series by having Odo, while interrogating a suspect, nearly walk out of the scene before turning around to say, "Oh, there was one other thing…"

"Second Sight": D

Commander Sisko becomes interested in a woman who suffers from a bizarre form of split personality.

Air date: November 21, 1993
Teleplay by Mark Gehred-O'Connell, Ira Steven Behr & Robert Hewitt Wolfe
Story by Mark Gehred-O'Connell
Directed by Alexander Singer
TV rating: 9.4

"I'm telling you, Dax, it was the same woman. The face, the voice. It was Fenna." —Sisko

With this installment, *DS9* gives us *Portrait of Jennie* as a *Star Trek* episode. Unfortunately, as *Trek* too often does, the beauty of the mystery is eschewed for a rational, technobabble answer with some faux jeopardy stuck in for good measure. *Portrait*, in both book and film form, works because the enigmatic woman becomes more interesting with each encounter. Here, the idea of "the mysterious woman who keeps disappearing" serves as an intriguing jumping off point, but it goes nowhere. There's simply no real story beyond the premise, just an explanation, as if the joy of the mystery is in the answer.

There's also a B story about an arrogant scientist's attempt to reignite a star, with Richard Kiley's flamboyant performance equally comical and galling. ("Must I remind you, Lieutenant Dax, some of us only have one lifetime.")

The A and B stories fold together by the end, but with neither story particularly satisfying in their own right, their unification falls short of providing a fulfilling climax. Fortunately, ideas from *Portrait of Jennie* would be better used in *DS9's* Season Four episode, "The Visitor."

Did you know? Robert Nathan wrote *Portrait of Jennie*, a story about a Depression-era artist and a mysterious young girl, in his mid-40s. Originally published in 1940 as a novella, CBS adapted the story into a radio play in 1946 and Vanguard Films turned it into a movie in 1948. With elements of romance, fantasy, mystery, and the supernatural, the book continues to haunt readers and inspire writers in the present. Nathan died in 1985 at age 91.

"Sanctuary": C

A group of refugees from the Gamma Quadrant claims that Bajor is the homeland they've long been searching for.

Air date: November 28, 1993
Teleplay by Frederick Rappaport
Story by Gabe Essoe & Kelley Miles
Directed by Les Landau
TV rating: 8.9

"Bajor simply cannot absorb three million refugees at this time." —Sorad

One of the recurring themes for *TOS* is that because something is different or unattractive, it doesn't mean it's wrong or unworthy. A recurring theme for *TNG* is, "How can we help this group of people who are struggling with a problem?" "Sanctuary" combines the two ideas into an immigration allegory that doesn't quite live up to the promise of either.

It all begins with a *Star Trek* faux pas: an attempt to explain how the universal translator works. The problem is that past (and future) precedents for communication between aliens on *Star Trek* can't be rationally and consistently explained and simply have to be accepted as an artistic liberty. As such, it's in *Star Trek's* best interest to limit references to the universal translator and not call attention to how it works. This episode, however, gets too cute, presenting aliens that give the improbable device trouble. (The *DS9* writers have since admitted that this is just a stall tactic because the real story is too short for a full episode.) The idea works in *TNG's* Season Five episode "Darmok" because *TNG* avoids the specifics of the technology. In contradistinction, "Sanctuary" awkwardly discusses it while raising more questions than it answers. How does the universal translator immediately identify the languages of other aliens we haven't encountered before? Why do the lip movements always look like English? Heck, in the *TNG* episode "First Contact," Riker spends most of the episode seemingly speaking English to a race of aliens who don't know he's not one of them. Does the U.T. create a holographic face to match the mouth movements needed for its translations? But I digress.

The story itself, once the communication issue is buried, moves along nicely and is enjoyable for what it is. It's especially a hoot to see William Schallert—last seen in *Star Trek* as Nilz Baris in *TOS's* "The Trouble With Tribbles"—as a Bajoran musician who opens the episode with a rendition of the Deep Space Nine theme. Ultimately, however, "Sanctuary" sidesteps offering a clear statement on the immigration issue, playing both sides of the fence and probably pleasing no one in the process.

Did you know? In this episode, Armin Shimerman's wife, Kitty Swink, plays a Bajoran Minister who denies the aliens' immigration request.

"Rivals": D+

A con artist opens a bar with a gambling machine that can alter the laws of probability.

Air date: January 2, 1994
Teleplay by Joe Menosky
Story by Jim Trombetta & Michael Piller
Directed by David Livingston
TV rating: 9.3

"My luck's running good today." —Martus

The idea of distorting the laws of probability to manipulate luck is an interesting notion, and the premise of this episode would easily fit into any incarnation of *Star Trek*. *DS9*, however, doesn't really flesh it out so much as sketch it out, outlining the general plot but neglecting to give it any real substance. The high concept, with all its possibilities, is used merely for petty gambling and sporting games, with the idea of borrowing a little good luck now at the expense of a lot of bad luck down the road wasted on comedic fodder.

The concept itself splits into two intersecting stories. On one hand, we're introduced to Quark's new rival, Martus, played by guest star Chris Sarandon. This plot goes next to nowhere, because Shimerman and Sarandon have no chemistry together, and the scriptwriters completely botch the pair's game of one-upmanship. On the other hand, we've got a sporting rivalry between Bashir and O'Brien that fares better thanks to the strong performances of the actors and a relationship that works well on screen. All the same, there's just not much here, and the only must-see feature of the episode is Bashir's racquetball attire.

Did you know? Martus was intended to be the wayward son of *TNG*'s Guinan, but when Whoopi Goldberg's schedule prevented her from appearing in this episode, all references to her character, Guinan, were removed from the script.

"The Alternate": C

The doctor who discovered Odo believes he may have found the shape-shifters' homeworld.

Air date: January 9, 1994
Teleplay by Bill Dial
Story by Jim Trombetta & Bill Dial
Directed by David Carson
TV rating: 8.9

"Dr. Mora thinks he may have discovered the origin of my people. Of me."
—Odo

This character-driven Odo episode works its way into an old-fashioned monster/mystery story, though it takes its own sweet time getting there before adding a twist near the end.

DS9 deserves credit for introducing the idea of Dr. Mora in previous episodes, with Odo even saying in "The Forsaken" that his hair is a copy of this doctor's. By seeding ideas like this, the new character comes across as more familiar and less contrived. And by meeting a character so important to Odo's development, we learn much about Odo—even when he's not on screen. Guest star James Sloyen, who previously played the title character in *TNG's* "The Defector," is excellent as the doctor, substituting for the actor the part was originally written for, René Auberjonois. (The size of the doctor's part and the complexity of Auberjonois's make-up made the double role impossible.)

Unfortunately, while the episode works well as a primer for Odo's backstory and provides tremendous insight into the shape-shifter's character, the story itself is *Trek* at its most vanilla, offering little excitement for fans of the franchise.

James Sloyan would go on to guest star on *TNG* as K'mtar in Season Seven's "Firstborn" before appearing as the title character in *VOY's* Season One episode "Jetrel" and reprising Dr. Mora in *DS9's* Season Five offering, "The Begotten."

Did you know? This is the last *Star Trek* episode to be overseen by David Carson, the director behind *TNG's* "Yesterday's Enterprise," *DS9's* "Emissary," and *TNG's* first feature film, *Generations*.

"Armageddon Game": B

The governments of two alien races believe there's only one way to ensure that their peace agreement lasts: anyone with knowledge of their past weapons, including O'Brien and Bashir, must die.

Air date: January 30, 1994.
Written by Morgan Gendel
Directed by Winrich Kolbe
TV rating: 8.6

"Don't worry, Chief, I'm going to get you home." —Bashir

This Bashir/O'Brien episode has an interesting premise, but the television budget forces the writer to scale back the possibilities of the story. Ideally, the action would begin at a lab on a planet, and Bashir and O'Brien would escape and go on the run. Instead, the action begins on a spaceship, so the show can use the one set for two purposes, before the two beam down to a planet and hide in one location. But the Bashir/O'Brien pairing always works, and it's fun to see the actors move the relationship forward.

Meanwhile, back on Deep Space Nine, Avery Brooks is outstanding as the guy in charge who's torn up over the apparent deaths of his officers but must bury his feelings while he performs the difficult tasks necessary to move forward. One of his tasks is informing Keiko, which gives us one of the finest Rosalind Chao performances of the series.

"Armageddon" was nominated for an Emmy for the two awful alien hairstyles, proving that these award shows have no taste. (Actually, it's possible the contrasting hairstyles were the cause of the aliens' war to begin with.)

Did you know? One of the alien ambassadors is played by Darleen Carr, an accomplished singer who provided a singing voice for Kurt von Trapp in *The Sound of Music* (1965).

"Whispers": B+

When Chief O'Brien returns from an away mission, he finds that everyone is acting strangely, and he's been locked out of key systems.

Air date: February 6, 1994
Written by Paul Robert Coyle
Directed by Les Landau
TV rating: 9.3

"I mean, the way they were acting, they might've been trying to pull off one of those surprise parties that I can't stand, only my birthday's not until September."
—O'Brien

This O'Brien mystery thriller is built around the considerable talents of Colm Meaney, who is in every scene. Reminiscent of *The Twilight Zone* and Philip Dick's short story "The Imposter," the story moves forward and backwards in unexpected ways. O'Brien makes headway, seemingly getting close to figuring out what's going on, only to have a lesser officer get in his way. Just as he's about to make it through this obstacle, a superior officer obstructs and redirects him! (Avery Brooks handles his supporting role especially well, giving just the right glances and imparting just the right intonations at opportune times to arouse the appropriate suspicion.) As a conspiracy seemingly coalesces and the paranoia begins to build, the writers float several plausible theories to explain what's happening but keep the viewer guessing until the final act. The end is a bit abrupt (and sad), but it's clear Paul Robert Coyle developed the mystery from its conclusion rather than vice versa, and the result is an end that makes perfect sense and satisfactorily answers all the questions raised throughout the course of the episode.

Did you know? A scene where one runabout chases another had to be cut from the episode because the writer mixed up the names of the two vessels throughout the sequence.

"Paradise": C–

Sisko and O'Brien are stranded on a world where technology doesn't function.

Air date: February 13, 1994
Teleplay by Jeff King, Richard Manning & Hans Beimler
Story by Jim Trombetta & James Crocker
Directed by Corey Allen
TV rating: 8.2

"Change doesn't come easily to you, Ben. I realize it. Believe me, I'm not expecting some sudden, miraculous conversion. Change will come by itself if you're open to it. But you do have to show us that you're open to it." —Alixus

This cult story features a strong performance from Avery Brooks as "Cool Hand Sisko" and a nice effort by guest star Gail Strickland, who gives her character, Alixus, plenty of smarm and smugness. Unfortunately, the part really needs the charisma and gravitas that only a special actor—such as David Warner and Ricardo Montalbán—can give. Devoid of such, the battle of wills between Sisko and Alixus lacks drama, and the climax lacks punch. Within its limitations, however, the episode works okay, moving at a nice clip while giving Kira and Dax the "find the missing crewmembers" B story. The latter is short, but the actresses are good together, and it's a nice diversion.

That said, the greatest problem with the episode might be the ambiguous conclusion which seems to vindicate the wrong character. It makes you wonder what the point of the episode is or if the writers ever decided upon one when they were writing it. Unfortunately, they waste a good opportunity to do a creepy horror climax akin to something in *The Stepford Wives* or *The Wicker Man*.

Did you know? In this episode, Strickland delivers one of more interesting lines of the season. Mixing up her prepositional objects, she says, "We can plow the crops and harvest the fields."

47

"Shadowplay": C

Odo and Dax discover a village where the inhabitants are disappearing one at a time.

Air date: February 20, 1994
Written by Robert Hewitt Wolfe
Directed by Robert Sheerer
TV rating: 9.5

"I've got twenty-two people who've disappeared without a trace." —Colyus

Comprised of three separate stories, this unfocused offering is a harmless but forgettable installment of a series still trying to find its footing.

The heart of the episode, both structurally and emotionally, is a planet-based mystery Odo stumbles upon that plays out like it could be a *TNG* Data story. Featuring several scenes with Odo and the various people of a village, it's a genuinely touching sci-fi yarn that takes advantage of some good guest stars, including 76-year-old Kenneth Tobey and ten-year-old Noley Thornton. Auberjonois, working well with the young and old alike, gives Odo a combination of stubbornness and goodness as he tries to find the answers the village needs, making his character all the more endearing in the process.

Meanwhile, the B story attempts to move the Kira/Bareil relationship forward, and the C story follows Jake as he stresses over how to tell his dad he doesn't want to join Starfleet. Neither of these offer any surprises but both serve as satisfactory counterpoints to the main story and lay some groundwork for future episodes to build on.

Did you know? For this episode, *DS9* reuses the village stage set designed for *TNG's* "Thine Own Self."

48

"Playing God": C−

While hosting her first Trill initiate, Lieutenant Dax discovers an expanding protouniverse that threatens the quadrant.

Air date: February 27, 1994
Teleplay by Jim Trombetta & Michael Piller
Story by Jim Trombetta
Directed by David Livingston
TV rating: 8.8

"Jadzia will be a wonderful host, Well, that is, she is a wonderful host in a Trill manner of speaking. I'm sure you'll learn a lot from her." —Bashir

The conventional *Star Trek* episode introduces a sci-fi premise and finds opportunities throughout the story for character development. This Dax episode inverts the formula, exploring the characters while finding opportunities to touch upon the sci-fi idea of a miniature universe. As a Trill story, it's somewhat interesting, expanding on the recharacterization of Dax put forth in "Rules of Acquisition" and introducing Arjin (Geoffrey Blake), who is sufficiently wussy enough to serve as her opposite and highlight their differences. The script develops parallels between Jadzia's experience of being mentored and her attempt at being a mentor—and has her come to terms with what each means. It's well played by Terry Farrell and adds interest to the character going forward.

As an exciting piece of sci-fi, however, the episode falls flat. The fascinating idea of a protouniverse is underdeveloped and given the NIMBY treatment. There's also a C story reminiscent of the "The Trouble with Tribbles," with alien rodents infesting the station, but it comes across as contrived and serves simply as a comedic runner.

Did you know? Terry Farrell and Geoffrey Blake played boyfriend and girlfriend in *Paper Dolls*, a soap opera that lasted 14 episodes in 1984.

"Profit and Loss": C

Quark puts everything on the line to win back his lost love, a Cardassian woman suspected of terrorism.

Air date: March 20, 1994
Written by Flip Kobler & Cindy Marcus
Directed by Robert Wiemer
TV rating: 8.8

"Of all the raktajino joints in all the stations in all the universe, she walks into mine." —Quark

Unlike "Necessary Evil," this episode doesn't depart from the style of the series to tell its story—other than some snappy film noir dialogue—but it does take the story of *Casablanca* (1942) and loosely adapts it into a Quark/Garak story, with Quark as Bogey and Garak as...well, Garak.

As a love story, it might be make-up man Michael Westmore's demented dream, but it comes across as a little silly, not to mention out of character for Quark. The plot itself, however, is interesting and thoughtful enough to entertain—just like it was the first time around—and Robert Wiemer directs it well, slowing down the pace in the second half for some lengthy scenes that are well played by Shimerman, Auberjonois, and Robinson.

Unfortunately, the whole thing is undermined by some gaping plot holes, and worse yet, we never do find out what the fallout of the conclusion is!

Did you know? While the cast and crew were preparing to shoot some scenes for this episode, a 6.7 magnitude earthquake struck southern California, sending everyone into a panic. Some of the actors, including Armin Shimerman and Andrew Robinson, drove home in their make-up to check on their families, getting some strange looks from other drivers along the way.

"Blood Oath": B

A trio of legendary Klingons prepare for a mission of revenge.

Air date: March 27, 1994
Written by Peter Allan Fields
Directed by Winrich Kolbe
TV rating: 8.4

"The Klingons have their own set of laws. This is justice to them." —Dax

By the 1990s, *Star Trek* had amassed such a rich back-story, many writers saw it as a curse. Gone were the days when they could easily invent a new aspect to the franchise on a whim to help tell a story or solve a script problem. But the curse could also be an asset. When somebody pitched a story to *TNG* about an unknown ambassador with mental problems, the writing staff realized it would be more dramatic to reuse an old, beloved character rather than invent one and borrowed Sarek from *TOS*. Here on *DS9*, when Peter Allan Fields pitched the idea of this story with new characters, Robert Hewitt Wolfe suggested they use the three Klingon headliners from *TOS* instead. The truth is the story itself is solid enough that it would probably work with Terry Farrell and three unknowns. But Kang, Kor, and Koloth, give the episode believability, nostalgia, and three guaranteed solid Klingon performances.

The episode itself is a Dax story with a well written script that cleverly hides its exposition inside her quest to prove herself to the Klingons. Basically, these three guys have found their equivalent of Osama bin Laden and plan to storm the compound, kill him, and eat his heart—in whatever order presents itself—and Dax wants in. But she discovers there's more going on than meets the eye. Farrell and Michael Ansara (Kang) are the cornerstones of the episode and give it everything they have, emotionally and physically, to make it a success. And while it does seem a little too easy for our heroes to storm the compound, which they do in broad daylight for the benefit of the cameras, the climax is appropriately action-packed and fun to watch—not to mention a special treat for *TOS* fans. The three Klingons are so wonderful as *Star Trek's* equivalent to "The Three Musketeers," it's easy to forget that this is the first— and last—episode they all appear in together. Each appears in a different *TOS* episode, with Kor appearing in "Errand of Mercy," Koloth appearing in "The Trouble with Tribbles," and Kang appearing in "Day of the Dove." The three actors give their characters such a rapport, it's easy to believe that they spent the thirty years after the original series hanging out together—even if it's not true.

John Colicos reprises Kor in Season Four's "The Sword of Kahless."

Did you know? John Colicos died March 6, 2000 at 71, William Campbell (Koloth) died April 28, 2011 at 87, and Michael Ansara died July 31, 2013 at 91.

51

"The Maquis, Part I": B+

When a Cardassian freighter explodes at Deep Space Nine, the Cardassians blame a rogue group of Federation colonists.

Air date: April 24, 1994
Teleplay by James Crocker
Story by Rick Berman. Michael Piller, Jeri Taylor & James Crocker
Directed by David Livingston
TV rating: 8.6

"Without any help from either one of us, they've managed to start their own little war out here." —Dukat

The politics from *TNG*'s Season Seven episode "Journey's End" spill over into *DS9* here, as both shows attempt to lay some exposition for the upcoming *VOY*.

DS9 does its part, putting forth a solid two-parter that simultaneously sets up future stories while being pretty darn entertaining in its own right. Both halves of "The Maquis" are Sisko episodes, and the first literally begins with a bang before turning into a tense political thriller. "Part I" doesn't spend a lot of money on effects, but it does create a large scope on a small budget by using the dialogue and tactical displays to make it seem like more is going on than we actually see. (The episode also steals an establishing shot of a colony from *TNG's* "Ensigns of Command.")

Meanwhile, a number of guest stars give the plot its moving parts, with Tony Plana playing a human conspirator, Bernie Casey playing a Starfleet attaché, Bertila Damas playing a Vulcan, Richard Poe playing a Cardassian, and Marc Alaimo reprising Gul Dukat. The latter is the breakout character, with Alaimo and Avery Brooks finally given time together to develop the relationship between their character, leading to many more scenes between the two in future episodes. As Dukat becomes more three dimensional, the series gains a more interesting antagonist, and here it puts Sisko (and the audience) in the difficult position of hearing two different viewpoints of what's going on, making the situation more difficult to gauge. As this is going on, the other guest stars contribute to the story in small ways without overstaying their welcome, with Casey's performance being the most memorable of the bunch, and Damas getting a short B story with Armin Shimerman involving a black market deal. (A Vulcan walks into a Ferengi bar and orders weapons. Insert your own punch line.)

The story continues in "The Maquis, Part II."

Did you know? Bernie Casey accepted the part of attaché Cal Hudson specifically so he could work with Avery Brooks, whom he had admired as an actor since seeing Brooks's work in *Spenser for Hire* (1985–1988) and *A Man Called Hawk* (1989).

"The Maquis, Part II": B

Sisko tries to stop the Maquis terrorists to prevent a new war with the Cardassians.

Air date: May 1, 1994
Teleplay by Ira Steven Behr
Story by Rick Berman, Michael Piller, Jeri Taylor & Ira Steven Behr
Directed by Corey Allen
TV rating: 8.3

"The Federation believes that it can solve every problem with a treaty, but out here, on the frontier, without the power of the Federation to back them up, a treaty is only a piece of paper." —Cal Hudson

Adding a couple more guest stars, "Part II" is even more talky than "Part I," although the writers keep the plot interesting by continually moving the story forward with the dialogue. Quark even gets to finish up his B story with the Vulcan gunrunner. And as the episode approaches its conclusion, the big money is finally thrown onto the screen in the form of a space battle with some nifty special effects for 1990s television.

The central character is again Sisko, with Avery Brooks pairing up with each of the major guest stars in a succession of scenes. These guests—including Natalija Nogulich as Admiral Nechayev—give Brooks some generous performances to play off of, and with each new scene, the plot becomes more personal and Brooks becomes more intense. (That said, I do have to wonder why Legate Parn comes all the way to Deep Space Nine for a two minute conversation where he basically says, "The Cardassian government doesn't really care about this.)

Following the two-parter, *TNG* takes the baton back for a Maquis episode its own, "Preemptive Strike," before passing it on to *VOY* for the show's pilot, "Caretaker." *DS9* itself would return to the subject matter in Season Three's "Defiant" and Season Five's "Blaze of Glory."

Did you know? Dukat's line that on Cardassia "the verdict is always known before the trial begins" is the basis for "Tribunal," an episode later in the season.

"The Wire": B

Bashir fights to save Garak from an experimental brain implant which is slowly killing him.

Air date: May 8, 1994
Written by Robert Hewitt Wolfe
Directed by Kim Friedman
TV rating: 8.0

"It's not your pride I'm worried about. It's that implant you're carrying around inside your head." —Bashir

The Bashir/Garak relationship is finally given an A story in this bottle episode that begins like an allegory for drug addiction before becoming a playful study of Garak's history. While Siddig El Fadil and Andrew Robinson have a blast with a script that allows their dialogue to carry the plot, Kim Friedman, the show's first female director, proves her mettle by building the intensity in gutsy crescendos and covering for the lack of budget with dramatic character pieces.

And though guest star Paul Dooley nearly steals the show as Enabran Tain, Garak's mentor, the episode is really a watershed moment for Robinson and his alter ego. In past episodes, Garak is merely a supporting player. Here, he and the actor who plays him become as important as the regulars.

Did you know? Paul Dooley, who began his entertainment career as a stand-up comedian in the 1960s, is best known for his fatherly roles in films such as *Breaking Away* (1979) and *Sixteen Candles* (1984) and in television shows such as *Dream On* (1990–1996), *My So-Called Life* (1994–1995) and *Grace Under Fire* (1993–1998). Behind the scenes, he has produced hundreds of television and radio commercials.

"Crossover": B–

An accident leaves Kira and Bashir stranded in a parallel universe where humans are slaves and Kira's double is in charge.

Air date: May 15, 1994
Teleplay by Peter Allan Fields & Michael Piller
Story by Peter Allan Fields
Directed by David Livingston
TV rating: 8.9

"The players are all the same, but everyone seems to be playing different parts."
—Kira

When "Mirror, Mirror" first aired in 1967, who would have thought we'd have to wait 27 years for a sequel?

Unlike sister-show *TNG*, *DS9* is quite comfortable from the get-go acknowledging the original *Star Trek* stories, and this episode kicks off a total of five *DS9* episodes set in the mirror universe first established in *TOS*. "Crossover," a Kira episode to say the least, might be the best of the bunch, with the cast, much like Shatner, Nimoy, and company before them, having a blast with their new roles. The fun spills into the episode, and the result is simultaneously an homage to the past and a foundation for the future.

Inside the new framework, director David Livingston creates a fresh look, with dark and brooding sets that are shot at new angles to accent the alternate reality. But he deserves a special award for "best direction of an actor in a dual role," as no other *Star Trek* episode doubles up a character so believably. It's easy to watch the episode and believe there were two Nana Visitors on set, with Visitor and Visitor working wonderfully with each other. That said, I'm not sure what it says about the *Star Trek* writers when they figure that having two of the same man, such as Kirk & Kirk in "The Enemy Within" or Riker & Riker in "Second Chances," would create conflict, but two of the same woman would lead to one falling in love with the other.

The mirror universe would return in Season Three's "Through the Looking Glass."

Did you know? The writers wanted Worf to appear in this episode, but Michael Dorn was tied up with *TNG*'s finale episode.

"The Collaborator": B

With the pending election of Bajor's new religious leader, Kira investigates if Vedek Bareil is responsible for the death of dozens of Bajoran freedom fighters.

Air date: May 22, 1994
Teleplay by Gary Holland, Ira Steven Behr & Robert Hewitt Wolfe
Story by Gary Holland
Directed by Cliff Bole
TV rating: 6.6

"It doesn't make sense. Vedek Bareil's an honorable man. He wouldn't hide from the consequences of his actions by covering them up." —Kira

What "Sins of the Father" is to *TNG* and the Klingons, "The Collaborator" is to *DS9* and Bajor. Beginning deceptively simply, this Kira mystery episode unfolds like an installment of *20/20* as it adds layers of complexity, taking an idea that seems preposterous and turning it into a landmark moment in *DS9* history. A Bajoran political whodunnit, the story works because the writers set up the stakes in a way that's personal: personal to Kira, who is forced to uncover the naked truth regarding her lover, and personal to us, thanks to Philip Anglim (Bareil) and Louise Fletcher (Winn) making it impossible for the viewer not to form competing hopes and expectations for the eventual reveal.

Like some of the best *DS9* episodes ("Sacrifice of Angels," "In the Pale Moonlight"), "The Collaborator" can be enjoyed either as a standalone episode or as part of a larger tapestry that continues the Bajoran political story introduced in the Season One finale. Unfortunately, for whatever reason, when it first aired, not many people watched it at all.

Bareil and Winn return to Deep Space Nine in Season Three's "Life Support."

Did you know? The day after this episode first aired, *TNG* concluded its run with "All Good Things…"

56

"Tribunal": B

Chief O'Brien is arrested by the Cardassian military and forced to stand trial.

Air date: June 5, 1994
Written by Bill Dial
Directed by Avery Brooks
TV rating: 7.7

"This trial is to demonstrate the futility of behavior contrary to good order. Everyone will find it most uplifting." —Kovat

It's so easy to create drama in a courtroom setting, the idea has become a universal television trope. With *Star Trek*, the writers have the added advantage of amplifying the drama by moving the trial to an alien court where all the rules are different and more dramatic, as in *Star Trek VI: The Undiscovered Country*. "Tribunal," marking the directorial debut of Avery Brooks, attempts to mine this territory for all its worth, creating a story with excitement, mystery, and humor.

Taking its cue from a throwaway line in "The Maquis, Part II" in which Dukat implies that a guilty verdict is a foregone conclusion before any case on his planet even goes to trial, the writers flesh out an Orwellian culture and develop the idea of O'Brien and Odo sorting through a justice system where the procedures are all out of order. The concept is played for both tears and laughs, and as an Odo episode, it's fabulous, with great interplay between Auberjonois, Fritz Weaver, and Caroline Lagerfelt as advisor, defender, and judge. Meanwhile, Meaney performs his part so well, it leads to many more "torture O'Brien" episodes in future seasons.

Unfortunately, there's a B story with Sisko and his station-mates that's not so good. The writers give them the task of figuring out what really happened in the past in an attempt to prove O'Brien's innocence. Featuring Avery Brooks directing himself, it plays out too quickly, tying into the A story with an overly-dramatic scene showing how easy it is to fly to Cardassia, land, and interrupt one their trials without any warning while dodging all the tough questions the story presents. Fortunately, future *DS9* episodes of the sort would cross the finish line in better fashion.

Did you know? Having graduated from Rutgers University with a Master of Fine Arts in both acting and directing, Avery Brooks was well prepared for his increased duties in this episode. "I had a double major," he says, "so it was just a matter of time before I made the turn."

"The Jem'Hadar": C

On a camping trip in the Gamma Quadrant, Sisko, Jake, Nog, and Quark encounter the ruthless soldiers of the Dominion, the Jem'Hadar. (Season finale)

Air date: June 12, 1994
Written by Ira Steven Behr
Directed by Kim Friedman
TV rating: 7.7

"No one ever escapes from the Jem'Hadar." —Eris

Beginning as a lighthearted Sisko, Quark, and sons camping trip, Season Two's finale takes a left turn, becoming reminiscent of *TOS's* "The Empath," to plant the seeds of a Dominion trio that will become so important in the future. As a piece of *DS9* history, the episode is a successful beginning to greater events. As an episode itself, however, it's a hodgepodge of average. Brooks and Shimerman are amusing, but Molly Hagan as our first Vorta is a disaster. Cirroc Lofton and Aron Eisenberg continue their good work as Jake and Nog, proving themselves capable of carrying a comic relief B story, but their rescue mission gone wrong is somewhat mundane. The Jem'Hadar themselves make a memorable debut, although this is more because of the visual effects than the performances of the actors. Fortunately, the episode's highlights—a face for the Gamma Quadrant and an unstoppable foe—would be expanded upon in the future while its lowlights—the Vortas' strange abilities and Molly Hagan—would be dropped, ensuring the Dominion thread would become only more interesting with time.

"The Jem'Hadar" was nominated for an Emmy for visual effects.

Did you know? The four-foot Enterprise-D model, manufactured for *TNG's* Season Three in 1989, makes an appearance in the episode as the U.S.S. Odyssey.

58

The Second Season in Review

Talk about going out with a bang! A few weeks after *TNG* went off the air for good, *DS9* aired its own season finale with a climax featuring the destruction of a ship that looks suspiciously like the Enterprise-D. As Jim Kirk might say, "Message, Spock?"

There's no doubt that when the first two seasons of *DS9* aired, the series was in the shadow of *TNG*, which still today remains the most popular of the *Star Trek* shows. But while *DS9* was preparing for Season Two, the news finally became official: *TNG*, like a sibling going off to college, was moving onto feature films while a new series, *VOY*, was about to be born. *DS9*, still in its infancy, was about to become a middle child. Happily, Season Two is nonetheless a year to be proud of, with the show making the most of its opportunities. With "The Maquis," *DS9* gives us an entertaining two-parter while fulfilling a request to help jumpstart *VOY*. Meanwhile, "Blood Oath" and "Crossover" borrow nostalgic elements from *TOS*, pleasing most longtime Trekkers. And throughout the season, *DS9* also builds a foundation for its own future, peppering in Dominion references before creating some faces for these Gamma Quadrant adversaries in the season finale.

Behind the scenes, producer Dan Curry replaces the departing Rob Legato in visual effects while Ira Steven Behr moves up the ladder, starting the season as "co-executive producer." Amidst the changes, Avery Brooks makes his *Star Trek* directorial debut with "Tribunal," before helming eight more episodes in the future. A second season also means more money for sets, and the show uses it to introduce a new medical lab and an expanded Promenade with additional turbolifts, doorways, and a wider walkway to finally allow two characters to walk side by side for "walk and talks."

All the while, the series steadily improves in preparation for becoming *Star Trek's* senior TV show: Jadzia's warmer, playful side comes to the fore, Bashir matures, and O'Brien steps into the role of the everyman dealing with a universe that often doesn't make any sense. The secondary characters begin to play an increasingly important part too, with Garak, Dukat, and Winn becoming almost as important as the regulars.

More importantly, *DS9* spends its second season finding its own style of *Star Trek* storytelling, experimenting with a semi-serial format while mixing in successful standalone episodes. "When we really started doing stories about our space station, and really made it unique to itself," Michael Piller later said, "that's when the series, I think, really became special." Standouts include "The Circle," "Necessary Evil," and "Whispers." And while there are also the occasional clunkers, such as "Melora" and "Rivals," there's no question this is a series gaining its footing. As Robert Hewitt Wolfe later said, "I think Season Two is where we found our stride. Any success we had in subsequent years was built on what we learned in the second season, with its successes and failures."

Season Three

Production Order
(with air date order in parentheses)

1. "The Search, Part I" (1st)
2. "The Search, Part II" (2nd)
3. "The House of Quark" (3rd)
4. "Equilibrium" (4th)
5. "Second Skin" (5th)
6. "The Abandoned" (6th)
7. "Civil Defense" (7th)
8. "Meridian" (8th)
9. "Defiant" (9th)
10. "Fascination" (10th)
11 "Past Tense, Part I" (11th)
12 "Past Tense, Part II" (12th)
13. "Life Support" (13th)
14. "Heart of Stone" (14th)
15. "Destiny" (15th)
16. "Prophet Motive" (16th)
17. "Visionary" (17th)
18. "Distant Voices" (18th)
19: "Improbable Cause" (20th)
20: "Through the Looking Glass" (19th)
21. "The Die is Cast" (21st)
22: "Explorers" (22nd)
23. "Family Business" (23rd)
24. "Shakaar" (24th)
25: "Facets" (25th)
26. "The Adversary" (26th)

The Third Season Cast

Commander Sisko: Avery Brooks
Major Kira: Nana Visitor
Odo: René Auberjonois
Chief O'Brien: Colm Meaney
Dax: Terry Farrell
Dr. Bashir: Siddig El Fadil
Jake Sisko: Cirroc Lofton
Quark: Armin Shimerman

Notable Guest Stars

Salome Jens
Kenneth Marshall
Andrew Robinson
Natalia Nogulich
Martha Hackett
Rosalind Chao
Mary Kay Adams
Max Grodénchik
Robert O'Reilly
Joseph Ruskin
Lawrence Pressman
Marc Alaimo
Brett Cullen
Jeffrey Combs
Jonathan Frakes
Philip Anglim
Frank Military
Dick Miller
Bill Smitrovich
Clint Howard
Louise Fletcher
Aron Eisenberg
Wallace Shawn
Paul Dooley
Tim Russ
Chase Masterson
Andrea Martin
Penny Johnson
Duncan Regehr
Lawrence Pressman

"The Search, Part I": C

In an attempt to head off a Jem'Hadar invasion, Sisko leads a diplomatic mission into hostile territory.

Air date: September 26, 1994
Teleplay by Ronald D. Moore
Story by Ira Steven Behr & Robert Hewitt Wolfe
Directed by Kim Friedman
TV rating: 9.3

"We have to convince them that the Federation does not represent a threat to them." —Sisko

Like the Season Two finale that precedes it, this unfocused season opener is about change, setting up the future of the series. Introducing a new ship and resolving Odo's mystery, it packs quite a punch for one hour. Unfortunately, many of the scenes, particularly early, come across as contrived and clumsy, with the invisible hand of the writers and director easily perceived moving the pieces around to get them into position for the future. (When the staff of the Grand Nagus is pulled out of storage just to provide motivation for Quark, you know the writers are reaching.)

The centerpiece of the episode, however, is the Defiant, a new vessel that has been developed to combat the threat of the Dominion and give the series a better way to travel and battle. It's a home run shot, injecting both the episode and the series as a whole with a tangible excitement every time it appears. (Unfortunately, the same can't be said for the Romulan officer that comes with it, but she won't last long.) As the episode approaches its climax, the drama only gets more intense, featuring a great Kira/Odo scene and an action packed conclusion.

Did you know? The Romulan officer is played by Martha Hackett. While the actor doesn't appear again on *DS9* after "The Search, Part II," director Kim Friedman brings her back to play Seska in *VOY's* "Parallax."

"The Search, Part II": B

Odo learns about his people while Sisko questions the price the Federation is willing to pay for peace with the Dominion.

Air date: October 3, 1994
Teleplay by Ira Steven Behr
Story by Ira Steven Behr & Robert Hewitt Wolfe
Directed by Jonathan Frakes
TV rating: 8.2

"I finally return home and they still treat me like an outsider." —Odo

Weaving together fantasy and reality within the fictional confines of the *Star Trek* universe, this episode of self-discovery is reminiscent of the 1980s *Twilight Zone* series, employing arguably the most creative use of the A/B story format in *Star Trek* history.

As an Odo episode, and a special one at that, it gives René Auberjonois the opportunity to move his story forward and add layers of depth to his shape-shifter's personality. Auberjonois and guest star Salome Jens, who stands out as a female Changeling, are extraordinary together, and their characters' chemistry reverberates throughout the remainder the series.

The Sisko station-story is equally compelling, with events continually spiraling out of control until the viewer exclaims, "How are they going to get out of this one?" The unpredictable answer might initially disappoint some viewers, with the conclusion, on the surface, coming across as deus ex machina, but with time to process the subtext, most fans gain a greater appreciation for the writing device Behr employs, with the answer to "What's on the other side of the hatch?" even more surprising than what ABC's *Lost* would come up with eleven years later.

Did you know? Before playing the female Changeling, Salome Jens previously appeared in similar make-up as an ancient humanoid in *TNG's* "The Chase," also directed by Jonathan Frakes.

"The House of Quark": B–

After taking credit for the accidental death of a Klingon in his bar, Quark is forced to marry the Klingon's widow and become the head of her house.

Air date: October 10, 1994
Teleplay by Ronald D. Moore
Story by Tom Benko
Directed by Les Landau
TV rating: 7.6

"The ceremony is complete. You are husband and wife." —Tumek

It's the old Steve Urkel gag again. Similar to Li Nalas becoming a hero by blind luck, Quark has his own "Did I do that?" moment, and it's used as a catalyst to trigger a humorous story with a bit of action, comedy, and heart—the typical Quark episode formula. This interesting take on Quark and the Klingon culture features guest star Mary Kay Adams as Grilka the widow and allows Robert O'Reilly to make his first *DS9* appearance as Gowron. Both actors are fabulous, but it's Armin Shimerman, bringing some more respectability to the Ferengi, who makes the whole thing work.

Meanwhile, a B story about Chief O'Brien trying to please his wife is short and forgettable, serving simply to move Keiko out of the picture to make room for more Chief O'Brien/Dr. Bashir scenes.

Grilka and her advisor, Tumek (played by *TOS* veteran Joseph Ruskin) return in Season Five for "Looking for par'Mach in All the Wrong Places."

Did you know? While wearing her Klingon make-up for "The House of Quark," Mary Kay Adams had an interesting experience. "At one point," Adams recalls, "we were taking a golf cart from one sound stage to another across a lot, and after a while I forgot I had all this stuff on my face and head. So I'm riding around on this golf cart, and people were passing, and I was waving. They were all looking at me strangely, and I wondered what the matter with them was. Suddenly I realized, 'Oh, of course, I'm a Klingon!'"

"Equilibrium": B–

Dax is plagued by disturbing hallucinations that allude to a hidden past.

Air date: October 17, 1994
Teleplay by René Echevarria
Story by Christopher Teague
Directed by Cliff Bole
TV rating: 7.4

"I don't need therapy, Julian. I need answers." —Dax

The *Star Trek* franchise, with over seven hundred television episodes, has drawn inspiration from a diverse palette of sources. "Equilibrium," however, is the only entry with a magic show as the root and catalyst for its story. Intrigued by the act of illusionist Jeff Magnus McBride, the *DS9* writing staff turned it into a story with McBride playing Joran, the most important character. While this might sound like a recipe for a flop—and it probably would have been, had the staff gone with their original idea of a traveling circus visiting the station—"Equilibrium" is a success because the magic act serves merely as a doorway to a darker, more interesting place with a surprising secret.

Picking up some threads from Season Two's "Playing God," the character-based episode features Dax, Sisko, and Bashir, with strong performances from Farrell, Brooks, and El Fadil, each of whom has become comfortable in their roles independently while collectively settling into in their relationships with each other. And with no money for location shooting, the script depends on them. The dream sequences and a visit to the Trill homeworld all take place on preexisting sets, with the homeworld's only appearance in *Star Trek* consisting of a matte painting, a redressed stage, and the cave set.

Eventually, we get a big reveal, and it works because it's not a tacked on conclusion or a throwaway resolution. It's a significant piece to the Trill puzzle that becomes incorporated into Dax's character and comes back into play in Season Three's "Facets" and Season Seven's "Field of Fire."

Did you know? Jeff McBride has opened for many famous acts, including Diana Ross, George Carlin, and Tina Turner.

"Second Skin": B

Kira is abducted and told she's really a Cardassian spy.

Air date: October 24, 1994
Written by Robert Hewitt Wolfe
Directed by Les Landau
TV rating: 7.8

"I don't know who you are or what you're trying to do, but it won't work. Whatever you think this is going to get you, you can forget it." —Kira

This Kira episode, with a hook reminiscent of *TNG's* "Face of the Enemy," spins its premise into a fun mystery with a satisfying payoff.

This time around, the plot is more of a mind game. For if "Face of the Enemy" is *Quantum Leap*, with Troi forced to play along with a ruse for the greater good, "Second Skin" is *Total Recall*, with Kira increasingly unsure of what's real and what's not. The major, much like the audience, disbelieves the whole premise of the episode from the start, but as the story unfolds, she must deal with the increasing amount of evidence indicating that she really is what she grew up hating while figuring out how to cope with her life being turned upside down. Nana Visitor's performance, taking Kira from angry and uncooperative to confused and broken, is one of her finest performances of the series, with "Second Skin" giving the actress her richest material since "Duet."

Meanwhile, Sisko and Garak get a B story about a trip to Cardassia. (This time, Sisko's trip to the planet isn't so easy!) Garak, of course, is always a delightful character. ("Ah, it was just something I overheard while hemming someone's trousers. I suggest we get away from here as quickly as possible.") But his pairing with Sisko is especially good, setting the stage for more great Sisko/Garak scenes to come, such as those in Season Six's "In the Pale Moonlight."

Unfortunately, if "Second Skin" does have a fault, it's that it's overly talky. Lawrence Pressman guest stars as Kira's Cardassian father, Ghemor, and while he's fine in the role, his character, like most Cardassians, sure likes to yap. Yet the episode still packs an emotional punch and is a fan favorite—leading to Ghemor's return in Season Five's "Ties of Blood and Water".

Did you know? To bring Ghemor to life, Lawrence Pressman turned to Nazi Germany for inspiration. "My original image of Ghemor was one of the old military elite in Germany who loathed Hitler," he says. "They were certainly willing to fight the war, but they were unwilling to fight according to Hitler's plans." For Pressman, who is Jewish and lost many relatives in the Holocaust, the acting decision seemed quite appropriate for *Star Trek*. "When I connect the loss of my father's family to a piece of the material, I think that's sort of a paradigm for what shows like these shows have done."

"The Abandoned": D

Odo attempts to raise an alien child found abandoned in the wreckage of a salvaged ship.

Air date: October 31, 1994
Written by D. Thomas Maio & Steve Warnek
Directed by Avery Brooks
TV rating: 8.0

"Odo, do you really think you can control him?" —Sisko

This Odo episode is the poor man's version of *TNG's* Season Two offering, "The Child," with a similar idea but without the heart. The real problem is that the writers want to keep viewers from forgetting about the Dominion, but they don't want to move the Dominion story forward—at least not yet. That leaves us with a difficult concept to pull off: a Dominion filler episode. It's something the show would do better in subsequent seasons, when the Dominion is better defined and offers more material. In the meantime, however, it's just awkward.

In fact, here it seems like director Avery Brooks and the writers are on different pages. Brooks lets the early scenes play out in a way that sets up "I Borg" (*TNG*) expectations. The writers, however, take it in a different direction, giving us a payoff that's something else altogether. (Perhaps the whole thing would play out better if the baby was a Vorta.)

Meanwhile, in a B story, Jake introduces his girlfriend to his father. Did I mention he's 16 and she's a 20-year-old casino woman who's built like an Orion slave girl? It's actually an interesting, if short, subplot with some great facial reactions from Jake and his father; although I do wonder if Commander Sisko (and the writers) would act the same way if we were talking about a 16-year-old daughter dating a 20-year-old man who seems to be falling out of his clothes. Still, I'm sure Cirroc Lofton and 16-year-old boys around the world are happy the writers decided to go with what they did, and many males probably appreciate the choice of actress—18-year-old Jill Sayre—although I can't help but wonder if Lofton hand-picked the actress himself. Regardless, it sure must have been interesting for Lofton and Sayre to shoot the "meet the Dad" scenes with "Dad" directing the whole thing! Unfortunately, it all distracts from the A story like a Dabo girl distracting us from a gambling game, which might be the point.

What's this episode about again? Oh yeah…overall, the episode isn't that good, even with Auberjonois trying his darnedest to make it so.

Did you know? This episode introduces Jake's literary talents, foreshadowing his future endeavors.

"Civil Defense": B

When O'Brien accidentally triggers a leftover anti-insurgency program, the station's computers believe that the crew is a rebelling mob attempting to seize the station and takes steps to contain them.

Air date: November 7, 1994
Written by Mike Krohn
Directed by Reza Badiyi
TV rating: 8.1

"It seems we've tripped some kind of automated security program the Cardassians left. We're locked in." —Sisko

This cute bottle episode is a derivative of *TNG's* "Disaster," which is a wise choice since the concept opens the door to both drama and comedy. The standstill plot, of course, is pure filler, but the circular story is delightful nonetheless, with the writers using the regulars well and even finding a way to work Dukat and Garak into the mix. In the A story, Kira, Dax, and Bashir are trapped in Ops before the Cardassians show up to steal the show. Meanwhile, in the B story, the two Siskos and O'Brien are trapped below. The C story includes the tried and true combination of Odo and Quark, although calling it a "story" is a bit of an exaggeration, since not much of note happens.

As the episode progresses, it's "out of the frying pan into the fire" with the action moving along swiftly at first before slowing down in the second half.

There are no great visual effects or breakout character moments, but the old "people are trapped in a room" story has worked on television since the medium was invented, and this is no exception. This kind of episode offers fans a chance to see familiar characters in unfamiliar situations, and pique the interest of causal TV viewers flipping through channels looking for something to watch, allowing the show to please old fans while making new ones. In fact, *VOY* would do its own version of "Civil Defense" with its penultimate Season Three episode, "Worst Case Scenario."

Did you notice? The belt Odo wears for the first six episodes of Season Three disappears in "Civil Defense." René Auberjonois originally requested the belt because he liked the one that went with his mirror universe costume in "Crossover." However, by the time of this episode he decided his new belt looked too "*Buck Rogers*-y" and asked for it to be removed from Odo's wardrobe.

69

"Meridian": C–

Jadzia falls in love with a scientist from a planet that shifts between her universe and a plane of pure energy.

Air date: November 14, 1994
Teleplay by Mark Gehred-O'Connell
Story by Hilary Bader & Evan Carlos Somers
Directed by Jonathan Frakes
TV rating: 8.5

"What if I just hold onto you? After all, we're not going to be together again like this for a long time and I was just getting used to this." —Dax

Sure, in the real world some people consider mixed race relationships or same sex marriages to be awkward. In *Star Trek*, however, it takes a little bit more to be considered weird. If your boyfriend isn't from another plane of existence or another time/space continuum, you've got a pretty normal relationship. Unfortunately for Dax, her relationship in "Meridian" is complicated even by *Star Trek* standards. (And we're not even talking about her symbiotic make-up.) It turns out there's a reason why so many fathers tell their daughters to avoid boys from noncorporeal dimensions.

The episode's interesting and creative concept, based on the 1947 Broadway musical *Brigadoon*, is a precursor to Season Five's "Children of Time." But unlike that episode, the story within the concept doesn't work so well here. Terry Farrell and guest star Brett Cullen are both fine actors who give it their best, and there's some pretty location shooting at the Huntington Botanical Gardens in San Marino. But without enough time to build up a realistic, genuine relationship that actually makes the viewer care, there is no real drama—no matter what tricks director Jonathan Frakes tries to pull out of his hat. In fact, the romance gets sidetracked by technobabble, becoming more about the planet than the characters.

There's also a B story that's just a comedic runner to fill time: Quark tries to steal Kira's likeness for a holosuite program. It's not bad, although it's mostly notable for introducing *Star Trek* fans to guest star Jeffrey Combs, who would go on to play various aliens on *DS9*, *VOY*, and *ENT*.

Did you know? Before appearing on *DS9*, Jeffrey Combs auditioned for *TNG's* Commander Riker. While the actor didn't land the part, he did impress his competition, Frakes, who sought out Combs to play a part in "Meridian."

"Defiant": B

Riker arrives on Deep Space Nine and steals the station's new ship, the Defiant.

Air date: November 21, 1994
Written by Ronald D. Moore
Directed by Cliff Bole
TV rating: 9.3

"Taking the Defiant only raises the stakes. The Cardassians are going to send a fleet after you. They are going to kill more people hunting you down than they ever did during those border raids." —Kira

Back in the day, there was a lot of excitement about Commander Riker crossing over onto *DS9* just as the first *TNG* movie was debuting in theaters. Turns out, it's a swerve, though I won't spoil it here. While this seems like a letdown at first, the end result vindicates the choice.

"Defiant" is a chase episode with Riker and the titular ship as the prey and the Cardassians as the predators. The twist, inspired by the 1964 film *Fail-Safe*, is that Sisko joins the Cardassians in their war room to help catch his ship. This gives Avery Brooks a chance to shine and gives *us* a peek behind the curtain at Cardassian politics, with Marc Alaimo returning as Gul Dukat and Tricia O'Neil guest starring as Korinas of the Obsidian Order, Cardassia's primary military intelligence agency. The set for the war room is especially savvy, with a large viewscreen with graphics helping to tell the story in a way that's far less expensive than shots of ships interacting in space.

With all the components working together in concert, Ron Moore's script progresses in a way where the story just keeps getting more and more interesting with each act. The result is a military thriller nearly on par with *TOS's* "Balance of Terror" and *TNG's* "The Enemy." The story even plants the seeds for a Riker sequel, but for whatever reason the idea was blacklisted by the show's producers in their notes to the writers—which is perplexing, since Frakes and Nana Visitor have mad chemistry with each other. Rest assured, however, the fallout of this episode reverberates into the future, with "Improbable Cause" picking up a loose thread from "Defiant" later in the season and Commander Eddington filling the void left by Riker the following season in "For the Uniform."

As for "Defiant," fans looking for a great Commander Riker episode might be disappointed, but fans of Frakes won't be.

Did you know? The Cardassian viewscreen that appears in this episode is actually a miniature. Similar to how weathermen interact with a green screen, the actors appear in front of it through the use of blue screen compositing.

71

"Fascination": C

Lwaxana Troi visits the station to attend the Bajoran Gratitude Festival just as an outbreak of passion occurs throughout the station.

Air date: November 28, 1994
Teleplay by Philip LaZebnik
Story by Ira Stven Behr & James Crocker
Directed by Avery Brooks
TV rating: 8.2

"People are acting very strangely today." —Kira

Lwaxana Troi's second visit to Deep Space Nine gives the writers a chance to do *DS9's* version of *A Midsummer Night's Dream*, an ensemble piece that's a departure from the series' norm. In fact, the offbeat script opens the door for new costumes, new lighting, and new music, making this lighthearted comedy a one of a kind offering.

Director Avery Brooks follows Shakespeare's lead, allowing the story, such that there is, to develop before increasing the pace and the silliness as the episode approaches its conclusion. Along the way, Jake chases Kira, Kira chases Bareil, Bareil chases Dax, and Chief O'Brien and his wife engage in some petty bickering that, despite its futuristic sci-fi setting, seems more realistic than most relationships on TV set in the present.

In the end, like a sitcom, everything returns to normal and nothing of lasting consequence happens. But as a lighthearted placeholder between more serious episodes, "Fascination" adequately serves its purpose.

Majel Barrett returns to reprise Lwaxana Troi in Season Four's "The Muse." Philip Anglim returns to put a period on Vedek Bareil on the other side of "Past Tense."

Did you know? Looking back at this episode, Avery Brooks remarks, "I guess it was over the top. But what is over the top, after all? If you're having a pint of Guinness and you see the foam pouring over the top, you think, 'That's great!'"

"Past Tense, Part I": A–

A transporter accident sends Sisko and Bashir to the year 2024, where the two are placed in a ghetto for homeless people.

Air date: January 2, 1995
Teleplay by Robert Hewitt Wolfe
Story by Ira Steven Behr & Robert Hewitt Wolfe
Directed by Reza Badiyi
TV rating: 7.4

"By the time we get dinner, it'll be time for breakfast. You'd think that before they lock thousands of people into a twenty-square-block area, they'd give some thought to how those people are going to get fed." —Bashir

At its heart, *Star Trek* is an exploration of and commentary on the evolving social interaction of mankind. As individuals, we are essentially the same as our ancestors who lived hundreds or thousands of years ago, born with the same genetic make-up, feeling the same emotions, and sharing the same potential. As a society, however, we are ever learning and changing, going through horrid phases such as slavery and the Holocaust while other times rising above our bigotry to put social structures in place that protect people from selfishness and hate. With the nature of *Star Trek* being essentially a study of how we treat each other, the shows are at their best when its characters are facing the worst.

Instead of borrowing bad circumstances from history or creating an allegorical copy, "Past Tense" invents its own setting: a homeless prison in the 21st century. The genius of the idea is that it's such a natural extension of human history, fitting snugly into our social patterns, it feels like a real (and heartbreaking) future, that might come to pass. Like most bad ideas that become reality and unlike the fictional dystopian futures that don't, the scenario in this episode is grounded with good intentions. The homeless need a place to live. The rest of us would like to walk down the street without being bothered by them. So why not kill two birds with one stone and move them to a sanctuary district? Then again, the roots of the Holocaust are essentially the same.

Through a time travel accident, Sisko, Bashir, and Dax are tossed into this setting, their rank and technology rendered moot. The two men, who are indeed homeless, get the A story, giving us a look at life inside the Sanctuary. Sisko, the history buff, serves as our guide while Bashir becomes an audience surrogate, asking the right questions to learn the rules of the situation and the basics of what's going on. Meanwhile, Dax, despite being an illegal alien, avoids the same fate, getting the B story with a wealthy man who takes a liking to her. This gives us a set of eyes outside the Sanctuary, allowing us to see from the perspective of those on the other side of its walls. O'Brien and Kira, still in their own time period, get the C story, as they try to figure out what happened to Sisko and company and what to do about it.

Overseen by the Iranian-born Reza Badiyi, "Part I" proceeds quietly for the most part while featuring location shooting at Paramount's New York Street backlot with a large number of extras. This style is enhanced by the absence of music, with only a few minutes of audible score in the entire episode. As the story unfolds, the premise plays on the existing stigma attached to being homeless; that it's the result of being stupid or immoral. To see Sisko and Bashir, the furthest thing from, dealing with this prejudice provides an insightful exploration into the social patterns of our present and provides us, through their interactions with the people of our near-future, with a mirror to look upon ourselves. And as the episode comes to its conclusion, Sisko makes a decision that's a watershed moment for the character and the series.

Did you know? While the cast and crew were shooting this episode, an article in the *Los Angeles Times* caught their attention:

Homeless Camp Weighed in L.A. Industrial Area
October 14, 1994

Determined to make Downtown Los Angeles friendlier to business, the Riordan Administration has launched a plan to shuttle homeless people to an urban campground on a fenced lot in the city's core industrial area.

The mayor's proposal, which has come under heated attack by some homeless advocates, calls for turning a vacant city block in the eastern part of Downtown into a homeless drop-in center, where up to 800 people could take showers and sleep on a lawn.

"If we're just looking to get people off the streets so we don't have to look at them, then that's what the city's proposing—an Orwellian poorhouse," said Alice Callaghan, director of Las Familias del Pueblo, a Skid Row social service center. "Building a large fence or a stadium is nothing but a prison."

"Past Tense, Part II": A

To restore the timeline, Sisko must pose as a hero from Earth's history.

Air date: January 9, 1995
Teleplay by Ira Steven Behr & René Echevarria
Story by Ira Steven Behr & Robert Hewitt Wolfe
Directed by Jonathan Frakes
TV rating: 8.0

"You want to make demands, I'll give you some demands. We tell them if they want the hostages back, they've got to shut down the Sanctuaries." —Sisko

For "Part II," Reza Badiyi passes the director's torch to Jonathan Frakes, and the setting shifts from outside to inside. If "Part I" is "The City on the Edge of Forever," "Part II" is *Die Hard* from Hans Gruber's point of view. And yet the two halves go together surprisingly well.

Sisko and Bashir again take center stage, sharing the A story with several of the characters previously introduced. Foremost of these is Biddie "B.C." Coleridge, the unstable instigator of the events, played by Frank Military. The performance is either brilliant or annoying, depending on your viewpoint. (In truth, it's probably a little of both.) In contradistinction to this is Webb, the "guy next door," played by Bill Smitrovich. Giving this character just the right blend of honesty and intelligence, Smitrovich makes him one of the most realistic and likeable characters to ever grace a *Star Trek* series. Veteran character actor Dick Miller, playing a security guard who doesn't know when to sit still, helps round out the ensemble, and the nature of the plot allows us to get to know all of them better, enhancing the drama of the situation and the power of the climax.

Meanwhile, Dax again gets the B story, although this time it's brief, written with the sole purpose of opening a door for the A story and padded out with a guest appearance by Clint Howard as a mentally-ill homeless man, marking Howard's first *Star Trek* appearance since playing a youthful-looking Balok in *TOS's* "The Corbomite Maneuver."

The C story, with time chasers O'Brien and Kira, is a blatant but funny comedic runner that's a bit of filler itself.

In the end, however, the joy of "Past Tense" is seeing our future and *Star Trek's* past collide, an idea that is elaborated on in the sixth *Star Trek* series, *ENT*. The greater meaning of the episode, however, lies in a timeless truth: that how we treat each other matters, and how we do so will shape our future.

Did you know? Frank Military went on to serve as a producer for several different shows, including *Jericho* and *NCIS*.

"Life Support": D

After a serious accident, Vedek Bareil struggles to help Kai Winn conclude a peace treaty with Cardassia.

Air date: January 30, 1995
Teleplay by Ronald D. Moore
Story by Christian Ford & Roger Soffer
Directed by Reza Badiyi
TV rating: 8.2

"You were able to replace some of his internal organs with artificial implants. Could you do something similar with the damaged parts of his brain?" —Winn

As proven by Darth Vader, the idea of gradually replacing parts of a man until he's no longer the original man is an interesting story idea. But it doesn't quite work here, being shoehorned into the ongoing Bajoran political thread last seen in Season Two's "The Collaborator." The real problem is that the essence of the story is overwhelmed by Kai Winn and the Treaty of MacGuffin, with Kira's reaction to Bareil's health mostly buried in the script. To make matters worse, a lighthearted Jake and Nog B story is thrown in as filler—the two get into a fight over girls. Neither story is particularly strong on its own, but together they're all the worse for having opposite tones.

In the end, "Life Support" feels like a filler episode with a serious consequence—an awkward dichotomy and rare misfire from teleplay writer Ron Moore.

DS9 continues to build the Bajoran political intrigue later in the season with "Shakaar."

Did you know? Shortly before this episode first aired, *VOY* made its debut, launching The United Paramount Network on January 16, 1995. *DS9* and *VOY* would continue to run concurrently for four and a half years.

"Heart of Stone": C

Trapped on a moon, Kira is caught in an expanding crystal formation that threatens to engulf her if Odo cannot set her free.

Air date: February 6, 1995
Written by Ira Steven Behr & Robert Hewitt Wolfe
Directed by Alexander Singer
TV rating: 8.3

"Your foot's been encased in some kind of crystal. And from the look of things the crystal is spreading." —Odo

The premise here is a sci-fi stand-in based on an idea from the film *Sometimes a Great Notion*, where a character gets his foot caught under a log in a river with the water on the rise. Another variation of the same idea is somebody getting his foot trapped in a railway track, with a train scheduled to arrive later in the day. In each instance, the idea works on a basic dramatic level because it puts life and death on the line with a countdown to doom. Ironically, the earth-bound ideas work better than the sci-fi equivalent because we can better identify and empathize with water and train accidents, giving them a more vicarious horror. But for this budget saving episode of *DS9*, the story had to be shot in a studio, and so an expanding man-eating crystal formation is used, because it can fit inside the cave set, even if it looks hokey. This sort of story, much like an elevator episode, opens the door for rich character interplay, and that's the whole point here. It's an Odo episode designed to get his feelings out in the open before the story earns its Shakespearean inspired title with its unexpected climax. (To fully understand it, viewers will have to have watched the first two episodes of the season first.)

Surprisingly, the episode is just as noteworthy for its B story, which begins as comedic filler but turns into something more. In a turning point for the character, Nog develops an interest in Starfleet. Aron Eisenberg, clearly excited about Nog's new ambition, embraces the part, and his enthusiasm makes it hard not to root for the character. With Avery Brooks's help, he turns what could have been a forgettable subplot into something more substantial for the writers to build on.

Did you know? This is the first episode in which Odo uses a weapon.

"Destiny": B–

An ancient Bajoran prophecy complicates an attempt to establish a permanent communications link through the wormhole.

Air date: February 13, 1995
Written by David S. Cohen & Martin A. Winer
Directed by Les Landau
TV rating: 8.1

"I am here with a warning from the Prophets. They don't want you to let the Cardassians come aboard the station. If you do, you will bring destruction on us all." —Yarka

Prophecies of doom have been popular throughout the history of man because they come prepackaged with the perfect elements for drama: there's a warning, a ticking clock, and the question of its legitimacy. For fiction writers, prophecies are particularly irresistible because there's total control. They can manipulate the story however they want and control how it all turns out.

This episode has fun with a Nostradamus-like prophecy that's never actually said in full and subtly changes throughout the episode. It's hinted that the prophecy comes from the wormhole aliens, which is a creative use of their previously established nature of existing outside of linear time. (It's also nice to see Sisko's "Emissary" status worked into the narrative of the story instead of simply being a title.)

As the plot unfolds, the writers avoid the predictable traps for stories of this type, such as having everyone disbelieve an old prophetic warning because they think the superstition is silly, only to have it come true in the end, or having the protagonist do everything he can to stop a prophecy from happening, which only makes it come true. The problem in either case is that we know the writer is pulling the strings and directing the story, and that negates any meaning or message from it all. The drama in "Destiny" doesn't really revolve around the outcome but instead how our characters react to it.

Interestingly, the writers cut Kai Winn a break by choosing another to be the antagonist, adequately played by Erick Avari. Louise Fletcher would be better, especially if Winn were to have an ulterior motive, and her character would need no introduction or back-story development. On the other hand, it's probably better to protect the character from being overused and overexposed.

The episode also includes a tacked-on B story for Chief O'Brien. He and a Cardassian scientist have to deal with their cultural differences. This doesn't actually go anywhere, but it's cute for what it is.

Did you know? A TV executive once told writer David S. Cohen that a friend considered "Destiny" his favorite episode of the series. "Go figure," Cohen said. "Hell, it's not even my favorite episode."

"Prophet Motive": C–

Quark and Rom are shocked when Grand Nagus Zek rewrites the Rules of Acquisition to create a kinder, gentler Ferengi culture.

Air date: February 20, 1995
Written by Ira Steven Behr & Robert Hewitt Wolfe
Directed by René Auberjonois
TV rating: 7.5

"There's something terribly wrong with the Nagus, and we have to help him before he gets us all killed." —Quark

This lightweight Ferengi comedy episode might sound like another vehicle for Wallace Shawn to showcase his talents as Grand Nagus Zek, but it's really a Quark/Rom episode. Their reactions to Zek's new fun-loving philanthropist attitude drive the story, presented by freshman director René Auberjonois. Unfortunately, the plot is uninspiring and predictable, and even with Armin Shimerman and Max Grodénchik doing everything they can to elevate the material, there's not much of significance to make it worthwhile.

Meanwhile, the B story, which is so insubstantial it feels like a C story, is about Bashir dealing with a nomination for an award he thinks he can't win. It's supposed to be an allegory for *TNG's* 1994 Emmy nomination for Outstanding Drama, with the cast and crew trying not to get their hopes up after the nomination was announced. Most viewers won't see the point of it, but the subplot is inoffensive, harmless, and forgettable—much like the episode as a whole.

Grand Nagus Zek returns in Season Five for "Ferengi Love Songs," with Auberjonois again serving as his director.

Did you know? The only *Star Trek* show to ever win an Emmy for Best Series is *Star Trek: The Animated Series*, which won it in 1975.

"Visionary": B

Following an accident, O'Brien begins shifting back and forth in time.

Air date: February 27, 1995
Teleplay by John Shirley
Story by Ethan H. Calk
Directed by Reza Badiyi
TV rating: 7.9

"Well, who am I to argue with me?" —O'Brien

With its Klingons and Romulans, time travel and technobabble, "Visionary" plays like a *TNG* episode, even featuring *TNG* vet Chief O'Brien. But as a *DS9* offering, it's a nice departure for the series and an improvement over *TNG's* similar Season Two episode "Timed Squared."

Embracing *VOY's* theory of time behaving irrationally ("Parallax"), the writers eschew explanations and opt for a tongue in cheek approach to paradoxes, allowing them to have fun with the premise and up the ante with each of O'Brien's time jumps. (In fact, "Visionary" features the only look at Deep Space Nine's destruction we'll ever see.) Yet, like *Back to the Future*, the script and direction keep things crystal clear so we never get confused over plot points, with a dense story that gives just about everyone a moment to shine, almost turning it into an ensemble episode.

Perhaps most interesting and bold of all, the writers throw us a curve with an ending that still has *Trek* fans debating its meaning —although in a practical sense, it really doesn't matter. Regardless, "Visionary" is one of *DS9's* more unique and memorable episodes.

Did you know? A tool Bashir uses to adjust an armband worn by O'Brien is actually a modified warp nacelle from a Romulan Warbird model.

"Distant Voices": C–

When Bashir is knocked unconscious, he travels through his own mind and is helped by different aspects of his personality, each represented by a different member of the crew.

Air date: April 10, 1995
Teleplay by Ira Steven Behr & Robert Hewitt Wolfe
Story by Joe Menosky
Directed by Alexander Singer
TV rating: 7.1

"I haven't picked any of you. I'm in a coma!" —Bashir

Comfortable in its role as a budget saving bottle episode, this Bashir episode doesn't even try to disguise its nature, tipping its hand early before playing out just as you'd expect. It's a "nightmare story," which, like an episode of the 1990s TV show *Herman's Head*, includes the *DS9's* regulars—and Garak—inside Bashir's head as parts of his personality.

Being more of a concept than a story, "Distant Voices" is dependent on Siddig El Fadil and director Alexander Singer to carry it. Both are nearly up to the task, with Fadil turning in an impressive performance as an aging man—doing a heck of a lot better job than Clayton Rohner's reverse role in *TNG's* Season One episode "Too Short a Season" —and Singer keeping things moving swiftly enough to keep the episode from becoming dull.

Interestingly, with the tease of Garak's holosuite program (which is never actually seen) the episode almost backs into a *Total Recall*-like story, where we're not certain where Bashir's reality ends and the fictional story picks up. Had the writer pursued this idea, "Distant Voices" might have made for one of the more memorable episodes of the season. However, the writers set the idea of the holosuite program aside, never connecting to the main narrative, leaving us with a simpler episode instead.

"Distant Voices" went on to win an Emmy for Bashir's make-up. Its plot device would return again in just a few episodes, with "Facets" finding a more creative way to pull it off.

Did you know? In the Season One episode "Q-Less," Bashir mentions that he mixed up a preganglionic fiber and a postganglionic nerve on his Starfleet exams, a mistake that cost him his position as valedictorian in his medical class. After writer Robert Hewitt Wolfe's wife, Celeste, who studied biology as a preveterinarian, groused about the fact that the two nerves look nothing alike, Wolfe took the opportunity to lampshade the mistake in "Distant Voices" by having a character echo her thoughts. Later, for Season Five's "Doctor Bashir, I Presume," Ron Moore expands upon the thread and works it into the narrative, finally putting the issue to rest.

"Through the Looking Glass": C

Sisko is taken to the mirror universe, where he must persuade the alternate version of his deceased wife to join the human rebels.

Air date: April 17, 1995
Written by Ira Steven Behr & Robert Hewitt Wolfe
Directed by Winrich Kolbe
TV rating: 6.9

"I think you'll find that random and unprovoked executions will keep your work force alert and motivated." —Intendant Kira

In this sequel to Season Two's "Crossover," *DS9* brings back the mirror universe and forever changes how it's used. Instead of being foremost a vehicle to allow some of the regulars to play against type, it's turned instead into a playground for the characters from our universe to frolic in.

"Through the Looking Glass" is a swashbuckling adventure that sees Sisko lead a band of rebels against an evil empire on the cusp of finishing a weapon that will crush the rebellion once and for all. If this sounds suspiciously like another franchise, don't worry: the show is sure to present it all with lots of talk and an extraneous Tuvok cameo to ensure that people know they're watching *Star Trek*. However, there's still more action than the usual *DS9* episode, including an *Empire Strikes Back*-esque climax with ray guns blasting back and forth.

Avery Brooks is excellent as a talker and a fighter, playing Sisko as emotionally affected by the reunion with his late wife but simultaneously dedicated to completing his mission—even if it means firing phasers with both hands. (He needn't worry. The broadly played villains can't hit the broadside of a barn.)

The mirror universe returns in Season Four's "Shattered Mirror."

Did you know? *Through the Looking-Glass, and What Alice Found There* is Lewis Carroll's 1871 sequel to *Alice's Adventures in Wonderland* (1865). It's most famous for introducing Tweedledee and Tweedledum.

"Improbable Cause" (1): B+

After a bomb destroys Garak's tailor-shop, Odo uncovers a tangled web of deceit.

Air date: April 24, 1995
Teleplay by René Echevarria
Story by Robert Lederman & David R. Long
Directed by Avery Brooks
TV rating: 6.9

"I've had enough of your dissembling, Garak! I am not Dr. Bashir, and we are not sparring amiably over lunch!" —Odo

Picking up loose threads from "The Wire" and "Defiant" and combining them, this Odo/Garak mystery episode begins with a literal explosion and becomes more intriguing with each successive scene, weaving in startling revelations throughout the story. It even tosses in an "informant" scene that seems to have been lifted right out of *The X-Files*.

Combining a character-driven plot with some intermittent fireworks, the episode's master stroke is its pairing of the station's inquisitive constable with its secretive tailor. With Odo specializing in uncovering the truth and Garak specializing in dancing around it, the dialogue between the two is always witty and exciting, with the two actors clearly enjoying their verbose characters' elaborate wordplay. Meanwhile, their relationship anchors a bigger story that develops around it, with much going on off-screen, helping a small-scale episode masquerade as a larger-scale event.

As director Avery Brooks builds the suspense and works his way to the climax, it's only natural to ask, "How will they get out of this one?" Interestingly, this was a question that initially stumped the writers, too.

"Improbable Cause" was nominated for an Emmy for hairstyling.

Did you know? Unable to come up with a satisfying ending to this episode, the writers opted to expand the story into a two-parter.

83

"The Die Is Cast" (2): A–

Garak interrogates Odo on the eve of a joint Romulan-Cardassian attack on the Dominion.

Air date: May 1, 1995
Written by Ronald D. Moore
Directed by David Livingston
TV rating: 7.0

"Odo, talk to me! Tell me something, anything. Lie if you have to but just say it, please!" —Garak

Named after a quote attributed to Julius Caesar that means that events have been set in motion that cannot be undone, this conclusion to "Improbable Cause" flips the script by having Garak be the authority figure while Odo hides the truth. Meanwhile, everything else seems backward as well, with an evil, large scale invasion fleet threatening mankind's enemies while Sisko and his station-mates become renegades, violating the orders of Starfleet command. Yet the balance between the personal, character-driven moments and the epic action is especially well handled by director David Livingston and sets the stage for more of the same in the future.

Along with great performances from the usual ensemble, guest stars Leland Orser (Colonel Lovok) and Kenneth Marshall (Eddington) develop their characters especially well, giving the A and B stories their added dimensions while giving birth to the question, "Is Eddington a Changeling?"

Did you know? The writers thought about calling this "Improbable Cause, Part II" but felt the title wasn't actually applicable to the episode itself. Thus, "Improbable Cause" and "The Die is Cast" make up *Star Trek's* first two-parter with two separate titles.

"Explorers": B

Sisko pilots a replica of an eight-hundred-year-old Bajoran solar ship to prove that Bajoran explorers could have made it to Cardassia without developing warp drive.

Air date: May 8, 1995
Teleplay by René Echevarria
Story by Hilary J. Bader
Directed by Cliff Bole
TV rating: 6.7

"It's almost like being on the deck of an old sailing ship, except the stars are not just up in the sky; they're all around us." —Sisko

Like "Heart of Stone," this episode features a sci-fi stand-in for an older, more earth-bound concept. In fact, the idea is so on the nose, it's more of a metaphor than an allegory. In 1947, Norwegian explorer Thor Heyerdahl, who believed the original inhabitants of Easter Island were migrants from Peru, sailed over 4000 miles across the Pacific in a primitive raft to prove that South Americans could have reached the Polynesian islands. Beyond this specific trip, the idea of early man using his ingenuity to cross oceans fascinates many people and is a natural parallel to space exploration, which is why it translates so easily into a *Star Trek* episode.

"Explorers" itself is almost a bottle episode that uses its premise to deliver a calm, lighthearted character-driven plot that features the two Siskos bonding on a father/son trip while giving us two striking visuals. The first is Commander Sisko's new beard, which is obviously fake, but has a Riker-like coolness nonetheless. The second is his solar ship, one of *Star Trek's* most memorable and gorgeous designs both inside and out, But the true joy of the episode lies in its execution: Avery Brooks and Cirroc Lofton have chemistry together and always give convincing and interesting performances as father and son, developing their characters and moving their relationship forward each time they're together, and the writers wisely put the episode's emphasis on the two actors while avoiding a false sense of peril for the sake of drama.

Balancing out the man versus nature A story is a more internal struggle in the B story. The arrival of the one person who outdid Bashir at Starfleet Medical Academy causes the doctor to question whether he's second best. The story is appropriately short and sweet, but the presentation itself transcends the material, and it even finds the time to work in a discussion about the advantages of sitting still over always having to be on the move. (Take that, *TNG* and *VOY!*)

Did you know? When the Europeans discovered America and the Polynesian islands, they noted something interesting. Natives in both places grew sweet potatoes. In fact, some Polynesians even called this vegetable "kuumala," which resembles "kumara," and "cumal," two of its names used in the western part of South America. Most anthropologists believe the sweet potato originated in South America before somehow making its way across the Pacific. But how did the vegetable make the 5,000-mile journey? Did its seeds hitch a ride on seaweed or somehow get lodged in the wing of a wayward bird? Perhaps some Polynesians made a journey to South America before returning home. Or perhaps somebody from South America made the same trip as Thor Heyerdahl.

Thor Heyerdahl (photo courtesy of the National Archives of Norway)

"Family Business": B–

Quark and Rom discover that their mother, Ishka, has illegally made a profit through a secret deal.

Air date: May 15, 1995
Written by Ira Steven Behr & Robert Hewitt Wolfe
Directed by René Auberjonois
TV rating: 6.9

"If you ask me, this society could use a little chaos." —Ishka

This is sort of a remake of Season Two's "Rules of Acquisition," but with a better script and a better performance from the lead guest star. Taking place largely on Ferenginar in its *Star Trek* debut, this women's liberation story is an improvement because the issue is more personal to Quark and explored in greater depth.

Like the best Ferengi episodes, the script simultaneously celebrates the culture (likely the only one where sons are uncomfortable with their mothers wearing clothes) and pokes fun at it ("That will be three slips of gold-pressed latinum for the use of the chair") while never letting the overall story get lost in the shuffle. Armin Shimerman and Max Grodénchik get the bulk of the scenes, and it's clear that by this point in the series the two know just how to work together and love doing it. They're joined by guest star Andrea Martin (Ishka), who finds her own lane and demonstrates that Mom loves each of her boys in different ways and knows just how to handle them. Sadly, there's no appearance from Wallace Shawn as Grand Nagus Zek, but this opens the door for Liquidator Brunt, the first of three recurring *Star Trek* characters played by the fantastic Jeffrey Combs. Director René Auberjonois pulls all the performances together so well, the dialogue carries the show, and most viewers won't even notice that the entire episode includes only about six minutes of music.

Meanwhile, a B story includes a mini sequel to the previous episode, following up on Sisko's promise to meet a pretty freighter captain. There's not much to it and what's there resembles the first half of *TNG's* "Lessons," but it's a nice building block for the future of the show.

All that said, "Family Business" doesn't stand out from the crowd. There are better Ferengi episodes, and nothing happens here that's too important or memorable.

Did you know? Armin Shimerman used to invite Max Grodénchik over to his house to rehearse scenes for upcoming episodes and decide how they were going to interact before having to rehearse with the cast and crew at large.

"Shakaar": C

Kira tries to retrieve some farming equipment from the stubborn leader of her old resistance cell.

Air date: May 22, 1995
Written by Gordon Dawson
Directed by Jonathan West
TV rating: 7.1

"Next time I start getting nostalgic for the old days, shoot me." —Lupaza

DS9 wastes little time in replacing Bareil in this Kira political episode that introduces Shakaar, a Clint Eastwood-like war hero, as the new Bajoran heartthrob who's everything Kai Winn isn't. Duncan Regehr plays the titular character, and he's okay, but the story itself is a paint-by-numbers redress of "Progress" with a more personal connection for Kira. There's also a B story that's just a harmless runner about O'Brien being "in the zone" as a dart player.

"Shakaar" has its moments: Nana Visitor and Regehr are good together, Louise Fletcher steals some scenes as Kai Winn, and freshman composer Paul Baillargeon delivers a score that's a welcome change of pace from the series norm. But the A and B stories both end abruptly, and the conclusion is ultimately unsatisfying and forgettable.

Shakaar returns in Season Four's "Crossfire." Kira's other Resistance colleagues return in Season Five's "The Darkness and the Light."

Did you know? This episode includes rare interior location shooting. When cold weather forced director Jonathan West to cancel many of the exterior shots he had planned at Bronson Canyon, he used the extra time to shoot scenes intended for the cave set in the canyon's real caves. Later, the needed exterior shots were rewritten so they could be shot on stage sets.

"Facets": B–

Dax performs a Trill ritual in which she gets to meet each of her past hosts by transferring their memories into her friends.

Air date: June 12, 1995
Written by René Echevarria
Directed by Cliff Bole
TV rating: 5.9

"If you don't mind, I'd like to borrow your bodies for a few hours." —Dax

Beginning with a creative premise that gives just about everyone a new part to play, "Facets" picks up a thread from "Playing God"—an episode about Jadzia the mentor—and gives us the flip side of the coin—Jadzia the mentored.

Unfortunately, the first half is slow going, with Terry Farrell interacting with each of the other actors in one-on-one scenes while they define the past parts of Dax's existence. Truth be told, it would probably be better to have Dax transfer her past personalities into all of her station-mates at once, since it would be fun to see them all interact and allow the episode to get to its real point more quickly. Instead, we spend twenty minutes wondering just where this is going before the story meanders into an Odo/Curzon dilemma that allows René Auberjonois to summon his inner Jimmy Durante.

Meanwhile, there's a B story that follows up on the Nog/Starfleet thread begun in earlier in the season in "Heart of Stone," though for whatever reason, it simply rehashes the same story as last time in a different form.

Nonetheless, the Dax transference idea is a fun concept that could only be done on *DS9*, and the actors are game—especially Farrell. There's always a danger in these sort of episodes that they will become less about Jadzia and more about the Trill's eccentricities (such as Season One's "Dax") or that her spotlight will be stolen by other actors (such as Season Two's "Invasive Procedures"), but Echevarria keeps the character in the forefront and plays to Farrell's strengths, giving her an internal struggle to resolve even while Auberjonois attempts to steal the show.

Did you know? In this episode, Curzon orders a couple tranyas, a drink last seen in *TOS's* "The Corbomite Maneuver."

"The Adversary": B+

A Changeling manipulates the crew of the Defiant. (Season finale)

Air date: June 19, 1995
Written by Ira Steven Behr & Robert Hewitt Wolfe
Directed by Alexander Singer
TV rating: 7.1

"We have seven hours before we enter Tzenkethi space. I want that Changeling found before then." —Sisko

This ensemble episode begins as a mystery before turning into the old "runaway train with a monster on board" story. (Okay, so most train stories don't do the monster part.) Most of the episode takes place on the Defiant, the stand-in for the locomotive, and the monster aspect is an extension the season's opening two-parter. As the suspenseful story moves swiftly along, the intelligent plot challenges the viewer while still featuring plenty of action, introducing the Defiant's engineering set and expanding on the character of Lt. Commander Eddington (Kenneth Marshall) along the way.

And yet even as the episode develops into an effective paranoid thriller, there's something different about it all that sets it apart from most other *Star Trek* episodes—in a good way. Behr & Wolfe, the Lennon & McCartney team of *DS9*, know how to keep the audience on its guard, teasing a swerve around every corner, and the plot is well served by its unpredictable nature. The writers' true genius, however, is finding a way to serve up enough of a conclusion to satisfy most fans while also developing enough of an abstract cliffhanger to entice people to return for the next season.

DS9 returns to pick up the loose threads of the episode in Season Four's "Homefront" and "Paradise Lost."

Did you know? A scene where the senior officers take blood samples from each other to determine which one of them is the Changeling was inspired by *The Thing from Another World*, a 1951 horror film based on Joseph Campbell's 1938 novella *Who Goes There?*

The Third Season in Review

While it wouldn't be fair to say Season Three is *DS9's* response to viewer feedback, it does have just enough tweaks to morph the show into something more in line with the causal Trekker's wishes. The showpiece is the Defiant, beautifully designed inside and out, which allows the series to dispense with the claustrophobic runabout scenes and gives the writers the ability to move the cast around the galaxy with ease. The result is more searching, exploring, and—utopia be damned—fighting. Equally important and working hand in hand with the new ship, the Dominion threat asserts itself while simultaneously becoming intertwined with Odo and the future of the space station. This leads to Sisko, with his snazzy new beard, finally being promoted to Captain, joining Kirk, Picard, and Janeway in the exclusive club, and all comes together to make *DS9* seem more *Star Trekish*. At the same time, because of the complexity of the Dominion's make-up and the rich story possibilities it presents, the nature of the series continues to move toward a more serial format, though rich episodic adventures continue as well.

It's all overseen by Ira Steven Behr, now an executive producer, taking over as *DS9's* showrunner to allow Rick Berman and Michael Piller to concentrate on *VOY*. Behr himself benefits from inheriting several key members from the defunct *TNG* series. Ron Moore and René Echevarria arrive to help strengthen the writing staff with their proven talent while Jonathan West, for the second time in his career, takes over as director of photography from Marvin Rush. West's style is similar to Rush's with one exception: West likes to keep the backgrounds in greater focus. But his contributions to the series go beyond photography: after directing one episode of *TNG* ("Firstborn"), he makes his directorial debut for *DS9* in Season Three's "Shakaar."

Meanwhile, several other familiar faces help direct as well. Avery Brooks and Jonathan Frakes helm three episodes each, while Auberjonois makes his directorial debut in "Prophet Motive" before following up with "Family Business."

In front of the camera, a special guest appearance by Frakes gives the series a temporary ratings boost while Auberjonois is given plenty to do as well, with meaty parts in "The Search," "The Abandoned," "Heart of Stone," "Improbable Cause," "The Die is Cast," and the "Adversary" Fortunately, the writers find a way to give at least one good episode to each of the other regular cast members as well, though it's clear at this point who their favorite is!

At the same time, the rich palette of background characters continues to be developed, with side characters like Garak and Nog becoming more integral to the series as a whole. Meanwhile, the series introduces Lieutenant Commander Eddington, Kasidy Yates, Leeta, and Shakaar—all of whom would play greater parts later.

Unfortunately, while Season Three would earn *DS9* another Emmy, with "Distant Voices" winning for make-up, getting new viewers to give the show a chance would continue to be a struggle. Yet like *TNG* before it, *DS9* gives *Star*

91

Trek fans an impressive Season Three that is simultaneously entertaining in its own right while also pointing the series in a fruitful direction. Clunkers are virtually non-existent, and episodes such as "Second Skin," "Past Tense," "Improbable Cause/The Die is Cast," and "The Adversary" are now considered classics.

Season Four

Production Order
(with air date order in parentheses)

1. "The Way of the Warrior" (1st)
2. "Hippocratic Oath" (3rd)
3. "The Visitor" (2nd)
4. "Indiscretion" (4th)
5. "Rejoined" (5th)
6. "Little Green Men" (7th)
7. "Starship Down" (6th)
8. "The Sword of Kahless" (8th)
9. "Our Man Bashir" (9th)
10. "Homefront" (10th)
11 "Paradise Lost" (11th)
12 "Crossfire" (12th)
13. "Return to Grace" (13th)
14. "Sons of Mogh" (14th)
15. "Bar Association" (15th)
16. "Accession" (16th)
17. "Rules of Engagement" (17th)
18. "Hard Time" (18th)
19: "Shattered Mirror" (19th)
20: "The Muse" (20th)
21. "For the Cause" (21st)
22: "The Quickening" (23rd)
23. "To the Death" (22nd)
24. "Body Parts" (24th)
25: "Broken Link" (25th)

The Fourth Season Cast

Captain Sisko: Avery Brooks
Major Kira: Nana Visitor
Odo: René Auberjonois
Chief O'Brien: Colm Meaney
Dax: Terry Farrell
Dr. Bashir: Alexander Siddig
Jake Sisko: Cirroc Lofton
Quark: Armin Shimerman
Worf: Michael Dorn

Notable Guest Stars

Marc Alaimo
Robert O'Reilly
Andrew Robinson
J.G. Hertzler
Penny Johnson
Tony Todd
Aron Eisenberg
Roy Brocksmith
Kenneth Marshall
James Cromwell
Max Grodénchik
John Colicos
Robert Foxworth
Susan Gibney
Brock Peters
Duncan Regehr
Casey Biggs
Jeffrey Combs
Chase Masterson
Rosalind Chao
Camille Saviola
Richard Libertini
Ron Canada
Craig Wasson
Majel Barrett
Michael Ansara
Salome Jens

"The Way of the Warrior": B+

When a Klingon fleet arrives on Deep Space Nine, Sisko recruits Lieutenant Commander Worf to uncover the Klingons' true intentions.

Air date: October 2, 1995
Written by Ira Steven Behr & Robert Hewitt Wolfe
Directed by James L. Conway
TV rating: 8.5

"First, it was the Cardassians. Then it was the Dominion. Now it's the Klingons! How's a Ferengi supposed to make an honest living in a place like this?"
—Quark

With its new title sequence, new version of the theme song, and new storytelling direction, Season Four's two-hour premier serves as a rebirth for a series that was already gaining strength down the stretch in Season Three. More importantly, "The Way of the Warrior" brings together all the successful ingredients that would go on to define *DS9* for its fans and spins them into a fun, exciting story that just keeps getting more interesting as it moves along.

The first half begins without a strong central theme, and viewers can be forgiven if they spend twenty minutes wondering where the writers are going. It's essentially a mystery story, moving from one character to another without focus until shaping itself into a military thriller involving the Klingons. That opens the door for Worf to step in, and the beauty of his involvement is that he

95

doesn't overwhelm the rest of the characters but actually makes them more interesting. In fact, if this was to be a one-time appearance for Michael Dorn on *DS9*, it would be a justifiable choice because of how he augments the other actors, bringing out their best. "Warrior" isn't even a pure Worf episode but flips back and forth between Worf and Sisko as the focal character of the ever-changing A story.

The second half is more action packed, with several battle sequences and a sense that events are spinning out of control, reshaping the future of the series and *Star Trek* as a whole. Yet it also retains its focus on the characters and their choices, nicely tying in Worf's story here to Sisko's in the original pilot. With this dynamic and the rich guest star performances from old favorites, including Andrew Robinson (Garak), Marc Alaimo (Dukat), and Robert O'Reilly (Gowron), "The Way of the Warrior" takes what looks on paper like a ratings stunt and turns it into a natural continuation of the series and a must-see for any *Star Trek* fan.

The episode was nominated for an Emmy for Outstanding Cinematography.

Did you know? Originally running two hours, "The Way of the Warrior" was separated into two one-hour parts for subsequent airings. To make room for the second part's "Last time on *Deep Space Nine*..." and its opening credits, three scenes were cut:

• Dax and Kira in a holoprogram
• Bashir and O'Brien eating sand peas at Quark's
• Odo and Quark discussing Quark's intention to defend his bar and the discovery of the missing disruptor pistol

"The Visitor": A+

An elderly Jake Sisko recounts a freak accident which caused his father to become lost in time.

Air date: October 9, 1995
Written by Michael Taylor
Directed by David Livingston
TV rating: 6.9

"It begins many years ago. I was eighteen, and the worst thing that could happen to a young man happened to me. My father died." —Jake

"The Visitor" is to *DS9* what "The City on the Edge of Forever" is to *TOS* and "The Inner Light" is to *TNG*—that special episode with so much universal appeal that it outshines virtually everything else, including the more expensive and ambitious two-parters, with its simplistic beauty. It was the first *DS9* episode to be nominated for the Hugo Award for Best Dramatic Presentation, and it topped a 1996 *TV Guide* list ranking the best *Star Trek* episodes of all time.

A Ben/Jake Sisko story (polished by an uncredited René Echevarria), "The Visitor" is a "love through the ages" tale that eschews romance to instead explore the love between a father and a son. For those of us who grew up tossing around a ball with Dad in the backyard, it's especially meaningful, but what really makes it unique is its imaginative structure. Like some of the episodes of the 1980s *Twilight Zone* series, instead of ending with a twist, it begins with one. Opening with an elderly Jake Sisko at the end of his life, the plot unfolds like a chess game in its late stages working its way backwards toward the beginning, a narrative tool that was obviously developed organically from the story, as no writer would sit down and spontaneously invent it at the beginning of the process. It's a daring choice, as it puts the weight of the episode on the shoulders of a guest star and asks him to carry the show, but it pays off. Tony Todd, beginning the episode in old age make-up, serves as a pinch hitter for Cirroc Lofton, taking over the part of Jake for much of the episode, and hits a grand slam. Todd, of course, had already secured himself free tickets to *Star Trek* conventions for life for his work as Worf's younger brother, Kurn. But his work as an older Jake Sisko here is his magnum opus. Sharing the stage with him as "the visitor" is Rachel Robinson, daughter of Andrew Robinson (Garak). While her understated performance is far less memorable than what her father brings to the show, it's the perfect complement to Todd's charismatic storytelling, giving the two futuristic characters a chemistry that reverberates throughout each scene they're in.

And then there are Avery Brooks and Cirroc Lofton. Brooks, playing a part reminiscent of Kirk in the "The Tholian Web," does the most with the least; his character appears infrequently, arguably becoming the titular character, yet

Brooks plays him with such emotion, his love for his son spills over into scenes he's not even in. Lofton, meanwhile, might be overshadowed as Jake Sisko by Todd, yet gives perhaps his greatest performance of the series.

Credit must also be given to the set decorators, make-up, and wardrobe teams who effectively create the illusion that we've broken the bonds of *Star Trek's* present and are catching a glimpse of a possible future. (Sadly, only the make-up team's work would go on to be nominated for an Emmy.) And with all the elements working together, they produce a synergy that can't be described in a recap or review. "The Visitor" is a must see, an episode that transcends *Deep Space Nine* and *Star Trek*, entertaining and moving nearly anyone who gives it a chance to do so.

Did you know? This episode's writers, Michael Taylor and René Echevarria, were friends who used to live across the street from each other in New York.

Did you also know? When O.J. Simpson agreed to an unrestricted interview with Katie Couric and Tom Brokaw about the murder of his ex-wife, NBC scheduled the discussion to air at the same time "The Visitor" was going to premier in many markets, including Los Angeles. The day before the interview was to happen, however, Simpson backed out, and the *DS9* producers breathed a sigh of relief.

The Greatest *DS9* Episodes

There will always be debate about which *DS9* episodes are truly the best, but here are some top ten lists that have been compiled over the years.

The Hollywood Reporter

1. "In the Pale Moonlight" (Season Six)
2. "Far Beyond the Stars" (Season Six)
3. "The Visitor" (Season Four)
4. "Emissary" (Season One)
5. "Homefront"/"Paradise Lost" (Season Four)
6. "Call to Arms" (Season Five)
7. "Duet" (Season One)
8. "Sacrifice of Angels" (Season Six)
9. "What You Leave Behind" (Season Seven)
10. "Soldiers of the Empire" (Season Five)

Empire Online

1. "Far Beyond the Stars" (Season Six)
2. "The Visitor" (Season Four)
3. "In the Pale Moonlight" (Season Six)
4. "Trials and Tribble-ations" (Season Five)
5. "The Way of the Warrior" (Season Four)
6. "Our Man Bashir" (Season Four)
7. "For the Uniform" (Season Five)
8. "Homefront"/"Paradise Lost" (Season Four)
9. "What You Leave Behind" (Season Seven)
10. "Duet" (Season One)

Den of the Geek

1. "The Visitor" (Season Four)
2. "Once More Unto the Breach" (Season Seven)
3. "It's Only a Paper Moon" (Season Seven)
4. "Far Beyond the Stars" (Season Six)
5. "Little Green Men" (Season Four)
6. "Trials and Tribble-ations" (Season Five)
7. "Our Man Bashir" (Season Four)
8. "The Way of the Warrior" (Season Four)
9. "Dr. Bashir, I Presume" (Season Five)
10. "Duet" (Season One)

New York Magazine

1. "Far Beyond the Stars" (Season Six)
2. "The Visitor" (Season Four)
3. "In the Pale Moonlight" (Season Six)
4. "Trials and Tribble-ations" (Season Five)
5. "The Way of the Warrior" (Season Four)
6. "Improbable Cause"/"The Die is Cast" (Season Three)
7. "Second Skin" (Season Three)
8. "The Sound of Her Voice" (Season Six)
9. "Sacrifice of Angels" (Season Six)
10. "For the Uniform" (Season Five)

The Internet Movie Database

1. "In the Pale Moonlight" (Season Six)
2. "Trials and Tribble-ations" (Season Five)
3. "The Visitor" (Season Four)
4. "Call to Arms" (Season Five)
5. "Duet" (Season One)
6. "The Way of the Warrior" (Season Four)
7. "Sacrifice of Angels" (Season Six)
8. "The Die is Cast" (Season Three)
9. "By Inferno's Light" (Season Five)
10. "Far Beyond the Stars" (Season Six)

My Personal Choices

1. "The Visitor" (Season Four)
2. "In the Pale Moonlight" (Season Six)
3. "Trials and Tribble-ations" (Season Five)
4. "Far Beyond the Stars" (Season Six)
5. "Past Tense" (Season Three)
6. "The Quickening" (Season Four)
7. "Emissary" (Season One)
8. "Duet" (Season One)
9. "Necessary Evil" (Season Two)
10. "Children of Time" (Season Five)

"Hippocratic Oath": C

Bashir and O'Brien are captured by a Jem'Hadar group that wants to break free of s drug used to control them.

Air date: October 16, 1995
Teleplay by Lisa Klink
Story by Nicholas Corea & Lisa Klink
Directed by René Auberjonois
TV rating: 7.7

"I'm sorry I couldn't find a nicer place to crash-land. Should we try again?"
—O'Brien

This Bashir/O'Brien episode takes the two characters, generally known for their friendly sparring, and attempts to drive a serious wedge between them by bringing back the Jem'Hadar—last seen in Season Two's opening two-parter—and giving the two officers opposite ideas of how to deal with them. Bashir thinks of the situation as a medical crisis, whereas O'Brien firmly believes they're in a POW story. This presents a problem for the writers, because to keep both characters appearing reasonable, the story has to shift back and forth between being a medical drama and an escape adventure. Without a strong central line, this A story is unable to build toward a satisfying climax, and ultimately the viewer is left wondering what the point is.

The B story fares better. The writers bring attention to the differences between *TNG* and *DS9* by having Worf stick his nose in Odo's business. Michael Dorn and René Auberjonois work together fabulously, with Dorn all but saying, "I'm frickin' Worf, dude!" and Auberjonois all but responding, "That's nice, but it's *my* show!" The whole story plays off their characters well, taking advantage of Worf's arrogance and Odo's pigheadedness, and is well handled by Auberjonois as the episode's director.

Did you know? René Auberjonois was originally scheduled to direct "The Visitor," but when the *Star Trek* producers learned Colm Meaney would be needed on the set of *The Van* while *DS9* was shooting its third episode of the season, the producers flip-flopped the production order of "The Visitor" and "Hippocratic Oath" to accommodate him. Auberjonois and David Livingston, keeping their same slots, switched assignments.

"Indiscretion": C

Kira and Dukat search for the six-year-old crash site of a Cardassian freighter that was carrying Bajoran prisoners.

Air date: October 23, 1995
Teleplay by Nicholas Corea
Story by Toni Marberry & Jack Trevino
Directed by LeVar Burton
TV rating: 7.2

"Captain Sisko is right. You are in love with the sound of your own voice."
—Kira

By this point, thanks to episodes like Season Two's "Necessary Evil" and "The Maquis," Cardassian politics have become so intertwined with Bajoran politics, there's no better pairing for a search and rescue mission than Kira and Dukat, even if it's something akin to Anne Frank teaming up with Adolf Hitler. And it even provides an interesting counterpoint to the previous episode. After seeing best friends driven apart, we see archenemies working together.

The plot itself develops into something reminiscent of *The Searchers* (1956) and gives Gul Dukat's character some depth. Marc Alaimo clearly relishes the opportunity, and his work on location at Soledad Canyon with Nana Visitor is striking and memorable. Unfortunately, there's an impenetrable firewall between Dukat and Kira that holds the episode back. It's simply impossible for their relationship to move past a certain point, and their "developing friendship" can only go so far. Director LeVar Burton tries to breeze past this point by focusing on the internal conflicts within the characters, and it helps, but only to a degree.

There's also a B story about Sisko and his significant other having communication problems. It's mostly a comedy runner, but it's well written and serves as a nice break from the more serious matters.

Dukat returns later in the season to pick up the loose threads of this episode in "Return to Grace."

Did you know? After being first mentioned in *TNG's* "Hero Worship" and subsequently name-dropped in *TNG's* "Interface," *Star Trek: Generations*, and *VOY's* "Elogium," the Breen finally make their debut in this episode.

"Rejoined": C

Dax and a Trill whom she was married to in their past lives must decide whether or not to ignore Trill taboo and continue their relationship.

Air date: October 30, 1995
Teleplay by Ronald D. Moore & René Echevarria
Story by René Echevarria
Directed by Avery Brooks
TV rating: 7.0

"Can you really walk away from me? From us? After all this time we're back together. Don't throw that away." —Dax

The idea of a Trill in a same-sex romantic relationship goes all the way back to *TNG's* Season Four episode "The Host," which introduces the species, but is finally fully developed here. The wonderful thing about the episode is that the conflict doesn't come from the relationship itself but is a product of external forces. It's sort of like a gay relationship in the U.S. military of the 1990s: people not only had to deal with an unjust system but faced pressures from those around them who didn't want to see them professionally hurt by coming out.

Unfortunately, while it's a good use of the Trill, the episode as a whole doesn't stand out beyond the unusual subject. Romantic relationships are not *Star Trek's* strong suit, particularly when one member of the couple is a debuting guest star. Director Avery Brooks gets some emotional performances out of Terry Farrell and guest star Susanna Thompson (Kahn), but it's difficult to build and conclude a story of this nature inside an hour and expect the audience to share the same feelings. To make matters worse, the love story is couched inside a generic and forgettable MacGuffin, a sci-fi story about creating another artificial wormhole.

Coming from two of *Star Trek's* best writers and one of *DS9's* better directors, it's a bit of surprise this one isn't more interesting.

Did you know? A production assistant took a call from a man who claimed *Star Trek* was messing up his kids by showing two women kissing. The man insisted it would have been better for the two women to shoot each other instead.

"Starship Down": C+

After an attack by the Jem'Hadar, the Defiant is left drifting in a hostile atmosphere.

Air date: November 13, 1995
Written by David Mack & John J. Ordover
Directed by Alexander Singer
TV rating: 7.1

"I hate the Gamma Quadrant." —Quark

Like "Civil Defense," this ensemble piece is a variation of an idea introduced in *TNG's* Season Five episode "Disaster": something happens to segregate the characters and force them to work through separate plotlines to survive and put things back in order.

In this case, the disaster happens to the Defiant, which becomes trapped in the atmosphere of a gas planet. This setting gives us some rich visual effects which, thanks to mid-1990s advancements in CGI, approach cinema quality. The various stories within the plot, however, are all quite basic. In contrast with the "fish out of water" theme in "Disaster" or the humorous aspects of "Civil Defense," this one plays out fairly straight with the characters not far out of their comfort zones: Worf ends up in charge of the ship and has trouble dealing with a couple engineers, Quark is trapped in a room with an alien (James Cromwell) he's been trying to cheat, Kira attends to a concussed Sisko, and Bashir is trapped in a turbolift with Dax. The nature of this sort of storytelling keeps things moving along briskly, with it necessary to continually cut from story to story. And there are highlights: Cromwell is fantastic, the engineers are goofy enough to be charming in their own right, and Kira's dialogue with Sisko is beautiful. There's also an extended wrap-up which serves the show well, giving us a more satisfactory conclusion than some of the rushed endings of *DS9's* past. Yet, while it's all very watchable, it doesn't break any new ground and feels mostly like another day at the office.

Did you know? Writer David Mack conceived this episode after watching *Das Boot*, a 1981 German submarine film.

"Little Green Men": C+

A malfunction on Quark's new ship causes Quark, Rom, and Nog to crash in Roswell, New Mexico...in 1947.

Air date: November 6, 1995
Teleplay by Ira Steven Behr & Robert Hewitt Wolfe
Story by Toni Marberry & Jack Trevino
Directed by James L. Conway
TV rating: 7.7

"All I ask is a tall ship and a load of contraband to fill her with." —Quark

This Ferengi comedy with Quark, Rom, and Nog is an homage to the old sci-fi invasion movies and doesn't take itself seriously. It even parodies *Star Trek* itself with Rom spitting out some hilarious technobabble to explain how he's going to force the ship out of warp. (Quark's response? "I have no idea what you're talking about! Just do it!") With its one joke concept, the lack of a B story, and a foregone conclusion, the episode needs ample padding, and it gets it. A convoluted introduction starts things off slowly before the writers bring back the "malfunctioning universal translator" delay tactic (previously used in Season Two's "Sanctuary") to further stall the "plot." The comedy, however, masks these storytelling flaws and turns what could be tedious into an enjoyable little character piece. Meanwhile, the 1940s look provides a nice change of pace, with it especially fun to see the outrageous looking Ferengi in a 20th century setting. Unfortunately, the episode's budget forces the writers to keep most of the action to a single room, limiting the plot's possibilities and eliminating any hope of a *Star Trek IV* parody. (We'll just never get to see Quark on the run looking for nuclear wessels.)

Did you know? Charles Napier guest stars in this episode as the square-jawed Lieutenant General Denning. It's his first *Star Trek* appearance since Season Three of *TOS* when he played Adam, the singing space hippie, in "The Way to Eden." (Yay, brother.) Napier died in 2011 at age 75.

"The Sword of Kahless": C

Worf, Kor, and Dax search for the Sword of Kahless, a relic said to be capable of reuniting the Klingon Empire.

Air date: November 20, 1995
Teleplay by Hans Beimler
Story by Richard Danus
Directed by LeVar Burton
TV rating: 6.9

"You know what I like about Klingon stories, Commander? Nothing. Lots of people die, and nobody makes any profit." —Quark

The Klingon equivalent of the search for the Holy Grail, this Worf/Kor/Dax episode is reminiscent of Season Two's "Blood Oath" but features a more internal conflict. While the premise might sound like *Indiana Jones and the Last Crusade*, it plays out more like Frodo's quest in *The Lord of the Rings*. Finding the sword is easy (perhaps too easy) but bearing it back to the ship is like taking the One Ring to Mount Doom. The thing isn't just a burden but a divisive force.

Featuring one character from each of *Star Trek's* first three live action shows, the episode is a treasure trove of *Trek* history, with references to quite a few past episodes, yet remains accessible to new fans by giving them enough information to get by. Director LeVar Burton plays up the biblical moments of the episode, from Kor's stories, well told by the lively John Colicos, to the finding of the Sword, which David Bell scores in a way that would make Howard Shore proud.

Unfortunately, the episode takes place almost exclusively in the cave set, giving it a limited look and scope, and the internal conflicts get tedious by the second half. And while it is fun to see Kor again, and it's great to see Worf finally get an A story, the episode ultimately falls short of its potential, although its conclusion does leave the story open to a sequel. (Perhaps someday there will be a *Star Trek* series that does "The Sword of Kahless II.")

John Colicos reprises Kor one last time in Season Seven's "Once More Unto the Breach."

Did you know? This episode was chosen to be included in a four-disc DVD collection devoted to the Klingons. The other episodes included are:

- *ENT's* "Broken Bow"
- *TOS's* "Errand of Mercy" and "The Trouble with Tribbles"
- *TNG's* "A Matter of Honor," "Sins of the Father," and "Redemption I & II"
- *DS9's* "The Way of the Warrior" and "Trials and Tribble-ations"
- *VOY's* "Barge of the Dead"

"Our Man Bashir": B

A transporter accident traps the senior staff of Deep Space Nine in Bashir's James Bond-like holosuite program.

Air date: November 27, 1995
Teleplay by Ronald D. Moore
Story by Robert Gillan
Directed by Winrich Kolbe
TV rating: 6.8

"We believe the holosuite memory core is holding the transporter patterns of five crewmembers. If you stop the program, their patterns might be lost.
—Eddington

With a title derived from a James Bond parody called *Our Man Flint* (1966), this comedic Bashir episode, conceived by script coordinator Robert Gillan, uses one of *Trek's* most ridiculous premises since "Spock's Brain" to allow everyone to cut loose and have fun in a spy spoof. Like *TNG's* Season Six episode "A Fistful of Datas," the show uses a malfunctioning holosuite as a way to step into a new genre, and in this case, it provides a vehicle for many of the regulars to play the episode's guest stars. While the science behind the premise is silly to say the least, the point of *Star Trek* is to entertain, and "Our Man Bashir" passes this test with flying colors.

The star of the show is the suave Alexander Siddig, who walks with ease from elaborate set to elaborate set, with each, in true Bond style, including complex moving parts. He's joined, but not upstaged, by Andrew Robinson who, as Garak, plays the perfect sidekick: the real life secret agent who treats the romantic notion of espionage with bemusement and a wink. ("I think I joined the wrong intelligence service!") Filling out the adventure are all the familiar characters from the genre: the sexy woman with an accent, the one-eyed hitman with a score to settle, the female scientist with a silly name (Honey Bare), the tuxedoed gambling mobster, and, of course, the megalomaniacal villain trying to destroy the world. Meanwhile, the B story features several characters trying to save those trapped in the holodeck, with the dark station providing a nice contrast to the bright, gaudy spy sets. Everything is played over the top, with director Winrich Kolbe shooting the holosuite adventure in a comic book style and Jay Chattaway giving it a bigger than life score that was nominated for an Emmy and still stands out as some of *Trek's* best music.

In fact, overall, "Our Man Bashir" might be *Star Trek's* greatest holodeck adventure of all time.

Did you know? "Our Man Bashir" was Robert Gillan's first sale.

107

"Homefront" (1): B+

Captain Sisko is recalled to Earth after a terrorist bombing reveals that Changelings have reached the planet.

Air date: January 1, 1996
Written by Ira Steven Behr & Robert Hewitt Wolfe
Directed by David Livingston
TV rating: 6.8

"That's why my people came here: to undermine the trust and mutual understanding the Federation is built on." —Odo

This Sisko episode, a follow-up to "The Adversary," was originally conceived as a season finale for Season Three but postponed at Paramount's request. But while it lacks the budget it might have otherwise have had, "Homefront" makes up for it with character and intrigue. The Earthbound story, evoking memories of the 1980s miniseries *V*, alternates between tense military scenes in San Francisco and Paris and deeply personal scenes in New Orleans. With Sisko involved with each, we get to see the military plot take shape from the inside while simultaneously getting the captain's reaction to the situation in a more personal setting, the equivalent of the Sisko family dinner table. It's a genius formula and a nice change of pace from the usual A/B format with different lead characters. Boasting several fine guest star performances, the episode might be most noteworthy for introducing Brock Peters as Grandpa Joseph Sisko. Already well known to *Star Trek* fans for his standout performance as Admiral Cartwright in the *Star Trek* movies, Peters tops himself as the stubborn, elderly patriarch of the Sisko family, stealing every scene he's in and expertly delivering some of *Star Trek's* greatest lines. ("Jake, the only time you should be in bed is if you're sleeping, dying, or making love to a beautiful woman.")

Unfortunately, *DS9* balances Peters' greatness with Herschel Sparber's suckitude. Playing the Federation's president, Sparber has all the charm and charisma of Droopy the dog. The shame of it is that the writing is fine, and had someone like Bernard Hill or Jack Tunney been cast, the part would have been an asset to the story. As is, guest star Robert Foxworth (Admiral Leyton) outclasses Sparber to such an extent, it's easy to wonder why Leyton isn't running the Federation instead…well, at least until we see the conclusion of this story in "Paradise Lost."

Overall, however, "Homefront" is an effective episode that moves the Dominion story forward while providing a nice change of scenery for the series.

Did you know? Brock Peters provided the voice of Darth Vader for an adaptation of the original *Star Wars* trilogy for radio. The actor, who shares my birthday, died in 2005 at age 78.

"Paradise Lost" (2): A

While Starfleet tightens security measures on Earth, Sisko and Odo discover that someone is deviously plotting to take over the planet.

Air date: January 8, 1996
Teleplay by Ira Steven Behr & Robert Hewitt Wolfe
Story by Ronald D. Moore
Directed by Reza Badiyi
TV rating: 6.8

"We do not fear you the way you fear us. In the end, it's your fear that will destroy you." —Changeling

This successful conclusion to "Homefront," also set on Earth, moves the military plot-thread to the forefront, this time handing the "guest star of honor" reins to Robert Foxworth (Admiral Leyton). The theme of the episode, five years ahead of its time, is the danger of cognitive distortions following a large-scale tragic event. It's easy to see Leyton as a 21st century politician, using fear and suspicion to push through a self-serving agenda and believing it's for the greater good. Caught up in the political demagoguery is Leyton's relationship with Sisko, with Avery Brooks and Foxworth stepping into the familiar Trek roles of "the Star Trek regular" and his "former mentor gone bad." With apologies to Jonathan Frakes and Terry O'Quinn, never is such a dynamic as exciting as in "Paradise Lost," with both actors knowing just how to play their parts and both characters knowing just how to deal with the other, leading to a sequence of scenes that leaves the viewer on the edge of his or her seat, wondering how it will all end.

Be that as it may, "Homefront" and "Paradise Lost" aren't the game-changing episodes they tease themselves to be. The writers have fun with some misdirection before the true danger takes shape—but the two-parter's significant message will always remain relevant.

The Changeling-infiltration drama continues in Season Five's opener, "Apocalypse Rising."

Did you know? A few years after *TOS* was cancelled, its primary producers, Gene Roddenberry and Gene Coon, teamed up to create a new series called *The Questor Tapes* about an android in search of his creator. When writing the pilot, Roddenberry envisioned Leonard Nimoy playing the lead, and the producer was especially gratified when the actor responded positively to an early draft and verbally agreed to join the project. Unfortunately, *Questor's* studio, Universal, would not let Nimoy audition and cast another actor in the part: Robert Foxworth. While the series ultimately did not sell, its development did lead to a rift between Roddenberry and Nimoy, with the latter falsely assuming it was Roddenberry who had rejected him.

"Crossfire": B

When Kira falls in love with her former resistance leader, Shakaar, Odo struggles to accept the relationship.

Air date: January 29, 1996
Written by René Echevarria
Directed by Les Landau
TV rating: 7.0

"People see you as the guy who always gets his man. Now you're becoming the guy who tears up his quarters and sits alone in the rubble." —Quark to Odo

This quiet, character-driven Odo episode continues the Odo/Kira unrequited love story first hinted at in "The Collaborator" and developed in "Heart of Stone."

"Crossfire" itself is a lot like high school. Poor Odo likes the cheerleader (Kira) but before he can muster up the courage to tell her, the dashing football player (Shakaar) begins trying to win her affection, and Odo is relegated to "good friend/third wheel" status. This gives us *DS9's* first love triangle, and for *Star Trek* it's a significant step. In fact, apart from soap operas, most TV shows had trouble presenting complex, evolving relationships before the 1990s because it was assumed that most viewers would miss episodes here and there for nights out or kids' piano recitals, and producers therefore put an emphasis on episodic storytelling with little character change. Then, when VCRs became popular enough, shows like *TNG* and *DS9* began to flirt with serial storytelling and character growth. Finally, in 2002, when DVDs and DVRs swept over the world, the boundaries were all but eliminated. Whereas the writers of *TNG* harbored no illusions that new fans would view complete past seasons, as season collections on video tape were expensive and bulky, by 2005 the writers of *Lost* knew that new fans would have no problem catching up and learning every nuance of the show, with DVDs being cheap, compact, and readily available. (And it wouldn't be long before streaming services would make binge-watching even easier.) But as for the latter half of the 1990s, what we have is a transitional period that's all the more interesting to watch because of such.

For "Crossfire," Echevarria provides a savvy script that includes and expands upon Odo and Quark's adversarial friendship while René Auberjonois plays the subtext to perfection. With such rich character interplay, there's no need for a B story or a "faux jeopardy" climax. The real star of the day is Odo's quiet dignity, and the character's need, like Spock and Data before him, to hide his true feelings when he's most vulnerable. The result is one of Auberjonois's best episodes and a setup for Season Five's "Children of Time."

Did you know? This episode, conceived by Robert Hewitt Wolfe, was inspired by *The Bodyguard* (1992).

"Return to Grace": C

Kira and Dukat chase a Klingon ship that destroyed an outpost hosting a Cardassian/Bajoran conference.

Air date: February 5, 1996
Teleplay by Hans Beimler
Story by Tom Benko
Directed by Jonathan West
TV rating: 6.5

"I am the only Cardassian left, and if no one else will stand against the Klingons, I will." —Dukat

This quick follow-up to "Indiscretion" brings back Dukat for another story about him and Kira working together—this time on a ship. And while it's a low-budget character-driven story, it uses tactical displays, anticipation, and a few well timed action sequences to make the episode seem bigger than it really is. At its heart, however, it's a story about Dukat's choices, letting Marc Alaimo, as Dukat, do what he does best: think out loud.

Along the way, "Return to Grace" opens up a lot of issues. We learn that Dukat believes the Cardassian occupation of Bajor was a mistake, that his actions and beliefs are making him an outsider on Cardassia, and that he finds Kira increasingly attractive. Meanwhile, we are reminded that the Klingons are no longer playing nice, and that their hostility not only threatens the Federation, but everyone else too. But instead of developing and exploring the issues, the script is content to pay some lip service to them before moving along and resolving the plot. (Sometimes I wonder if *Star Trek* writers missed the day in scriptwriting school when students were taught that on TV it's better to show than tell.)

It is fun, however, to see Kira and Dukat together again, with Nana Visitor and Alaimo continuing to work well together and the ship-based sets serving as a nice counterpoint to the location shooting in "Indiscretion." But perhaps "Return to Grace" is most notable for introducing Casey Biggs as Damar, Dukat's right hand man. Biggs is able to take a simple gesture and somehow make it specific and interesting in its own right, laying a foundation for a character initially presented with no background, and his breakout performance ensures that we'll see a lot more of Damar in the future.

Did you know? Ziyal, introduced in "Indiscretion," is reprised in "Return to Grace" by guest star Cyia Batten and given a more substantial part. The producers, however, were not happy with the actress's performance here and recast Ziyal for the character's next appearance in "For the Cause." Batten nonetheless returns to the *Star Trek* fold as a Terrellian pilot in *VOY* and an Orion slave girl in *ENT*.

111

"Sons of Mogh": C+

Worf's brother comes to Deep Space Nine and asks to be killed.

Air date: February 12, 1996
Written by Ronald D. Moore
Directed by David Livingston
TV rating: 7.3

"Regulations? We're not talking about some obscure technicality, Mr. Worf. You tried to commit premeditated murder." —Sisko

Star Trek finishes up with Worf's brother, Kurn, in this Klingon episode that also features the beginning of Worf's relationship with Dax. It's a daring episode that's more about Worf and his choices than anything else. Using Kurn as an example of a true Klingon, the episode contrasts the brothers to illustrate how Worf is different and is on his own unique path. *TNG's* "Sins of the Father," also written by Ron Moore, begins in a similar fashion but morphs into a celebration of Worf's Klingon side. Here, the emphasis is on Worf's human side and his future outside the Empire.

As a study of Worf's character, the episode is a success. As a Kurn episode, it's a disappointment. Tony Todd (Kurn) is fine, though it's certainly not his best performance of the season, but his only purpose in the episode is to give Worf something to play against, and the way Kurn's story is tied up at the end is a cop-out.

Did you know? In a 1998 interview, Michael Dorn said "Sons of Mogh" was probably the highlight of his experience on *DS9*.

"Bar Association": B–

Rom organizes a union to combat Quark's unfair labor practices.

Air date: February 19, 1996
Teleplay by Robert Hewitt Wolfe & Ira Steven Behr
Story by Barbara J. Lee & Jenifer A. Lee
Directed by LeVar Burton
TV rating: 6.7

"I'm not dumb, and you're not half as smart as you think you are." —Rom

A Ferengi comedy with a serious subject matter, "Bar Association" tackles labor/management issues better than most shows set in the present. The catalyst for the plot, a four-word pitch from the Lee sisters—Rom starts a union—might sound like a B story or a comedy runner, but the idea proves to have enough depth to carry an episode. It's interesting to see the union organize and go on strike, and hear the diverse opinions about the situation from the *DS9* regulars. And Armin Shimerman is in his element playing the owner under siege, which allows the writers to throw in some funny gags. He even gets to play Quark's more serious side when the Ferengi government—which treats organized labor like Wal-mart—discovers what's afoot and blames Quark for letting it get out of control. And then there's Sisko, who is dragged into the situation like Teddy Roosevelt being dragged into the coal strike of 1902. You can tell Avery Brooks is having a ball yelling at his castmates and playing the one sane guy on the station.

Through it all, however, the essence of the episode rests on the shoulders of Max Grodénchik. For the first time, Rom is the center of the story, and Grodénchik makes the most of the opportunity, instilling Rom with a passion and a new direction that raises the character to a new level.

Director LeVar Burton shoots it all nicely, including a complicated scene with multiple Quarks and a jaw-dropping uncut Steadicam shot that begins with Rom on the Promenade before moving up to the second level for a walk and talk scene with O'Brien and Worf.

All that said, this is an episode that will mean more to someone who has to deal with its issues and will mean less to someone who doesn't.

Did you know? This is an episode Armin Shimerman recalls fondly. "My favorite moment from my own acting is in that one. There's nothing extraordinary about the writing; it was just everything that I want to do as an actor. I just felt I hit one hundred percent 'in the zone,' so I'm very proud of that work."

"Accession": D+

Two hundred years after his disappearance, a Bajoran poet emerges from the wormhole claiming to be the real Emissary.

Air date: February 26, 1996
Written by Jane Espenson
Directed by Les Landau
TV rating: 6.5

"No more ceremonies to attend; no more blessings to give; no more prophecies to fulfill. I'm just a Starfleet officer again. All I have to worry about are the Klingons, the Dominion, and the Maquis. I feel like I'm on vacation." —Sisko

DS9 returns to Bajoran politics and prophecies for this Sisko/Kira story that's sort of a poor man's "Destiny." The episode flirts with a lot of meaty material: Sisko passes the Emissary torch to another, Kira questions her future, a religious leader brings back an archaic idea, the Bajorans have differing opinions of how to handle this, and there's even a murder. (And if that's not enough, Opaka, the former Kai, makes her last appearance in the series.) Yet most of the issues go unexplored, and there's a lack of energy behind what we do see. It's as if everyone is getting a bit tired of Bajoran spiritual beliefs and are now just going through the motions. Even the B story, about the O'Brien family dealing with change, is forgettable in its own right.

Guest star Richard Libertini, playing Akorem Laan, the new Emissary, does the script no favors. He's a weak antagonist with no gravitas. Had David Warner played the part, as was originally intended, it's likely he and Avery Brooks would have given the Akorem/Sisko adversarial relationship enough sparks to carry the episode. But Warner's wife didn't want "Accession" to disrupt a vacation, so her husband declined. What we're left with as a result is underwhelming.

Did you know? In the early 1960s, Richard Libertini and Paul Dooley were a stand-up comedy duo. Dooley appears in four episodes of *DS9* as Enabran Tain, but this is Libertini's only *Star Trek* appearance. He died in 2016 at age 82.

"Rules of Engagement": C

The Klingons try to extradite Worf after he accidentally destroys a transport full of Klingon civilians.

Air date: April 8, 1996
Teleplay by Ronald D. Moore
Story by Bradley Thompson & David Weddle
Directed by LeVar Burton
TV rating: 5.8

"The truth must be won. I'll see you on the battlefield." —Ch'Pok

Star Trek returns to the drama of a courtroom setting with a story that's similar to "Court Martial," the classic *TOS* episode, but with Worf as the central figure. An ensemble piece, the episode uses most of the *DS9* regulars as witnesses to flesh out the backstory. Directed by Dorn's buddy LeVar Burton, the most notable aspect of the episode is a diegetic twist. As introduced in Spike Lee's 1995 film *Clockers*, when a witness describes an event, we see a flashback that includes the character offering narration—as if on the witness stand—directly into the camera as he or she progresses through the scene from the past. The technique is initially jarring but serves the episode well, being used for both drama and comedy, giving an average story some memorable moments.

Dominating the episode is guest star Ron Canada, a former news anchor who sinks his teeth into Ch'Pok, an advocate for the Klingon Empire who serves as the episode's antagonist. More three dimensional than most Klingons, Ch'Pok isn't so much an adversary for Worf as he is for Sisko. And while we all know who's going to win the contest, Canada's smugness makes the foregone conclusion quite satisfying—like a good episode of *Law & Order*.

Unfortunately, the story behind the trial itself doesn't make much sense. We're supposed to believe that the Klingon Empire is upset with Worf for firing on a ship in the middle of a battle and that the Federation would extradite an officer to an enemy for doing so. It would seem to be more of an issue if it was the other way around.

Did you know? Burton enjoyed this episode's novelty. "That device the writers employed was, for a director, a lot of fun to play with. When I read that, I got excited, because it's not often that you break that fourth wall and have characters directly address the camera."

"Hard Time": B+

After being falsely convicted of espionage on an alien world, Chief O'Brien returns to Deep Space Nine with the memories of a virtual twenty-year prison sentence implanted in his brain.

Air date: April 15, 1996
Teleplay by Robert Hewitt Wolfe
Story by Daniel Keys Moran & Lynn Barker
Directed by Alexander Singer
TV rating: 5.7

"Chief, I know this is going to be hard for you to accept, but you haven't been in prison. What you experienced was an artificial reality, an interactive program that created memories of things that never actually happened." —Kira

This extraordinary O'Brien character piece serves as a dark mirror of sorts to *TNG's* "Inner Light," exploring such a powerful life-changing experience that it challenges the boundaries of conventional television.

Like *DS9's* Season Two episode "Necessary Evil," "Hard Time" features a *Lost/This is Us*-like structure, alternating between the past and the present, with the twist—known in advance—being that the past never actually happened. Sticking to essentials, the episode doesn't waste time explaining how O'Brien was caught by the aliens, what he really did, or even who these aliens are. The story is instead about the aftermath, with Chief O'Brien attempting to rebuild his life while simultaneously harboring a dark secret. This puts the episode on the shoulders of Colm Meaney while O'Brien runs the gamut of emotions. And whether appearing confused, sad, angry, or frustrated, Meaney is always compelling, passionate, and believable, and he turns the episode into his most memorable outing.

Craig Wasson, coming across like a Bill Maher impersonator, is nearly as good as O'Brien's fictitious friend Ee'Char, essentially playing the setup man, giving O'Brien something to work off of. Wasson plays a cliché role: the friend who turns out to be imaginary. But the beauty here is that instead of revealing this at the end as a sucker punch, writer Robert Hewitt Wolfe makes no secret of Ee'Char's nature from the beginning. What's important isn't what we think of Ee'Char but what O'Brien thinks of him.

Still, twenty years in a virtual prison seems a bit overboard. After all, O'Brien is part of the future of the series, and the events of this episode would seem to have messed him up too drastically for the character we know and love to ever return. Perhaps ten years would have been better. Either way, the idea of a "virtual experience" to punish criminals is a fascinating sci-fi idea. The punishment itself is better for the family of a criminal than a true sentence because it doesn't take a loved one away, and it simultaneously benefits society by avoiding the incarceration expenses of jails, guards, food, and medical care.

116

It can even be argued that it benefits the punished as well, giving him a physically safe environment for his penance. Best yet, there are no appeals to worry about, and nobody has to look the prisoner in the eye on a daily basis to see what is happening to him. But what is the end effect? That, of course, is what this episode is all about.

Unfortunately, the *DS9* writers do feel it necessary stick in a rebuttal of what they mistakenly believe is Gene Roddenberry's *Star Trek* philosophy: O'Brien comments how he was taught that humanity had evolved and outgrown hate and rage, but he believes this might be wrong. In fact, the idea behind *Star Trek* has never been that our emotions change with successive generations; it's instead about how we mature as a society, and why punishments such as that in this episode are cruel and unneeded.

But that's a minor quibble. "Hard Time" is a *DS9* standout and one of the best dark *Star Trek* episodes ever.

Did you know? "The Inner Light" and "Hard Time" share something beyond the idea of implanted memories: both include guest star Margot Rose. She plays Kataan's wife in the first and the alien who administers O'Brien's punishment in the second.

"Shattered Mirror": C

When Jake's mom from the mirror universe takes Jake into her own reality, Captain Sisko must follow to help his boy escape.

Air date: April 22, 1996
Written by Ira Steven Behr & Hans Beimler
Directed by James L. Conway
TV rating: 6.5

"This time, I will deal with the rebels myself." —Worf

This sequel to Season Three's "Through the Looking Glass" is an unabashedly simplistic comic book adventure featuring the Siskos in the mirror universe. Ben, Jake, and Jake's mirror-mom find themselves in a shoot 'em up story that puts subtlety and character development on hold to celebrate *Star Trek's* space-pirate side. The adversaries, seen in the B story, are Worf and Garak, giving Michael Dorn and Andrew Robinson a chance to ham it up and quote Darth Vader. In fact, the whole episode, much like *A New Hope*, features cookie cutter storytelling as we cut back and forth between both sides, with everything leading to a big space battle at the end that includes, appropriately, movie quality special effects.

Unfortunately, while the mirror universe setting was fresh and exciting when it was introduced in 1967, by this point it's no longer such a novel idea. The three Siskos have chemistry together, and perhaps it might have been more interesting to see them sharing a more emotional adventure on Deep Space Nine.

The mirror universe would get a rest in Season Five before coming back into play in Season Six with "Resurrection."

Did you know? James L. Conway would go on to direct *ENT's* "In a Mirror, Darkly."

118

"The Muse": F

A mysterious woman helps Jake write a novel, and a pregnant Lwaxana Troi asks Odo to help her escape her husband.

Air date: April 29, 1996
Teleplay by René Echevarria
Story by René Echevarria & Majel Barrett Roddenberry
Directed by David Livingston
TV rating: 5.3

"The dialogue is sharp, the story's involving, the characters are real...the spelling is terrible!" —Captain Sisko

The famous line, "It was the best of times, it was the worst of times," perfectly describes the Jake Sisko episodes from Season Four of *DS9*. "The Visitor" is, perhaps, the best of the series. "The Muse" might be the worst. Built on an idea that only a writer would think TV-worthy—a mysterious lady gets turned on by watching someone write—the A story never gets off the ground. In fact, it begins to meander by the second act. If the cast and crew set out to create an episode with the same vibe as *TNG's* Season Two finale, "Shades of Gray," they could hardly have been more successful, with "The Muse" somehow duplicating the depression and tedium.

The B story, with Odo and Lwaxana Troi (the latter making her last appearance on *Star Trek*) is built around an interesting cultural choice: the Tavnians hide the concept of gender from their children by segregating them at birth and having someone of the same sex raise them—until the secret is revealed when the young turn sixteen. Just imagine the horror the teenage girls go through when they learn about the male gender. ("They want to do *what* to me?") Lwaxana, or Laxwana, as guest star Michael Ansara first pronounces her name, is pregnant with a half-Tavnian boy and the father wants to take the baby away when it's born, so you can guess why she wants Odo's help. Unfortunately, instead of dealing with the problem, the story makes a morally questionable end run around it. The result is an episode that feels like it has two C stories, and the viewer waits in vain for something interesting to happen, disappointed when nothing does.

Let's just say that writer René Echevarria will probably never cite this one as "a far, far better thing that I do, than I have ever done."

"The Muse" was nominated for an Emmy for costume design.

Did you know? Before playing Laxwana's Tavnian husband here, Michael Ansara previously guest starred on *TOS* and *DS9* as Kang the Klingon in "Day of the Dove" and "Blood Oath," respectively. Later in 1996, he would reprise Kang one last time in *VOY's* "Flashback." Ansara died in 2013 at age 91.

"For the Cause": B

Sisko suspects the woman he's dating, Kasidy Yates, might be a Maquis smuggler.

Air date: May 6, 1996
Teleplay by Ronald D. Moore
Story by Mark Gehred-O'Connell
Directed by James L. Conway
TV rating: 5.6

"All I know is that you betrayed your oath, your duty, and me." —Sisko

Like a fine magic act, this Sisko/Maquis episode uses suspense and misdirection to build up anticipation before ultimately delivering a memorable finish.

Featuring the Maquis for the first and only time in Season Four, the whodunnit story gives the rebel group a new face and its most iconic speech, even if it takes a while to get there. But the real meat of the episode falls on Sisko's plate. Playing to Avery Brooks's strengths, "For the Cause" gives the captain conflicting professional and personal feelings, illustrating his thoughts and decisions through actions rather than words. In fact, all the major players here are tight lipped, apart from the aforementioned speech, unwilling to confide in others and let us in on what's going on in their heads. It's left to us to speculate on their motivations and ruminations and fill in the blanks. It's something that limits character development, but it also heightens the drama.

There's also a throwaway B story that's much more simplistic: Garak and Ziyal go on a date. The premise relies upon the actors to make it work, and Andrew Robinson is as good as ever. Tracy Middendorf, on the other hand, is nothing special in her debut as Ziyal. Fortunately, Ziyal's part in the episode is minor, and on the whole, "For the Cause" is quite fun. Season Five would give us a follow-up, "For the Uniform."

Did you know? As it turns out, Tracy Middendorf was allergic to her Cardassian make-up. As a result, the producers were forced to recast Ziyal again for the character's return in Season Five.

"To the Death": B

Following a hit and run attack on Deep Space Nine by a band of rogue Jem'Hadar, Sisko and his crew are joined by the Dominion on a mission to locate the rebels.

Air date: May 13, 1996
Written by Ira Steven Behr & Robert Hewitt Wolfe
Directed by LeVar Burton
TV rating: 6.0

"So let me get this straight, we're going to help the Jem'Hadar fight the Jem'Hadar?" —Dax

This ensemble piece follows the tried but true mantra that it's easier to get to know your enemy by working with them than against them. Here, we get a road trip with the servants of the Dominion, with most of the episode taking place on board the Defiant, giving us ample opportunity to compare and contrast Starfleet and the Jem'Hadar. Mess up with the Jem'Hadar, and they kill you. Mess up with Starfleet, and you get sent to your room. But what really drives the story and makes it work are the small character moments that develop organically from opposite sides working together, which, ironically, was supposed to be the premise of *VOY*. It gives the regulars and the guest stars alike a chance to have some fun with their parts.

"To the Death" also proves the perfect opportunity to reintroduce the Vorta—this time with Jeffrey Combs (Weyoun) ensuring it's done right. Combs would improve later on—here he plays the race a little too tentatively—but he's much better than Molly Hagan ("The Jem'Hadar") or even Dennis Christopher ("The Search, Part II") and provides a strong foundation for the future of the race. In addition, the episode serves as the perfect primer for a major story arc to come in future seasons, beginning with the Season Five finale, "A Call to Arms."

Did you know? This episode uses elements introduced in *TOS's* "All Our Yesterdays."

121

"The Quickening:" A

Dr. Bashir attempts to rid a planet of a plague caused by the Dominion.

Air date: May 20, 1996
Written by Naren Shankar
Directed by René Auberjonois
TV rating: 5.7

"Trevean was right. There is no cure. The Dominion made sure of that."
—Bashir

Way back in the 20th century, every once in a while a *Star Trek* episode would come along that had just the right elements to ensnare TV viewers who were just flipping through channels looking for a diversion—people who didn't really care about *Star Trek* and wouldn't normally give it a chance. They watched for a few minutes, intending to change the channel, but instead of losing interest, they became drawn into the story. Eventually, thoughts of changing the channel were set aside, and when the hour was over, they suddenly realized they'd just enjoyed a *Star Trek* episode.

This is how most new fans were made in the days before streaming platforms, and why episodes like "The Quickening" are so important to *DS9*. This understated Dr. Bashir medical drama represents the perfect alchemy of writing, direction, and acting, and it can be enjoyed equally by those who have seen every *Deep Space Nine* episode and those have seen none.

Like an episode of *Dr. Quinn, Medicine Woman*, the drama takes place in a quaint village with a seemingly insurmountable problem. René Auberjonois, overseeing a core cast supplemented by 70 extras, directs on location for the first time and crafts a mood that draws the audience into a relationship with the villagers to forge an interest in their lives and an empathic concern for their future. With this foundation in place, Dr. Bashir becomes the most important and sympathetic character in the episode, with the audience emotionally invested in his work and his feelings, reacting vicariously to his failures and successes—as if there's a real-life medical crisis he's trying to solve. Meanwhile, writer Naren Shankar touches on a wide array of ideas, including assisted suicide and the notion that we can't end suffering with the wave of a magic wand but we might be able to end it with patience and hard work.

Credit must also be given to the cast, including the late Michael Sarrazin and Ellen Wheeler, as well as Terry Farrell. But it's Alexander Siddig's show, and his amazing performance as Dr. Bashir, in concert with Shankar's script, makes this the definitive Dr. Bashir episode and one of *Star Trek's* great achievements.

Did you know? Auberjonois's first location shoot was a rough one. One night, a particularly bad storm washed the sets away and delayed production by three days while they were rebuilt.

"Body Parts": C

When Quark is told he is dying, he auctions off his body parts.

Air date: June 10, 1996
Teleplay by Hans Beimler
Story by Louis P. DeSantis & Robert J. Bolivar
Directed by Avery Brooks
TV rating: 5.1

"I'm going to die. Don't you worry about that. I just want to find the right way."
—Quark

"Body Parts" takes a comedic premise and turns it into a fine story about what being a Ferengi means to Quark. With Jeffrey Combs (Brunt) playing the antagonist, Shimerman has fun playing up expatriate issues that the writers usually reserve for Worf. Of course, you're never going to have a Quark episode with the depth of "Sins of the Father," but it does make for a nice change of pace. Combs himself is fine as Quark's adversary, though his character's motivation for becoming a thorn in Quark's side is sketchy at best, coming across as contrived as a comic book villain's stupid plan to conquer the earth.

Meanwhile, a B story with Kira and the O'Briens is introduced to work Nana Visitor's pregnancy into the show. Unfortunately, it makes Keiko even more of a third wheel than before.

Director Avery Brooks, knowing he's working with two stories with predictable endings, plays up the visual whimsy to compensate for the lack of surprise. In the end, however, "Body Parts" is simply an average offering sandwiched between two more ambitious and memorable episodes.

Did you know? From this episode onward, Andrew Robinson is credited as Andrew J. Robinson. The J stands for Jordt, his grandfather's first name.

"Broken Link": B

Odo is plagued by an unknown ailment as the Federation and the Klingon Empire move closer to war. (Season finale)

Air date: June 17, 1996
Teleplay by Robert Hewitt Wolfe & Ira Steven Behr
Story by George A. Brozak
Directed by Les Landau
TV rating: 6.2

"You caused my illness so that I'd be forced to come home." —Odo

While there are *Star Trek* episodes that include illnesses and life-threatening situations, this character-based Odo episode is the first to be about a regular in the latter stages of deteriorating health for which his loved ones can do nothing. It's one of the saddest parts of human existence, and a reminder of our mortality. To see it happen to Odo, alien as he is, is heartbreakingly effective as a piece of drama—for we know deep down, he's as human as us.

The first half of the story sees Odo battling to hold onto his dignity while literally falling apart, not wanting the attention or pity of the others. Each scene Auberjonois shares with his fellow castmates is gold, with director Les Landau mining little moments for all their worth,-including a precious moment between Odo and Quark. The second half shifts into a sequel to the Founders storyline last significantly seen in the previous season finale, "The Adversary." More of a legal matter than a medical issue, it nonetheless carries on the mood of an impending funeral with guest star Salome Jens playing the part of the Changeling leader with a heavy weight of sadness on her shoulders. It's also particularly interesting to see her character interact with Garak because her powerful determinedness meeting Garak's indomitable spirit is like the irresistible force meeting the immovable object!

A sidestory about the Klingon Empire is played in a way that's reminiscent of George Orwell's *Nineteen Eighty-Four* (or the Apple Macintosh commercial based on the book), which successfully creates a threat at a distance.

As a season finale, it all adds up to a decidedly low-key affair. But as an Odo episode, it's a standout and a key to his future character development.

The Changeling leader returns in Season Six.

Did you know? "Broken Link" was the first *Star Trek* season finale to be conceived by an outside writer.

The Fourth Season in Review

DS9 continues to change and evolve in Season Four, most notably sporting a faster rendition of its theme song along with a new opening sequence designed by Dan Curry. Meanwhile, the Klingons return to a position of importance, with Worf's return to television being one of the medium's most notable stories of 1995. For a show built on a foundation of Bajoran politics that had been laying the groundwork for three-pronged Dominion stories, it's another ball in the air to juggle, and the question is whether one will fall to the ground. Yet even with studio pressure to drop the Bajoran stories, and with the Klingons and Jem'Hadar increasingly getting more screen-time, Season Four still finds time to keep the everyone in the mix.

Behind the scenes, the show's producers are more willing than ever to let *Star Trek's* own talent run the asylum. LeVar Burton replaces Jonathan Frakes in the show's director rotation, overseeing five episodes, supervising producer David Livingston directs four, René Auberjonois and Avery Brooks direct two apiece, and director of photography Jonathan West directs one as well, with their total making up more than half the season.

Meanwhile, Siddig El Fadil, a working actor needing a simpler name for forgetful casting directors, changes his billing to Alexander Siddig for his acting credits. "Siddig El Fadil is still my real name," he clarifies. "but for an actor it wasn't so suitable."

In front of the camera, Bashir finally gains the rank of full lieutenant, Dax becomes a lieutenant commander, and Kira gets a new uniform with reduced shoulder pads, an altered neckline, and a darker color to accent her femininity and allow her to move more freely.

But the biggest news to *Star Trek* fans would be a mid-season announcement: *Star Trek's* first in-house baby was on the way, courtesy of Siddig and Nana Visitor.

Quality-wise, Season Four is certainly one of *Star Trek's* best, with the "The Visitor" topping many lists as *DS9's* greatest episode, and standouts such as "Our Man Bashir," "Hard Time," and "The Quickening" filling out a season with only one real flop, "The Muse."

In the end, about the only thing missing is Avery Brooks's hair.

Season Five

Production Order
(with air date order in parentheses)

1. "Apocalypse Rising" (1st)
2. "The Ship" (2nd)
3. "Looking for par'Mach in All the Wrong Places" (3rd)
4. "Nor the Battle to the Strong" (4th)
5. "Trials and Tribble-ations" (6th)
6. "The Assignment" (5th)
7. "Let He Who is Without Sin..." (7th)
8. "Things Past" (8th)
9. "The Ascent" (9th)
10. "Rapture" (10th)
11. "The Darkness and the Light" (11th)
12. "The Begotten" (12th)
13. "For the Uniform" (13th)
14. "In Purgatory's Shadow" (14th)
15. "By Inferno's Light" (15th)
16: "Doctor Bashir, I Presume" (16th)
17: "A Simple Investigation" (17th)
18. "Business as Usual" (18th)
19. "Ties of Blood and Water" (19th)
20: "Ferengi Love Songs" (20th)
21. "Soldiers of the Empire" (21st)
22. "Children of Time" (22nd)
23: "Blaze of Glory" (23rd)
24. "Empok Nor" (24th)
25. "In the Cards" (25th)
26: "Call to Arms" (26th)

The Fifth Season Cast

Captain Sisko: Avery Brooks
Major Kira: Nana Visitor
Odo: René Auberjonois
Chief O'Brien: Colm Meaney
Dax: Terry Farrell
Dr. Bashir: Alexander Siddig
Jake Sisko: Cirroc Lofton
Quark: Armin Shimerman
Worf: Michael Dorn

Notable Guest Stars

Robert O'Reilly
J.G. Hertzler
Marc Alaimo
Casey Biggs
Rosalind Chao
Mary Kay Adams
Joseph Ruskin
Danny Goldring
The Cast of *TOS*
Charlie Brill
Max Grodénchik
Monte Markham
Chase Masterson
Andrew Robinson
Aron Eisenberg
Penny Johnson
Louise Fletcher
James Sloyan
Duncan Regehr
Kenneth Marshall
Paul Dooley
Melanie Smith
Robert Picardo
Dey Young
Steven Berkoff
Lawrence Pressman
Jeffrey Combs
Cecily Adams

"Apocalypse Rising:" B–

Sisko leads an undercover team in an attempt to expose a Changeling impersonating a Klingon leader.

Air date: September 30, 1996
Written by Ira Steven Behr & Robert Hewitt Wolfe
Directed by James L. Conway
TV rating: 5.6

"So let me get this straight: all we have to do is get past an enemy fleet, avoid a tachyon detection grid, beam into the middle of Klingon headquarters, and avoid The Brotherhood of The Sword long enough to set these things up and activate them in front of Gowron." —O'Brien

Don't be fooled. Despite its pretentious title and season opening slot, "Apocalypse Rising," a loose sequel to "Broken Link," is a simple caper/assassination story that's fine as an episode but hardly the spectacular season kickoff *DS9* fans are used to.

The plot itself is like a polyjuice potion infiltration mission, complete with dramatic and comedic possibilities that are both taken advantage of. And while it comes across as standard paint-by-number storytelling, the direction and acting are good enough to carry the idea from start to finish with plenty of excitement and few slow spots. Still, there are better Klingon episodes ("The Way of the Warrior" being one of them) and the show does a better caper story with its Season Seven episode, "Badda-Bing, Badda-Bang."

The Changeling infiltration arc continues later in the season with "In Purgatory's Shadow."

"Apocalypse Rising" was nominated for Emmys for cinematography and make-up.

Did you know? J.G. Hertzler, who plays Martok, first guest starred on *DS9* as a Vulcan in the show's pilot. He would go on to play a lost Changeling in Season Seven's "Chimera" before appearing as a Hirogen fighter on *VOY* and a pair of Klingons on *ENT*. Because he's been billed under different names for different parts, credited as J.G. Hertzler, John Noah Hertzler, and Garman Hertzler, there are some fans who have mistakenly assumed there are several Hertzler brothers who have landed parts on *Star Trek*.

"The Ship": C–

Sisko fights to keep the wreckage of a crashed Jem'Hadar fighter.

Air date: October 7, 1996
Teleplay by Hans Beimler
Story by Pam Wigginton & Rick Cason
Directed by Kim Friedman
TV rating: 6.0

"We found a wrecked ship and a dead crew, and we found it first." — Sisko

A good example of a premise gone wrong, "The Ship," inspired by the Battle of the Alamo, is nonetheless a fan favorite.

It's easy to see what the writers are going for here: Sisko and company are trapped in an enemy ship, and the captain is forced to make tough decisions while his crew bickers among themselves. Two problems: first, Sisko really isn't trapped on the ship, regularly leaving it to negotiate with a Vorta, and the crew's bickering comes across as arbitrary and forced.

The Vorta race itself suffers another setback. With Weyoun unavailable, the show goes in a different direction, giving us a sexy Vorta female, complete with lip gloss and cleavage, played by Kaitlin Hopkins. ("Maybe she lost an earring," Dax comments.) She has all the charisma and leadership abilities of a Wal-mart checkout clerk, basically letting Sisko walk all over her as she acts unsure of herself. Fortunately, the character is never seen again, though the actress reappears as a fake Kathryn Janeway in Season Six of *VOY*.

The ship itself, which is cleverly brought to life by an upside-down set, includes a surprise story point, though this is really just there to serve as a MacGuffin. With some work, this twist could have made the episode better. For example, if the ship is hiding a Changeling defector, this would explain the crash, add layers to the plot, and create an interesting relationship between the Changeling, the Jem'Hadar, and the Vorta. As is, the surprise is underwhelming and anticlimactic, leading to nowhere.

Despite all this, "The Ship" includes some great location work and some fine acting by Brooks, Farrell, and Meaney, who each give it enough emotional scenes to resonate with viewers.

Did you know? F.J. Rio, who guest stars in *DS9's* "Starship Down" and "The Ship" as Ensign Muniz, would go on to play a Benkaran prisoner in *VOY's* "Repentance" and a Vissian chief engineer in *ENT's* "Cogenitor."

"Looking for par'Mach in All the Wrong Places": C+

Worf helps Quark deal with Quark's Klingon ex-wife, Grilka.

Air date: October 14, 1996
Written by Ronald D. Moore
Directed by Andrew J. Robinson
TV rating: 5.7

"This is ridiculous! I'm surrounded by corpses, my shoes are dripping in blood, and you want me to feel romantic?" —Quark

With a title based on an old Johnny Lee song (because, I assume, the Shakespearean random title generator was broken), this lighthearted Quark/Worf episode serves as a sequel to Season Three's "The House of Quark," bringing back Mary Kay Adams as Quark's ex-wife for *Star Trek's* version of *Cyrano de Bergerac*. (Dax thoughtfully catches viewers up to speed on the prequel and explains that "par'Mach" is the Klingon word for love.)

The whole thing is really just a low-budget filler episode, but it benefits from having a gorgeous Klingon set left over from "Apocalypse Rising" and rich character interplay, including a B story about O'Brien and Kira trying to avoid a relationship. With Quark and Worf paired up for the first time, and Kira and O'Brien entering into new territory as an accidental couple (with Keiko naively unaware of what's going on), it's the perfect story for Andrew J. Robinson, an award winning stage director, to oversee as he makes his *Star Trek* directorial debut.

Did you know? After appearing as a child in *TOS's* "Miri" and playing the cadet in *Star Trek III: The Search for Spock* who asks Admiral Kirk if there will be a ceremony when the Enterprise returns to Earth, Phil Morris finally gets his first credited *Star Trek* part in this episode as Quark's Klingon adversary, Thopok.

"...Nor the Battle to the Strong": B–

Attempting to aid a Federation hospital, Jake and Dr. Bashir are caught in the middle of a battle between a Federation colony and a Klingon army.

Air date: October 21, 1996
Teleplay by René Echevarria
Story by Brice R. Parker
Directed by Kim Friedman
TV rating: 5.0

"It takes courage to look inside yourself, and more courage to write it for other people to see." —Captain Sisko

Calling Gene Roddenberry a visionary is hardly original, but when it comes to television, most people don't know just how far ahead of the curve he was. Back when most people thought of TV as *I Love Lucy* and *The Honeymooners*, Roddenberry imagined other possibilities. He came up with the idea of a show on a cruise ship, with regulars as the crew and guest stars as the passengers. Also, having seen the expansion of the airline industry firsthand as a commercial pilot, he thought a show about travel would be a big hit and could help people better understand how to visit foreign countries. And tapping into his World War II experience, he even had the idea of a show taking place during wartime, following a team of doctors and their support staff working just beyond enemy lines.

TV wasn't ready for these ideas in the 1950s or the 1960s, but eventually, other producers were able to turn the concepts into hits, and *Star Trek* reruns would, ironically, have to compete against them. In fact, the two most watched shows of the 1970s were *Star Trek* and *M*A*S*H*. So it's somewhat fitting that in the 1990s, the two concepts would be merged for an episode of *DS9*: "Nor the Battle to the Strong."

The biblically named Jake Sisko episode is one of *Star Trek's* most unique offerings, interspersing hospital-like medical emergencies with personal conversations between Jake, Dr. Bashir, and the guest stars. The formula provides ample opportunity for drama and character development, and while some of the others ham it up around him, Cirroc Lofton, in the most significant episode of his career, plays it straight and carries the episode with a compelling performance full of texture. It's especially interesting to see his interaction with Alexander Siddig, with Jake being on the brink of beginning his adult life and the young Dr. Bashir serving as a role model of sorts. It's a mentoring relationship that is seen less often than the more traditional father/son story.

And what of Jake's father? For once, he's away from the action, awaiting the good or bad news. Avery Brooks is great in this unusual B story, perhaps playing off his real feelings. With his minimal part in the episode, he would have been the perfect choice to direct it, and surely he would have loved

133

working with Lofton and exploring the meaty subject matter. Instead, the director reins go to *ER* veteran Kim Friedman, which works out just as well, since she knows just how to shoot the hospital-like sequences.

It all adds up to a *Star Trek* installment that breaks new ground while remaining true to the roots of the franchise, honoring the creator along the way.

Did you know? The title for this episode comes from the Bible, appearing in the book of Ecclesiastes, Chapter 9, Verse 11: "I returned, and saw under the sun, that the race is not to the swift, nor the battle to the strong, neither yet bread to the wise, nor yet riches to men of understanding, nor yet favor to men of skill; but time and chance happeneth to them all."

"The Assignment": D+

An alien possesses Keiko and forces Chief O'Brien to carry out mysterious instructions.

Air date: October 28, 1996
Teleplay by David Weddle & Bradley Thompson
Story by David R. Long & Robert Lederman
Directed by Allan Kroeker
TV rating: N/A

"Listen carefully, Miles. I have taken possession of your wife's body. I will hold it hostage until you do everything I tell you to, accurately and without question."
—Keiko

Reminiscent of "Power Play" but executed in a more personal, intimate way, this Chief O'Brien episode gives Rosalind Chao her most significant part since Keiko's introduction in *TNG's* "Data's Day." She plays it sufficiently creepy, clearly enjoying the opportunity to step out of her normal "blah" role. Unfortunately, there's not much of a plot to the episode beyond the premise, and the writers stretch it out a little too far, although working Rom into the plot is a nice touch, and the story introduces what would turn out to be a significant part of the series, with its adversary returning to become a major force in Seasons Six and Seven.

In truth, however, "The Assignment," like most of the early Season Five episodes, is just a low budget placeholder, with the show saving money for the next episode, the most unique in *Star Trek's* history.

Did you know? With Jay Chattaway and Dennis McCarthy unavailable, Gregory Smith stepped in and provided the musical score for this episode. He would go on to score "Honor Among Thieves" and "Field of Fire" before providing some uncredited music for the series finale. In 2006, he conducted a new recording of the *Star Trek* theme song for the remastered version of *TOS*.

"Trials and Tribble-ations": A

When Temporal Investigations arrives on Deep Space Nine, Sisko recounts how he and the crew of the Defiant traveled back in time to the 23rd century, hopping aboard the original Enterprise to prevent the assassination of Captain James T. Kirk while everyone was having "trouble with tribbles."

Air date: November 4, 1996
Teleplay by Ronald D. Moore and René Echevarria
Story by Ira Steven Behr, Hans Beimler & Robert Hewitt Wolfe
Directed by Jonathan West
TV rating: 7.7

"I lied to Captain Kirk! I wish Keiko could have been there to see it." —O'Brien

If there is one episode of *Star Trek* that can be called the greatest technological achievement of the franchise, it's this one, the brainchild of writer René Echevarria. Yet it's not the special effects that make it such a beloved part of the *Star Trek* canon, it's the episode's heart. Just as "All Good Things," the *TNG* finale, celebrates *TNG* by capturing the spirit of its entire run in one episode, "Trials and Tribble-ations" is a celebration of *TOS*; a love letter to the fans that not only captures the feel of the Kirk era but also the charm. Part of the reason for this is simple: if you're going to revisit one classic *TOS* episode, choosing "The Trouble with Tribbles" is a no-brainer. It's the most famous and fun of them all, and almost everyone loves it. Throw in some new optical effects (which would later be done for all the episodes of the original series) and it opens the door for the best kind of nostalgia trip: where everything seems bigger and better than it really was. It may not be the original series as people knew it in the 1960s, but it's how we want to remember it.

Striking just the right balance between old footage, new footage, and a hybrid of the two, the episode surpasses *Forrest Gump* by using the "new characters in old footage" trick as part of the plot (such that there is) as opposed to simply a gimmick. And while the story is hardly perfect in terms of plotting and pacing, which is to be expected, considering the constraints of a tale of this nature, it fulfills its purpose, which is really just to serve as a clothesline to hang some gags on. Assembled together, the various scenes effectively create the illusion that we really have stepped into *Star Trek's* past, with the original Enterprise crewmembers acknowledging the presence of the *Deep Space Nine* characters just enough times to make us feel like one of the *DS9ers* could actually walk up to Jim Kirk or Mr. Spock and interact with them. (Well, actually…let's just say that "Lieutenant" Sisko pays off the whole premise by doing just what every fan of *TOS* would do in his place.)

It's the result of a behind-the-scenes crew pouring more work into a *Star Trek* episode than ever before, chasing down details to make sure all the elements work so perfectly together, they all disappear into the story. I could tell you that they used old style camera lenses, lighting, and film stock. Or that they manufactured perfect facsimiles of Enterprise interiors, complete with vintage wall intercoms, turbolift controls, and blinking lights. I could even mention that they found some original Klingon uniforms stored away in a box, which saved the worried costume designer from having to duplicate their unique look. But really, none of this is necessary to know to enjoy the episode. As fans, we need just sit down, watch, and enjoy stepping into *Star Trek's* past with our *DS9* friends; laughing with Chief O'Brien while taking a ride with him on an old style turbolift, ducking for cover with Dr. Bashir during an old school fistfight with the Klingons, and marveling along with Sisko and Dax as Captain Kirk and Mr. Spock suddenly walk their way. And if we notice David Gerrold, the writer of the original "Tribbles" episode, in one of his "Gump" style cameos, so much the better. (Check him out as the gray-haired man who passes Sisko and Dax when the Enterprise goes to red alert.) But in the end, "Trials and Tribble-ations" is not about new computer technologies or even the hard work of the behind the scenes team, but what they achieve together. There may be better *Star Trek* episodes than this one, but when it comes to nostalgia and magic, "Tribble-ations" towers over the rest, standing out as one of the great wonders of television. It's an amazing confluence of two generations and, by allowing us to live vicariously through the *DS9* characters, about the closest most of us will ever get to really visiting the Enterprise.

"Trials and Tribble-ations" was nominated for Emmys for art direction, hairstyling, and visual effects and went on to win the 1997 Hugo for Best Dramatic Presentation.

Did you know? While discussing possibilities for what would eventually become "Trials and Tribble-ations" at a pizza parlor, the *DS9* producers suddenly spotted Charles Brill, a guest star from "The Trouble with Tribbles." They didn't approach him there for fear of complicating negotiations that are supposed to involve an agent, but it did cement their ideas and lead to Brill's return to *Star Trek*.

"Let He Who is Without Sin...": F

While on vacation, Bashir and Leeta break up while Worf joins a radical group determined to start a political revolution.

Air date: November 11, 1996
Written by Robert Hewitt Wolfe & Ira Steven Behr
Directed by René Auberjonois
TV rating: 7.0

"I see. Ruin the vacations of a few hundred thousand people to bolster the moral fiber of the Federation." —Dax

And here we get a confluence of awful, as the writers take one bad idea (Bashir and Leeta partake in a bizarre Bajoran breakup ritual) and marry it with another (Worf wants to spoil everyone's fun).Director René Auberjonois, augmenting the stage sets with location shooting at Malibu, finds a way to make the story somewhat watchable, playing up the humor and shock value of the characters' actions, but it mostly comes across as a bad episode of *The Love Boat*. The characters play caricatures of themselves, spouting trite dialogue as if the teleplay was a piece of fan fiction that was somehow mistaken for the script, and the plot takes forever to develop before we wish it would just go away.

The one bright spot is guest star Monte Markham, who plays the charismatic leader of the New Essentials, a group that comes across as a futuristic version of the Tea Party. His point of view, however—that vacations are a bad idea—isn't really worthy of an episode.

Did you know? While this episode was being shot in September of 1996, Nana Visitor gave birth to Django el Fadil.

"Things Past": C

In a dreamlike state, Sisko, Odo, Dax, and Garak find themselves stuck in the past and accused of planting a bomb.

Air date: November 18, 1996
Written by Michael Taylor
Directed by LeVar Burton
TV rating: 6.0

"Go beneath the surface! Conduct a real investigation!" —Odo

This episode, reminiscent of *TOS's* "Spectre of the Gun," is a companion piece to Season Two's "Necessary Evil," returning us to the dark days when the Cardassians ran *Deep Space Nine* and exploring Odo's past in a roundabout way. The plot goes in circles for a while, coasting on the mystery of the premise, before finding a direction in the second half and turning into a satisfying Odo character piece, making us wonder why Sisko, Garak, and Dax are such a large part of this thing to begin with. Overall, however, it comes across as a poor man's "Necessary Evil," with the same dystopian cinematography and a similar surprise revelation, but without the great plot and story structure of its predecessor.

Worth watching? Yes. A special *DS9* episode? No.

Did you know? While in production, this episode was jokingly christened "Nightmare on Odo Street."

139

"The Ascent": C+

When Odo and Quark are stranded on a planet, their only hope is to carry a heavy transmitter to the top of a mountain.

Air date: November 25, 1996
Written by Ira Steven Behr & Robert Hewitt Wolfe
Directed by Allan Kroeker
TV rating: 6.0

"Quark, wake up. We've got a mountain to climb." —Odo

Odo and Quark finally get an A story together in this dialogue-driven relationship study that begins with the same basic idea as the Quark story in "Starship Down" before becoming a mountain story reminiscent of Frodo and Sam's ascent of Mount Doom in *The Lord of the Rings*. Featuring location shooting at Mount Whitney, the tallest mountain in the conterminous United States, it provides a unique setting for *Star Trek* and gives the writers plenty of opportunity to include dialogue in the style of *Waiting for Godot*. (Think of it as Vladimir and Estragon trying to destroy the Ring of Doom.) The beauty of the premise is that unlike "Heart of Stone," which has danger in the form of a sci-fi metaphor, the danger in "The Ascent" is much more familiar, making the peril seem all the more real and the dialogue feel all the more dramatic.

Meanwhile, Jake and Nog move in together in the B story, leading to lifestyle clashes that are played for laughs. The *Star Trek* equivalent of *Perfect Strangers*, it's just a forgettable subplot thrown in by the writers to get Nog back on *Deep Space Nine*. Unfortunately, it doesn't work well with the A story and drags the episode down as a whole.

Did you notice? Jake's story that Nog proofreads shares the same title as *DS9's* second episode, "Past Prologue."

"Rapture": C

Sisko must choose between his faith and his life after he begins having visions that threaten his health.

Air date: December 30, 1996
Teleplay by Hans Beimler
Story by L.J. Strom
Directed by Jonathan West
TV rating: 6.0

"The baby I'm holding in my hands now is the universe itself. And I need time to study its face." —Sisko

Star Trek's version of *Field of Dreams* falls short of the mark due to budget and point of view issues, but remains popular with fans due to its subject matter.

With Sisko facing an uncontrollable compulsion, "Rapture" is a more spiritual episode than the usual *Star Trek* fare and strikes a chord with viewers looking for more depth in Sisko's Emissary role. Unfortunately, the budget limits scenes to the station and the cave sets and only allows for only a couple of guest stars. So instead of sharing Sisko's visions along with him, we only hear about the experiences after they happen. Apart from being a less exciting way to tell the story ("You should have been there, it was great!") it puts a barrier between Sisko and the audience, and forces us to view the story from the perspective of an outsider. It's like taking *TNG's* "Inner Light" and replacing all of Picard's experiences with Patrick Stewart telling us about how amazing they were.

Still, "Rapture" is a landmark episode for Sisko as the Emissary, and Brooks throws himself into the part with such vigor, it's infectious.

Did you know? A scene with Sisko carving shapes into a melon is included as an homage to a mashed-potato scene in the 1977 film *Close Encounters of the Third Kind*.

"The Darkness and the Light": B–

A hidden enemy systematically murders Kira's old Resistance comrades.

Air date: January 6, 1997
Teleplay by Ronald D. Moore
Story by Bryan Fuller
Directed by Michael Vejar
TV rating: 6.0

"I was a soldier. You're just a bitter old man out for revenge." —Kira

This loose sequel to Season Three's "Shakaar" is a well executed murder-mystery that somewhat succeeds despite its simplicity.

Director Michael Vejar returns to the *Star Trek* fold for the first time in nine years (joining the directors' rotation from here on out) and uses his steady hand to play up the suspense and surprises in Ron Moore's teleplay. There's nothing groundbreaking, and as mysteries go, the episode is underwhelming. But Vejar and Moore understand that the episode isn't really about the mystery or the murderer at all; it's about Kira. Exploring her emotions in a new situation while staying true to the character's roots, "Darkness" evolves into a powerful character piece reminiscent of Season Two's "Duet".

Guest star Randy Oglesby gets only one scene but makes the most of it, making it almost a shame we don't see more of him. Unfortunately, budget issues stemming from cost overruns in "Trials and Tribble-ations" ensure this one stays in its box, keeping it from becoming more ambitious.

Did you know? Randy Oglesby plays seven different *Star Trek* aliens, including the Xindi designer of a super-weapon on *ENT*.

"The Begotten": B

Odo discovers an infant Changeling and tries to teach it to shape-shift.

Air date: January 27, 1997
Written by René Echevarria
Directed by Jesus Salvador Trevino
TV rating: 6.2

"Constable, why are you talking to your beverage?" —Worf

This character-driven Odo episode is sort of a remake of Season Three's "The Abandoned," with Odo again exploring parenthood. Yet here the story works better because of a richer plot (a sequel to Season Two's "The Alternate") and two notable guest stars. There's James Sloyen, who returns as Odo's father-figure, and then there's a glass of goo, making its debut as Odo's adoptive son. Both are wonderful and set the stage for Auberjonois to carry the show with what might be his best performance as Odo, who must confront his past, present, and future on the most personal of terms.

Meanwhile, Kira prepares to give birth in a comedy runner that throws together O'Brien and Shakaar, with the latter making his final appearance, for some awkward scenes played for laughs. ("Next time you have a baby, leave my girlfriend out of it.") It's really just a filler-plot to set up the birth of the child, and it's kept appropriately short, doing what it has to while not overstaying its welcome.

Did you know? This is the first episode of the series in which Dax doesn't appear.

143

"For the Uniform": B

Sisko obsessively pursues the Maquis leader who betrayed him.

Air date: February 3, 1997
Written by Peter Allan Fields
Directed by Victor Lobl
TV rating: 6.0

"Can't you see what's happening to you? You're going against everything you claim to believe in. And for what? To satisfy a personal vendetta?" —Eddington

A sequel to Season Four's "For the Cause," this Sisko episode explores the ideas of obsession and stubbornness, turning the captain into a combination of Ahab from *Moby Dick* and, as acknowledged in the episode, Javert from *Les Misérables*. (With Victor Hugo unable to direct, they settle for Victor Lobl instead.) It's a personality that suits Sisko, and the antagonist's arrogance and smugness ensure that the audience's sympathies stay with the good guys regardless.

Most of the episode takes place on the Defiant, with the writers throwing in a couple of wrinkles. First, a 3D "holo-communicator" takes the place of the viewscreen, which allows the bad guy, well played by Kenneth Marshall, to interact with Sisko on the ship as opposed to through a TV screen. It's not a piece of technology that's suitable for regular use by the writers because it requires careful exposition to make clear the antagonist hasn't actually beamed *onto* the ship, and that sort of explanation isn't something they want to have to do every episode. But investing some time in this for one episode serves "Uniform" well. Second, damage to the Defiant leads the crew to operate the ship manually, complete with Nog having to relay messages between the bridge and engineering. The two ideas work in concert with each other to create an electric environment which is all the more special for not overstaying its welcome.

Kenneth Marshall's character and the Maquis both return one more time in Season Five's "Blaze of Glory." Meanwhile, the success of "For the Uniform" inspires the writers to go dark again and push the envelope even further in Season Six's "In the Pale Moonlight."

Did you know? The holo-communicator is used once more in the series in "Doctor Bashir, I Presume."

"In Purgatory's Shadow" (1): B

Garak and Worf investigate a message that suggests Garak's mentor is still alive.

Air date: February 10, 1997
Written by Robert Hewitt Wolfe & Ira Steven Behr
Directed by Gabrielle Beaumont
TV rating: 6.7

"We must escape and warn Captain Sisko before that Changeling carries out his mission." —Worf

This follow-up to Season Three's "Improbable Cause"/"The Die is Cast" is the opening of a two-parter itself, a Garak episode that finally answers some questions about his past. It's an ambitious offering with some big surprises, though most of the material is just exposition to set up "By Inferno's Light." Still, it's great to see Garak in an A story with Robinson at his best. He deftly delivers zingers early—"You know, I think that actually helped my back!"— before nailing a touching, heartfelt scene near the end.

The remainder of the episode features diverse character interplay, with Dukat and his daughter, now played by Melanie Smith, getting a B story that doesn't really go anywhere...yet.

It all leads to an inevitable "To be continued," with one of *DS9's* most dramatic cliffhangers.

Did you know? Derek Garth, one of *DS9's* lighting and rigging technicians, died in a car accident at age 50 in 1996. "In Purgatory's Shadow" is dedicated to his memory.

145

"By Inferno's Light" (2): B+

As Garak, Worf, and Bashir attempt to escape from a Dominion prison, Deep Space Nine prepares for a Dominion invasion.

Air date: February 17, 1997
Written by Ira Steven Behr & Robert Hewitt Wolfe
Directed by Les Landau
TV rating: 6.2

"Five years ago, no one had ever heard of Bajor or Deep Space Nine. Now all our hopes rest here." —Gowron

This exciting conclusion to another midseason two-parter owes thanks to a clever setup in two different ways. From a long-term standpoint, it benefits from a Dukat storyline that has threaded its way through the episodes since the beginning, and a Dominion storyline which has been carefully cultivated over several seasons. Both have thrived in *DS9's* semi-serial format, and here, in a stroke of genius, they are combined. From a short-term standpoint, the story is fortunate to follow "In Purgatory's Shadow," an episode that puts everything in position for "Inferno" to jump straight into its drama. "Part I" sets up the pins. "Part II" knocks them all down.

Eschewing a big special effects battle show, this one creates excitement from character development, switching back and forth between the Alpha and Gamma Quadrants. On the Alpha side, we have Sisko and his crew in a military thriller that generates political intrigue through the decisions of the Federation, the Dominion, the Cardassians, the Klingons, and the Romulans. Full of twists and turns, the events put into motion here will go on to affect the remainder of the series. On the Gamma side we get a prison escape story featuring Garak and Worf. It's a plot that lacks movement for the most part but disguises the flaw with some fine acting by Andrew Robinson as Garak battles claustrophobia and some fine fighting by Michael Dorn as Worf kicks some Dominion ass. The internal and external struggles bring out the best in the two, and the writers use the opportunity to ease another Klingon character into the fray.

In the end, the episode delivers a satisfactory conclusion while still leaving us excited for what is yet to come, with an over the top closing musical tag ("dum-dum DUM!") perfectly summing it all up.

Did you know? After finishing his work on this episode, Robert O'Reilly (Gowron) took a break from acting. The reason? Just after midnight on January 1, 1998, his wife gave birth to triplets—Jack, Joseph, and Michael. O'Reilly next appears in Season Seven's "When It Rains…"

146

"Doctor Bashir, I Presume": B+

When Dr. Zimmerman arrives on Deep Space Nine, he discovers a secret about Dr. Bashir.

Air date: February 24, 1997
Teleplay by Ronald D. Moore
Story by Jimmy Diggs
Directed by David Livingston
TV rating: 5.6

"There's going to be a formal investigation which will lead to my eventual dismissal from the service." —Bashir

Robert Picardo (The Doctor from sister-show *VOY*) guest stars as Dr. Zimmerman, creator of the Emergency Medical Hologram, in this Bashir episode with a science fiction secret. The unique story structure cleverly uses Zimmerman as a catalyst for both the A and B stories, which, much like the best Doctor episodes on Voyager, balance comedy with drama. It's the perfect sort of cameo for Picardo, who plays Zimmerman with a similar acerbic sarcasm as his holographic counterpart, but throws in a subtle downplay of the attitude that comes across as more human. His character, however, is really just there to get us into the true story, one about Dr. Bashir, his parents, and their secret. This sci fi concept is something on the horizon that *Star Trek* has never thoroughly explored before, and it's an interesting story and character idea wrapped up in one package, explaining Bashir's established behaviors and personality while creating a more interesting character for future episodes.

Brian George and Fadwa El Guindi play Dr. Bashir's parents, and they're probably the best guest stars to play relatives on *Star Trek* since Worf's parents in *TNG's* "Family." Siddig himself, reportedly unhappy with the script and the way it was sprung on him, spends the episode looking sulky and thoroughly dissatisfied, but it works well for his performance, being appropriate for what his character is going through. In fact, the part where he explains his past, despite being just dialogue, is one of *DS9's* most compelling character moments.

The seriousness is tempered with the comedy of Dr. Zimmerman putting the moves on Leeta in a B story. It's just a short comedy runner with a tangent that gives Rom and Nog some backstory.

Did you know? The title of this episode is in reference to the famous quote, "Dr. Livingstone, I presume?" Henry Morton Stanley, a reporter for the *New York Herald*, reportedly spoke these words in 1871 when he succeeded in finding Dr. David Livingstone, a Scottish missionary and explorer of Africa who had lost contact with the outside world for six years. After exchanging greetings, Stanley joined Livingstone in exploring the region.

147

"A Simple Investigation": B

Odo falls for a mysterious woman who is targeted for murder.

Air date: March 31, 1997
Written by René Echevarria
Directed by John Kretchmer
TV rating: 5.2

"Tell me, Arianna, what's a nice woman like you doing with a dataport?" —Odo

With *Star Trek* once again drawing inspiration from *The Bodyguard*, this "simple" Odo episode sees our favorite Changeling become interested in a woman under his protection. While hardly an original plot, the episode itself is a solid filler offering with some touching character moments. And while *Star Trek* romances between regulars and the short-term guest stars usually aren't that interesting, writer René Echevarria finds a way to make it work here, with René Auberjonois and Dey Young (Arissa) throwing themselves into the script and building some chemistry.

It's just too bad they couldn't squeeze this episode in earlier in the season. With Odo being more human, the physical scenes between the two would be much more interesting.

Did you know? Dey Young also appears in *TNG's* "The Masterpiece Society," playing a scientist who works with La Forge, and *ENT's* "Two Days and Two Nights," playing an alien who attempts to seduce Captain Archer.

148

"Business as Usual": C+

Quark's cousin offers him a job as a weapons dealer.

Air date: April 7, 1997
Written by Bradley Thompson & David Weddle
Directed by Siddig El Fadil
TV rating: 5.3

"I am here to buy weapons. Are you here to sell them?" —Regent of Palomar

Testing the limits of Quark's greed, this lighthearted episode has its moments, even if it amounts to little of substance. The structure of the story is simple but effective: the exposition is laid out, consequences are established, and a dilemma is created. It's like an episode of *Leave it to Beaver*, if the Beaver fell in with weapon smugglers and was worried about 28 million deaths. It's a good opportunity for the show to bring in some tough guy character actors, and it's a lot of fun to see Quark deal with them. It's also fun to see him try to weasel his way out if his dilemma, even if the ending is a bit of a cheat with a resolution shown off screen.

Meanwhile, there's a comedy runner comprised of Chief O'Brien's baby being fussy. (It is what it is.)

Rookie director Siddig El Fadil overdoes the clever directing at times, with extreme angles and lots of movement that call too much attention to the shooting style and distract from the story. But with an episode that's somewhat tongue-in-cheek to begin with, it's something he can get away with.

The best way to sum it all up is that it's like a good Ferengi episode with only two Ferengis.

Did you know? One of the weapons Quark sells is a Breen CRM-114, a reference to the CRM-114 device found in the B-52 bombers in the 1964 film *Dr. Strangelove or: How I Learned to Stop Worrying and Love the Bomb*.

"Ties of Blood and Water": C+

A Cardassian that Kira has grown close to comes to the station to spend his final days with her.

Air date: April 14, 1997
Teleplay by Robert Hewitt Wolfe
Story by Edmund Newton & Robbin L. Slocum
Directed by Avery Brooks
TV rating: N/A

"I...I was thirsty. I'm...I'm sorry." —Ghemor, after reaching for a glass of water and knocking it over

Caring for a loved one who needs continuing assistance can be a thankless job. It's a selfless act that deserves acknowledgement and praise. It does not, however, make for compelling television. There are two inherent flaws for a story of this type. First, the characters lack mobility because one has to tie the other down. And second, the plot lacks movement because there's nowhere to go with it. Nonetheless, the actors give it a go as Avery Brooks directs this episode that brings back Ghemor for a sequel to Season Three's "Second Skin" and explores his relationship with Kira as patient and caregiver.

To disguise the story's fundamental problems, the episode employs a complex narrative structure. Along with the A story about Kira and Ghemor, there are flashback scenes that are used to draw parallels between the last days of Ghemor and the last days of Kira's father, with Kira's past experiences influencing her present decisions. It's a witty structural idea *DS9* pulls out once in awhile ("Necessary Evil, "Hard Time") and it seems to work every time, which is probably why future TV shows such as *Lost* and *This is Us* borrow the formula. Meanwhile, the B story plays up the military and political consequences of Ghemor's defection from Cardassia, reminiscent of the time when the United States granted medical asylum to Iran's overthrown Shah, Mohammad Reza Pahlavi, while giving us some tense Dukat/Sisko sequences.

But in the end, it's Kira's relationship with Ghemor that forms the heart of the show, with Visitor and Lawrence Pressman making the most of it, mining a daring subject matter for any show but one that's doubly so for a science fiction program with so many other options.

Did you know? For his reprisal of Ghemor, Pressman was happy to be guided by director Avery Brooks. "Avery's a man who keeps to himself," he says. "He doesn't chat easily. But as a director he was right there and extraordinarily helpful. Somebody said to me, 'Avery talks jazz.' And it's true. What's more, it's brilliant jazz, wonderful stuff. He gives you images, and he does it through eye contact with you, so you get the feeling of what he wants."

"Ferengi Love Songs": C

Quark discovers that Grand Nagus Zek is having a secret relationship with his mother.

Air date: April 21, 1997
Written by Ira Steven Behr & Hans Beimler
Directed by René Auberjonois
TV rating: 4.8

"Wait a minute, what's the Nagus doing in my closet?" —Quark

DS9 returns to Ferenginar for another Ferengi comedy directed by René Auberjonois. The premise is solid. (I wish I could go back in time and pitch the idea of the Grand Nagus hooking up with Quark's mom, because it would have been an easy payday). Some of the gags are funny, with Quark discovering Zek hiding in the closet especially hilarious. But there are problems that undermine the success of the episode as a whole. The first is that Quark's mom has been recast, with Cecily Adams taking the place of Andrea Martin. It's sort of like replacing Tom Hanks with Pauly Shore. Adams tries to play the part as Martin did, but she just doesn't have the same comedic timing, and it's especially disappointing that we don't get to see Martin and Wallace Shawn together.

The second problem is that the silly Ferengi A story is saddled with a silly Ferengi B story: Rom and Leeta have a comedic breakup en route to their comedic decision to tie the knot. It's a trope that's appeared on television too often, including its appearance in *TNG's* "Data's Day".

Happily, the Ferengi would fare better in their next big episode, Season Six's "The Magnificent Ferengi."

Did you know? Cecily Adams, born in 1958, is younger than the actors playing her sons, with Armin Shimerman born in 1949 and Max Grodénchik born in 1952.

"Soldiers of the Empire": B–

After Worf becomes the first officer of a Klingon Bird-of-Prey, he is caught between loyalty to his commander and loyalty to the crew.

Air date: April 28, 1997
Written by Ronald D. Moore
Directed by LeVar Burton
TV rating: 5.2

"Make your jokes. Hold off fate for another day if you can, but this ship and all the souls within its hull are cursed." —Kornan

Following up the cliché Ferengi comedy is this cliché Klingon honor episode, with LeVar Burton directing Michael Dorn again for this standalone story featuring Worf, Dax, Martok and a crew of Klingons aboard a Bird-of-Prey. It's basically that old sports story where an outsider joins a loser team and tries to turn the culture around—except this version has Klingons in place of athletes. It's the sort of story that might come off as hokey, but veteran writer/Klingon expert Ron Moore makes the old plot work, ensuring that no moment feels dishonest or inauthentic. It especially helps that Dorn and Farrell know their characters like the back of their hands by this point, and the histories of Worf and Dax give Moore and the actors plenty to draw from. As the episode moves along, it balances out character-driven scenes that define the "players" with suspense and action, building the story like a crescendo. In the end, it's all about Martok, with J.G. Hertzler deftly playing the old has-been "coach" of a team that no one believes in. As Hertzler sinks his teeth into his meatiest role to date, he plays each scene with the perfect amount of grit and weariness, and even though the plot itself is as old as the hills, we still can't help but wonder how it's all going to end. Is it as good as *TNG's* "Redemption"? No. Klingon stories by this point have lost their freshness and have become somewhat redundant. But "Soldiers" is still pretty darn good.

Did you know? J.G. Hertzler found performing with one eye challenging. "I had no depth perception, so I would walk into walls," he later admitted. "And I didn't see anything on one side from my nose over, so people would walk up to me and start talking, and I didn't know who it was. I couldn't turn abruptly, or I'd knock them over."

"Children of Time": A

Sisko and the crew of the Defiant discover a planet populated by their own descendants.

Air date: May 5, 1997
Teleplay by René Echevarria
Story by Gary Holland & Ethan H. Calk
Directed by Allan Kroeker
TV rating: 5.5

"This settlement was founded by the crew of a Starfleet vessel that crashed on this planet two centuries ago. I realize this is going to be hard for you to accept, but that ship was the Defiant. Two days from now, when you leave here and try to pass through the energy barrier, you'll be thrown back in time two hundred years. You'll be stranded here and become the founders of this settlement. We are your descendants." —Miranda O'Brien

With its high concept and sweet title, this episode almost always cracks those *DS9* Top Ten lists of favorite episodes, and deservedly so. Unwilling to coast on the killer premise (and unable to use the station), writer René Echevarria uses each character to develop the story, giving each of them a personal issue and character arc as the beats of the episode unfold. It's not always a lot—O'Brien's part, in particular, is pretty simplistic—but sometimes it's mind-boggling. Either way, Echevarria fits all the pieces together so well, you'd never know he was weaving together two separate story pitches.

The heart of the story is the Kira/Odo relationship, which moves forward in probably the most bizarre fashion in the history of television. (The show certainly can't be accused of falling back on an old cliché, like sticking them in a broken elevator.) The continued development of this relationship itself is brilliantly handled by Auberjonois and Visitor, even if the actors were unsure of what to do with the script. (Visitor, by her own admission, disliked the writing and later said she no idea how to play it.) In the end, it's their uncomfortable lack of chemistry itself that's so interesting—and gives the writers more to work with in the future.

Still, the episode is not without its contrived points. The premise needs Kira to be healthy enough to be active, but sick enough to be dying. The solution? She's given a hidden sickness with no symptoms that will leave her dead in days if the crew can't escape. The episode also needs future-Odo to be able to interact with Kira without the present-Odo's interference. So present-Odo conveniently can't hold his form on this planet and is confined to a container.

Speaking of future-Odo, it would be nice to have a scene that shares a little more of his backstory. (In fact, there was going to be a scene where Odo tells Kira that after being stranded on the planet and watching all of his friends die, he left the colony to be on his own. But the scene was cut, and it's too bad, because it's interesting in its own right, and it explains a lot.)

Nonetheless, the premise itself is so strong, it would probably work for any of the *Star Trek* shows, and it certainly works here.

Did you know? This episode includes location shooting at Ahmanson Ranch, near Ventura, California. Unfortunately, on the day of the shoot there were gale force winds, forcing the crew to use equipment trucks as wind-blocks. Meanwhile, it was so cold, the crew wore snow jackets while the actors struggled through their scenes in shirt-sleeves.

Ahmanson Ranch (photo by Tyson Johnson)

154

"Blaze of Glory": C

When Sisko intercepts a message about a Maquis attack, he asks Eddington to help stop it.

Air date: May 12, 1997
Written by Robert Hewitt Wolfe & Ira Steven Behr
Directed by Kim Friedman
TV rating: N/A

"If you can't have victory, sometimes you just have to settle for revenge."
—Eddington

It's the old "enemies having to work together" story with Sisko and Eddington in a sequel (or coda) to "For the Uniform." Like "Indiscretion," which shares the same theme, the nature of the plot lends itself to dialogue, with most of the action taking place near the end. That's good for the budget—with sets from "Children of Time" reused, albeit with different lighting—but leads to an underwhelming Sisko episode, being more talky than exciting.

Still, there's something compelling about Eddington, which is probably why he keeps returning. Part of the reason might be that Kenneth Marshall is like him in many ways: he's talented and dependable, but he just doesn't have the look a leading man. Yet through Eddington, he's able to turn his everyman qualities into assets that shine in a way they otherwise wouldn't. We believe that this short, old, bald guy can be a charismatic leader, or at least that he wants to be.

Is it enough to make "Blaze of Glory" a standout episode? No. Though it includes a humorous B story where Nog tries to win the Klingons' respect, it lacks any elements to make it special. Personally I would have introduced a whole Eddington family. They almost go there, but they don't go far enough, and that's too bad because it would redefine the character, forcing us to reassess his life, and make the ending all the more poignant. In the end, however, Marshall's last appearance is much like himself: solid but unremarkable.

Did you know? In a scene at Quark's bar, the way Nog rocks his chair is an homage to Henry Fonda's character in *My Darling Clementine* (1946).

The Essential Eddington Episodes

- "The Search, Parts I & II"
- "The Die is Cast"
- "The Adversary"
- "For the Cause"
- "For the Uniform"
- "Blaze of Glory"

155

"Empok Nor": C+

Scavenging an old Cardassian space station for equipment, O'Brien and his team discover they are not alone.

Air date: May 19, 1997
Teleplay by Hans Beimler
Story by Bryan Fuller
Directed by Michael Vejar
TV rating: 4.9

"I'm not a tailor. Not for the moment anyway." —Garak

This suspenseful episode gives us O'Brien and Garak in a murder-mystery without much mystery before evolving into a story with shades of "The Most Dangerous Game." And while pairing up these two characters for the first time, the show introduces us to the writers' new playground: Deep Space Nine's abandoned sister-station, Empok Nor, with its nature giving *Star Trek* a new setting at no new expense. (Don't tell anyone, but the sets for Empok Nor are actually the regular *DS9* sets with new lighting.)

Star Trek, as far back as *TOS's* "The Man Trap," has often struggled with horror stories, but here director Mike Vejar is up to the task, handling the timing with expertise. The episode builds its suspense nicely before delivering "jump" moments at just the right times. Meanwhile, having a sister-station not only saves money but story time. There's no need to orient the viewer to the new setting. We know the Promenade is the Promenade and Ops is Ops.

All the same, "Empok Nor" will never be mistaken as one of *DS9's* best. It's a low-budget filler episode that doesn't lend itself well to repeat viewings. But it does succeed in doing what it sets out to do.

Deep Space Nine's sister-station reappears in Season Six's "The Magnificent Ferengi."

Did you know? In this episode, one of the Starfleet officers refers to a Cardassian as a "spoon-head," a line that wasn't scripted or preapproved by the producers. As one of the writers later said, "The guy is basically making a racist slur." Interestingly, as a fictitious slur, the line presented no problem for the stations the episode would air on, unlike real-life derogatory terms for real-life people. Yet for those involved in creating *Star Trek* content, the line sparked intense debate, with some believing it was inappropriate language for a Starfleet officer, and others concerned about such a comment being thrown out flippantly with no one on screen voicing disapproval. In the end, however, Ira Behr and Rick Berman elected to leave the line in, as they felt it illustrated the pressure of the situation and was appropriate given the circumstances.

"In the Cards": B

While the Dominion negotiates with Bajor, Jake and Nog try to acquire a baseball card.

Teleplay by Ronald D. Moore
Story by Truly Barr Clark & Scott J. Neal
Directed by Michael Dorn
TV rating: 4.5

"All I have to do is get him this card. How hard can that be?" —Jake

This one is sure different! Reversing the standard formula, a lighthearted A story threads its way through a darker B story.

Much like how *Star Wars* takes the lowest of the characters, the droids, and follows their adventures through a backdrop of drama and importance, Jake and Nog's hunt for a baseball card winds its way through scenes with higher profile characters, including Kai Winn and Weyoun. It's a solid piece of work by Ron Moore and expertly pulled off by Lofton, with his easy going manner and goofy grin being just what the story needs. The beauty of the plot is that Jake and Nog drive the action, interrupting the evil geniuses with their scavenger hunt. It allows each actor to have his or her moment, and it's funny *because* of them rather than at the expense of them. The script also has fun lampooning technobabble, convoluted time travel plots, and even some of *Star Trek's* own philosophy that Moore originally penned himself. It's all brought together in a coherent way by Michael Dorn, who directs his first *Star Trek* episode with a sure hand, showing off his talent behind the camera.

Did you know? Serving as this episode's MacGuffin, the Willie Mays rookie baseball card, featuring a painted image of "The Say Hey Kid," is #305 from the 1951 Bowman collection. In 2007, one sold for $93,412.

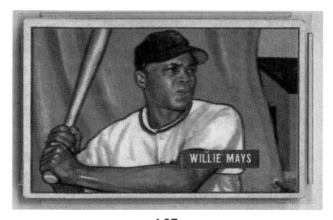

"Call to Arms" (1): A

When Sisko attempts to prevent Dominion ships from entering the Alpha Quadrant, the Dominion responds by launching an assault against the station. (Season finale)

Air date: June 16, 1997
Written by Ira Steven Behr & Robert Hewitt Wolfe
Directed by Allan Kroeker
TV rating: 5.2

"First we reclaim Terok Nor, and then onto Bajor." —Dukat

This season ending cliffhanger is another tense military thriller, which builds the suspense in the first three quarters with dialogue-driven character scenes before cutting loose with the action in the last quarter of the hour. It's sort of *DS9's* version of "The Best of Both Worlds," illustrating the eve of battle through the mood of the characters before taking the plunge. But the story has more complexity, with *Star Trek* having evolved in the seven years since, introducing Bajor, Cardassia, and the Dominion, each with their own agenda.

As a standalone episode, it's not the best of Season Five. Despite its richness in character, with almost all of the recurring guest stars related to the war making an appearance, and its major story developments, some of which happen off screen to save time and money, it doesn't tie them all together in a way that's as satisfying as "The Quickening" or "Trials and Tribble-ations." There's a diversity of ideas—such as Lita choosing a wedding dress, Jake writing about the station, and Weyoun and Gul Dukat having a disagreement— which don't fit together well enough to have us on the edge of our seat as one scene leads to another. But it is, of course, grossly unfair to complain about "Call to Arms" not being one of the greatest *Star Trek* episodes ever when it is, without a doubt, a fine piece of entertainment that qualifies as a *DS9* gem. Throughout the hour, there's a feeling that important decisions are being made with consequences that will be felt for many episodes to come. And by the end, there's a feeling that the series has come full circle, taking us right back to the pilot, but with a reversal of fortune—an open-ended cliffhanger that sets the table for the next season. For departing writer Robert Hewitt Wolfe, it's a great finish to an impressive body of work. For *DS9*, it's a heck of a way to finish a heck of a season and an effective opening to *Star Trek's* longest multi-parter yet.

"Call to Arms" received the International Monitor Award for Best Electronic Visual Effects in Film and Television Media.

Did you know? After writing "A Fistful of Datas" with Brannon Braga for *TNG*, Robert Hewitt Wolfe went on to cowrite 26 episodes with Ira Steven Behr for *DS9*. Following "Call to Arms," he would write one more episode for the series: Season Seven's "Field of Fire."

The Fifth Season in Review

With such great episodes as "Trials and Tribble-ations," "For the Uniform," "In Purgatory's Shadow"/"By Inferno's Light," "Doctor Bashir, I Presume," "Children of Time," and "Call to Arms," Season Five is *DS9* in its prime. Yet the season actually gets off to a slow start before catching fire. The reason? "Trials and Tribble-ations" eats the first quarter of the budget! Most would say it's worth it, however, including the producers who were happy with its ratings during sweeps week. And while it's ironic that the season's best episode honors a different series, only *DS9* could pull it off with such perfect humor and love.

That comes thanks to a behind the scenes crew that's largely the same as Season Four, including Herman Zimmerman, who was honored in 1997 with the inaugural award for excellence in production design from The Society of Motion Picture and Television Art Directors. But while several veteran directors would return to helm episodes, including LeVar Burton, René Auberjonois and Jonathan West, several new directors would be sprinkled in, including Alexander Siddig, Michael Dorn, Andrew Robinson, and Allan Kroeker. The latter, less known to most Trekkers than the others, would go on to become one of *Star Trek's* aces, overseeing every *DS9* season finale from Season Five on, as well as the series finales for *VOY* and *ENT*.

Season Five also includes something new in front of the camera, with *DS9* adopting new uniforms designed for *Star Trek: First Contact*, though the gang has to wait until "Rapture" to break them out to give the film the honor of introducing them.

So for the cast and crew, it's good times, though by the end of the season it's the new station commander who's the talk of the town. Jeffrey Combs, recalling the wrap party, remembers his wife approaching Avery Brooks. "He was at the bar looking very together, very cool, wearing shades, and my wife said to him, 'So, I guess my husband has taken over your station.' And Avery paused and then said, 'Yeah, but I think I'll get it back.'"

Season Six

The Sixth Season Cast

Captain Sisko: Avery Brooks
Major Kira: Nana Visitor
Odo: René Auberjonois
Chief O'Brien: Colm Meaney
Dax: Terry Farrell
Dr. Bashir: Alexander Siddig
Jake Sisko: Cirroc Lofton
Quark: Armin Shimerman
Worf: Michael Dorn

Notable Guest Stars

Andrew Robinson
Jeffrey Combs
Marc Alaimo
Aron Eisenberg
J.G. Hertzler
Casey Biggs
Barry Jenner
Brock Peters
Melanie Smith
Phil Morris
Max Grodénchik
Salome Jens
Chase Masterson
Philip Anglim
Tim Ransom
Faith C. Salie
Iggy Pop
Cecily Adams
Brad Greenquist
Cyril O'Reilly
Penny Johnson
Nick Tate
Leslie Hope
William Sadler
Stephen McHattie
James Darren
Louise Fletcher
Wallace Shawn
Rosalind Chao
Michelle Krusiec
Debra Wilson

"A Time to Stand" (2): B

With the Dominion winning the war against the Federation, Sisko and his crew prepare for a special mission.

Air date: September 29, 1997
Written by Ira Steven Behr & Hans Beimler
Directed by Allan Kroeker
TV rating: 5.4

"It's only a matter of time before the Federation collapses and Earth becomes another conquered planet under Dominion rule." —Dukat

While the Season Five finale teases a big battle show to follow, "A Time to Stand" spends most of its time in the periphery of hostilities until the end. With the battles happening off screen, the bulk of the episode is comprised of small-scale scenes between the characters, interspersing a mix of new and old pairings like Kira and Odo, Weyoun and Jake, Dukat and Kira, and Ben and an admiral from Starfleet. Guest star Barry Jenner, making his debut, takes a novel approach to playing the latter: he doesn't act like a dick, immediately vaulting his character ahead of every admiral preceding him for the "most liked figurehead" award.

As the episode progresses, the regrouping of the protagonists and the occupation of Deep Space Nine serve as alternating A and B stories, giving the story two rails to ride upon that don't intersect. And as the episode nears its end, the action picks up with a daring undercover mini-mission, setting the table for the next episode.

It's all the sort of storytelling *DS9* can do in its sleep, with the show finally fully embracing a serial format and making the most of it. There are better standalone episodes, but "A Time to Stand" does what it needs to and does it well.

Did you know? This episode is dedicated to the memory of Brandon Tartikoff, the former chairman of Paramount Pictures. While running the studio in 1991, Tartikoff foresaw the cast of *TNG* moving on to feature films to replace Kirk and company, and requested the creation of a new series about a father and son in a frontier-like environment. Tartikoff died in August 1997 of Hodgkin's lymphoma. He was 48.

"Rocks and Shoals" (3): B

Sisko and his crew are stranded on a planet with the Jem'Hadar.

Air date: October 6, 1997
Written by Ronald D. Moore
Directed by Michael Vejar
TV rating: 5.2

"I'm going to order the Jem'Hadar to attack your position tomorrow regardless of whether you agree to my terms or not." —Keevan

Reminiscent of "The Ship," but better, "Rocks and Shoals" is another "Sisko as a troop leader" episode. It's supposedly part of the season opening six-pack, but could just as easily have been made as a standalone episode. Sisko and most of the regulars, along with Garak and Nog, are part of an A story where they and an enemy ship have crashed on a planet. Only working together can the protagonists and antagonists safely escape. The result is combat crosscut with political drama.

The script itself isn't anything special, just running through the motions, but the acting, including the performances of guest stars Christopher Shea (Keevan) and Phil Morris (Remata'Klan), and the directing, utilizing location shooting at a quarry in Sun Valley, elevate the story, giving it a unique feel and feature film-like look. And while most of the episode features Sisko making the tough decisions, in the end we learn more about his enemy, the Vorta and the Jem'Hadar, than him, better defining what the Federation is up against.

Meanwhile, back on the station, Kira and Odo share a short B story where Kira begins to question her new role on the station. It's a completely internalized conflict, with the antagonists, Dukat and Weyoun, absent from the episode. What it really represents is a message from the show's writers: "Yes, we've got a lot going on, but we're not going to forget about Bajor." It's probably not something Paramount was interested in—the executives still believed episodes about Bajoran politics were bad for ratings and begged the show to focus on something new—but the way *DS9* placates the studio by adding elements such as Worf, the Dominion, and the war while simultaneously remaining true to its core and its roots with stories about Bajor, Sisko, and the wormhole is quite a balancing act to behold.

Did you know? "Rocks and Shoals" is an informal name for the military laws of the United States Navy that were in place for much of its early history. The nickname derives from a reference in Article 4, Section 10: "The punishment of death, or such other punishment as a court martial may adjudge, may be inflicted on any person in the naval service who intentionally or willfully suffers any vessel of the Navy to be stranded, or run upon rocks or shoals."

"Sons and Daughters" (4): D+

Worf's son, Alexander, has difficulty learning how to be a Klingon officer, much to the embarrassment of his father. Meanwhile, Dukat tries to use his daughter to get closer to Kira.

Air date: October 13, 1997
Written by Bradley Thompson & David Weddle
Directed by Jesus Salvador Trevino
TV rating: 4.8

"I wasn't the kind of son you wanted, so you pretended that you had no son."
—Alexander

Worf's son and Dukat's daughter return for appearances in separate stories that are really more about Worf and Kira.

The A story, set aboard a Klingon ship, is a remake of the Western *Rio Grande* (1950), a film about a fort commander and a new recruit who turns out to be his hapless son. It takes *Star Trek* fans into uncomfortable territory, because most fans can appreciate the side of Alexander that is so un-Klingon-like, and it's difficult to watch him suddenly, for unexplained reasons, want to be a warrior while turning into *Star Trek's* version of Steve Urkel. The point of the transformation, of course, is to set up a dilemma for Worf, creating a conflict between his responsibilities as First Officer and his instincts as a parent. But we appreciate Worf's sense of duty as well, and in the end he just comes across as both a bad officer and a bad parent. In fact, it's General Martok, who has some good one-on-one scenes with both Worf and Alexander, who seems to be only one who knows what he's doing.

Guest star Marc Worden takes over the part of Alexander from *TNG's* Brian Bonsall. Worden is five years older, but the age situation isn't really an issue, as Klingons are aliens and there's no reason they couldn't develop differently than humans. The real problem is that Worden acts and speaks so differently than Bonsall, it's difficult to imagine they're playing the same character.

Dukat's daughter, Ziyal, on the other hand, is still played by Melanie Smith, who returns for her first episode of the season. In a station-based B story, she's there basically to serve as the innocent child while Dukat and Kira step into the roles of divorced parents who love her dearly but have issues with each other. Dukat wants to use his daughter to bring him and Kira closer together while Kira is upset that this seems to be happening. It's the perfect direction to take Dukat's character, with the writers having established him as the master manipulator with a fancy for Bajoran women. For him, winning Kira after winning the station back would be the ultimate redemption, and it's interesting to see how Marc Alaimo plays it—with Dukat about as close as he'll ever be to having it all.

165

Still, there's a war going on, and as an episode set within it, "Sons and Daughters" falls a bit flat. Alexander returns for one last appearance in "You Are Cordially Invited." Ziyal returns in "Favor the Bold."

Did you know? Between Alexander, Ziyal, and Quark's mom, *Star Trek* employs enough actors to field a full baseball team.

Playing Alexander...

• Jon Steuer
• Brian Bonsall
• James Sloyan
• Marc Worden

Playing Ziyal...

• Cyia Batten
• Tracy Middendorf
• Melanie Smith

Playing Quark's mom...

• Cecily Adams
• Andrea Martin

Melanie Smith (photo by James Cannon)

166

"Behind the Lines" (5): B+

The female Changeling leader arrives on the station to pay Odo a visit. Meanwhile, Captain Sisko is promoted to desk duty.

Air date: October 20, 1997
Written by René Echevarria
Directed by LeVar Burton
TV rating: 5.1

"The Federation is losing this war. We can't sit by and do nothing." —Kira

After a couple of filler offerings, this Odo episode returns us to the war story and, for the first time in Season Six, gives the station the A story. With Weyoun and Dukat trying to bring the war to a close, the regulars on the station—Kira, Odo, Jake, Rom, and Quark—secretly try to disrupt the Dominion's plans and expand a rift between the Jem'Hadar and the Cardassians. Unfortunately, the resistance cell develops its own internal issue. At about the worst time, the Changeling leader, reprised by Salome Jens, suddenly waltzes through the door and attempts to rekindle her relationship with Odo. Odo, of course, knows she's manipulative and abusive, and he knows she's responsible for the war against the Alpha Quadrant. But he's like an addict who can't resist temptation, and throughout the episode, she breaks him down. Like someone giving in to drugs or alcohol, Odo begins to lose himself, and Auberjonois plays it perfectly. What's especially wonderful is that this bit of character exploration is a natural extension of the groundwork he's laid in previous episodes, going all the way back to Season One. And it also sets up some great acting from Nana Visitor, with Kira running the gamut of emotions that every friend or spouse of an addict knows too well. In the end, we sympathize with both of them, with some anger and hurt mixed in as well.

And then there's the B story with Sisko. The Defiant is sent on a dangerous mission...and Sisko has to wait in his new office until it returns. That's because he's been promoted to Admiral Ross's right-hand man, and Dax is now serving as captain of the ship. It's fascinating, if odd, to stay with Sisko while the Defiant leaves and carries out its mission off-screen, finally enabling us to see a mission from an admiral's "sit and wait" point of view. (It probably saves the show a pretty penny, too.) In the end, it works with the A story to create a character-driven episode that feels more action-oriented and epic than it really is.

Did you know? This is Salome Jens's first appearance on *DS9* since the Season Four finale. She later commented, "Everybody thinks the female shape-shifter is so evil. But I love the character. She was looking at everyone saying, 'You're crazy fighting. Where I come from there's no fighting. You can be anything you want.'"

167

"Favor the Bold" (6): B+

Captain Sisko convinces Starfleet Command to launch a fleet of starships to retake Deep Space Nine.

Air date: October 27, 1997
Written by Ira Steven Behr & Hans Beimler
Directed by Winrich Kolbe
TV rating: 6.0

"Odo, we are way, way past 'sorry.'" —Kira

Taking its title from a Latin proverb, this flip-side to "Call to Arms" is an ensemble piece that features preparations for a Federation invasion fleet while Weyoun and Dukat prepare to clear out a minefield blocking the wormhole. Like "Call to Arms," it's composed mostly of small character moments, showing us what everyone is thinking heading into the looming confrontation. With *DS9's* character depth, this allows the episode to cruise along without too much story movement, hopping from Sisko to Odo to Rom to Kira to Dukat, and so on, with small moments for the others such as Garak, Nog, Jake, Lita, Admiral Ross, and Ziyal. (Even the Changeling leader gets in on the action, literally getting some action.) What's great about this sort of episode is that the large number of characters makes the story seem even bigger than it is, as if it's spilling off the screen affecting millions of lives, which is just how a war story should come across.

Ace director Winrich Kolbe returns for the first time in two seasons to pull it all together and give it the perfect pacing. Once again, the station gets the A story while Sisko and the Federation get the B story, though the stories, at last, begin to intersect, thanks to Morn, of all people. Throughout the hour there's a sense that the characters are committing themselves to their choices. When Kira tells Odo that they are "way, way past sorry," it doesn't just describe their own relationship but where the show has gone as a whole. The Dominion's attitude toward Rom, Kira's actions toward Damar, and the impending invasion all represent decisions that one way or another threaten to alter lives for better or for worse. By the end, it's clear that everything is about to change, and the only question is, "What will it change to?"

Did you know? The Latin expression "audentis Fortuna iuvat," meaning "Fortune favors the bold," appears in the *Aeneid*, an epic poem written by Publius Vergilius Maro between 29 and 19 BC.

"Sacrifice of Angels" (7): B+

Sisko and the Federation continue in their effort to retake Deep Space Nine.

Air date: November 3, 1997
Written by Ira Steven Behr & Hans Beimler
Directed by Allan Kroeker
TV rating: 6.4

"I need a miracle. Bajor needs a miracle." —Sisko

Despite several episodes of groundwork, it actually takes a little bit of time for this payoff episode to kick into gear. But once it gets going, it's a thriller, complete with *Star Wars*-like ship battles and powerful character-based moments that tear the heart out. At the center of the story is the station commander. But in this case. it's not Sisko but Dukat! Introduced as a simple antagonist in the pilot, by this episode he's as interesting as Sisko himself. It's fascinating to see how he reacts to the events that unfold and how he treats the diverse characters assembled around him, each with their own agenda, as he attempts to protect and preserve what's important to him. While "Sacrifice" can accurately be called an ensemble piece, Dukat is its heart, and it represents Marc Alaimo's finest piece of work on the series.

And what of Sisko? He's given the B story, heading up the Federation invasion fleet, a part Brooks plays well. The actor is, however, upstaged through no fault of his own. In between shots of him standing on the bridge of the Defiant barking orders, the true excitement happens in the exterior shots of the ships in battle, a visual feast surpassing anything *Star Trek* has given us to this point, including the feature films. For the first time in the show's history, the ships battle using all three dimensions of space, diving, swooping, and flying in all directions as each side attempts visible strategies to win.

The climax to it all is a literal version of deux ex machina, but by tying it into the pilot and series finale, the writers turn what could be perceived as a cop-out into something that feels more like a well-planned, organic part of the show.

Still, while "Sacrifice" is a good episode itself, as a finale to a multi-episode story, it has its flaws. Previous episodes make a big deal out of the Jem'Hadar running out of white and emphasize a daring mission to destroy a key Dominion sensor array. Incorporating these details into the plot of "Sacrifice" would tie everything together, giving the finale a more epic feel..

Yet, the episode itself and the multi-part story from "Call to Arms" to "Sacrifice of Angels" both stand out as *DS9* successes and are must-sees for *Star Trek* fans.

Did you know? This is the first *Star Trek* episode to rely entirely on CGI for its battle scenes, with two visual effects houses, Digital Muse and Foundation Imaging, splitting up the workload to make it more manageable.

169

"You Are Cordially Invited...": D+

Worf and Dax tie the knot.

Air date: November 10, 1997
Written by Ronald D. Moore
Directed by David Livingston
TV rating: 6.5

"There's nothing more romantic than a wedding on DS9 in springtime."
—Bashir

For Worf and Jadzia's wedding episode, writer Ron Moore takes one bad idea, a bachelor party for Worf full of pain and anguish and marries it with another: Jadzia must prove herself to Martok's shrewish wife to join her house. There's also a short C story where Odo tries to avoid Kira, which is resolved off-screen of all things. They're all played for laughs, with a genuine funny moment as Dax does a ridiculous dance with Nog. But despite showcasing *Star Trek's* first marriage of regulars, the ideas don't offer much originality. We know how everything is going to go before it goes. (*TNG's* "Data's Day" is similarly predictable but gets away with it because of its tongue-in-cheek attitude, turning it into more of a parody.) The truth is if something comes from the pen of Ron Moore, we expect...well, more. (Perhaps René Echevarria, with his penchant for bringing out Worf's sensitive side in episodes like "Birthright Part II," would have been a better choice to write this one.) Thankfully, "Cordially" is the last time we have to see Alexander—who continues here to be recharacterized as the family klutz. And with Ron Moore, even one of his poorer offerings is better than 90% of what's on television.

Did you know? The producers of *DS9* considered including the crew of the Enterprise-D as guests at the wedding, but most of the actors were unavailable.

Did you notice? Shelby, from *TNG's* "The Best of Both Worlds," is referenced here as the captain of the Sutherland.

"Resurrection": C

The mirror universe's Bareil Antos visits Deep Space Nine and becomes interested in Kira.

Air date: October 17, 1997
Written by Michael Taylor
Directed by LeVar Burton
TV rating: 5.1

"I'll tell you one thing, Major. You'd better brace yourself. You're in for a rough ride." —Quark

This is a throwback to early season characters and formulas, with a predictable, mundane romantic story for Kira and mirror-Bariel before an asinine ending. It's a perfectly acceptable hour of entertainment, but it's also one of the most forgettable episodes of *DS9's* run. (It doesn't help that Odo, after admitting feelings for Kira, is mostly absent from this episode.) Still, the story doesn't try to be a "big event" and succeeds on its own merits. The bottom line, however, is that the mirror universe, originally created in *TOS*, is getting old by this point, and the prime universe *DS9* has fashioned is far more interesting.

Did you know? Although Michael Taylor is credited with writing this episode, the bulk of the work was done by Ira Steven Behr and Hans Beimler.

Ira Steven Behr (photo by Keith McDuffee)

171

"Statistical Probabilities": C+

When a group of eccentric genetically engineered people visit the station, Bashir takes an interest in their dark predictions for the future.

Air date: November 24, 1997
Teleplay by René Echevarria
Story by Pam Pietroforte
Directed by Anson Williams
TV rating: 5.1

"Well, I'd love to stay and chat about our impending doom but...." —Bashir

If a *Star Trek* writer ever got together with Samuel Beckett and Isaac Asimov to write a play, it would probably look something like this. With its simple settings, repetitive material, and emphasis on character, much of "Statistical Probabilities" seems more like what you'd expect to see on a stage than in *Star Trek*, but it works nonetheless as a simple Bashir episode and as an appropriate follow-up to "Doctor Bashir, I Presume."

The plot stems from the arrogance of those who think they know better than others, a cornerstone trait of humanity. From sports to the economy to politics or technology, there are always those who claim that statistics and past experience will allow them to predict the future with 100% accuracy and get testy with those who doubt what they have to say. Yet even the most intelligent of people inadvertently make assumptions that turn out to be false. It's the contrast between Bashir's "non linear dynamics," where the accuracy of a prediction becomes more reliable the further in the future you go, like the prediction that flipping a coin over and over will lead to similar occurrences of both heads and tails, and the butterfly effect, where small actions by individuals in the present can have enormous consequences in the future. "Statistical Probabilities" looks at both sides of the issue and has a lot of fun in the process, with Anson Williams (Potsie from *Happy Days*) directing the first of his six *Star Trek* episodes.

Unfortunately, it is difficult to buy that Starfleet would trust three mentally unstable individuals with detailed intelligence reports or that Deep Space Nine would allow Weyoun and Damar to sneak around the station for clandestine meetings. But the episode remains a compelling character study nonetheless.

The new guest stars in this episode, nicknamed "the Jack-pack" by the writers, return for Season Seven's "Chrysalis."

Did you know? Tim Ransom (Jack) played Dana Scully's boyfriend in the pilot episode of *The X Files*, but all his scenes were left on the cutting room floor.

"The Magnificent Ferengi:" C

When Quark's mother is captured by the Dominion, Quark leads a team of Ferengi in a rescue effort.

Air date: December 19, 1997
Written by Ira Steven Behr & Hans Beimler
Directed by Chip Chalmers
TV rating: 5.0

"A child, a moron, a failure, and a psychopath. Quite a little team you've put together." —Brunt

The original idea for this episode was to have the Grand Nagus captured by the Dominion, leading to all the recurring Ferengi characters banding together to save him. And what a perfect formula for a Ferengi comedy! Unfortunately, Wallace Shawn was unavailable, forcing the writers to use Quark's mom in place of the Nagus. It doesn't make much sense. (Why would the Dominion *want* Quark's mom?) But no matter. The episode isn't really about the captive anyway. Like *The Magnificent Seven*, the classic 1960 Western film, it's about the diverse set of characters who gang up together to accomplish a mission. And Quark's motley crew, comprised of himself, his brother, his nephew, his cousin, Brunt, and Leck (with the latter making his debut), is about as diverse as they come.

Then there's the antagonist: a Vorta played by rock star Iggy Pop. With his Midwestern accent, he sounds nothing like the Vorta that have appeared before, yet Pop's got a deadpan delivery and charming awkwardness that work for the race.

As the story progresses, finding its way to Deep Space Nine's sister-station, Empok Nor, the Ferengi do everything wrong, and there are quite a few genuinely funny moments as a result. (The writers even work in the *Weekend At Bernie's* gag after the "magnificent" group accidentally kills its prisoner.) But as is often the case with Quark, there are genuine heroic moments as well, turning what could have been an all-out farce into a semi-serious episode.

In the end, the eclectic ingredients somehow come together to form a successful episode, and the Ferengi continue to redeem themselves, making their poor introduction in *TNG's* "The Last Outpost" an ancient memory.

Did you know? *DS9* producer Ira Steven Behr originally wanted Iggy Pop to play the part of a crazy man in Season Three's "Past Tense," but Pop was touring in Spain at the time. Fortunately, when production started on "The Magnificent Ferengi," the musician was available.

173

"Waltz": B

Sisko is severely injured and trapped alone on a deserted planet with Dukat, who becomes increasingly unstable.

Air date: January 5, 1998
Written by Ronald D. Moore
Directed by René Auberjonois
TV rating: 4.9

"Benjamin, just a few hours ago I was a prisoner on my way to trial, and you were my dear old friend come to visit me in my cell. Now look at us. I'm free, and you're a prisoner of your own battered body." —Dukat

Picking up some threads from "Sacrifice of Angels," this Dukat/Sisko story is one of *Star Trek's* versions of an elevator episode: the two characters are stuck on a planet (the cave set) waiting for rescue. The point, of course, is to allow the dialogue to carry the show, and Moore, Alaimo, and Brooks bring the goods, resulting in one of *Star Trek's* better bottle episodes.

The interesting thing here is that it starts off as if Moore is trying to make Dukat saner than when we last saw him, as if to wipe away the end of "Sacrifice." Then the writer proceeds to bring alive the voices in his head through a chorus of personalities played by Weyoun, Damar, and Kira. It's a device that illuminates Dukat's mind in a unique way that even a monologue could not achieve. Within this construct, Weyoun represents Dukat's feelings of inadequacy, Damar represents his pride, and Kira represents his self doubt. As the episode progresses, we move from Dukat's need for validation to his self-satisfaction at finally defining himself, which leaves us realizing he's even crazier—and more dangerous— than we first thought.

While all this is going on, there's also a short B story with the Defiant about the search for Sisko that includes a classic fake-out moment.

Dukat returns later in the season in "Wrongs Darker Than Death or Night," but his next encounter with Sisko isn't until the series finale.

Did you know? Marc Alaimo was flattered to have this episode devoted to his character. "Stories like that are usually reserved for the regulars," he says, "but I'm very grateful that they trusted me enough to write an episode like this because it meant they liked and respected my work. It gave me a lot of responsibility, and I was glad to see that everything actually worked when it was all put together. It really is a really terrific piece."

"Who Mourns for Morn?" C

After hearing that Morn has died, Quark suddenly finds himself in the middle of a dispute among Morn's old acquaintances.

Air date: February 2, 1998
Written by Mark Gehred-O'Connell
Directed by Victor Lobl
TV rating: 5.3

"I want Morn's money. I need Morn's money. I deserve Morn's money."
—Quark

Another "Who Mourns for Adonais?" this ain't, with news of Morn's death only serving to set up a station-based treasure hunt for Quark, with some hammy character actors showing up at each turn. It's essentially a remake of "The Nagus," a comedy that's as broad as the day is long and predictable as the sun rising in the morning. But for a middle of the season filler episode between the seriousness of "Waltz" and "Far Beyond the Stars," it works just fine, with the "Quark gets in over his head" stories never getting old.

Anchoring the guest cast are Brad Greenquist and Cyril O'Reilly as a pair of alien brothers serving as the episode's heavies. Director David Livingston lets the two actors have at it, and they steal the show with their quirky, hilarious shtick. But Armin Shimerman is old hat at this sort of outing and holds his own, handling Quark with just the right blend of humor and seriousness. (Meanwhile, Mark Allen Shephard, who usually plays Morn, has an interesting cameo: he plays a Bajoran who, at the request of Quark, keeps Morn's seat warm!)

In the end, the offbeat episode might not be the greatest offering of the season, but it's probably the best episode about Morn, and it did earn an Emmy nomination for make-up.

Did you know? After playing Morn in the pilot as a one-shot deal, Mark Allen Shephard went on to reprise the barfly in 92 more episodes of *DS9* and even appears in *TNG's* "Birthright" and *VOY's* "Caretaker" as well. The actor is also a talented artist, with over twenty of his paintings appearing on the walls of the *DS9* sets.

"Far Beyond the Stars": A

Experiencing a vision from the Prophets, Sisko sees himself as Benny Russell, a sci-fi writer in the 1950s struggling in a world of racism and segregation.

Air date: February 8, 1998
Teleplay by Ira Steven Behr & Hans Beimler
Story by Marc Scott Zicree
Directed by Avery Brooks
TV rating: 4.8

"If the world's not ready for a woman writer, imagine what would happen if it learned about a Negro with a typewriter." —Herb

For this period piece, *Star Trek* dispenses with its usual metaphor and addresses a social issue head on through a *Quantum Leap*-like plot device. (The device itself is a sequel to "Rapture," but the means into the story itself isn't what's important here.) Following up an alien-heavy episode that earned honors for outstanding make-up, *DS9* dispenses with prosthetics and cosmetics here, with all the actors—including those who play Odo, Quark, Worf, Martok, Nog, Dukat, and Weyoun— appearing as their human-selves for this side-universe story about racism in the 1950s that blends the future and the past. It's sort of the reverse of *The Wizard of Oz*. Sisko goes from a fantasy world to more realistic place, meeting familiar faces that aren't so heavily made up. But it's also a refreshing change of pace and a sincere homage to the science fiction writers that laid the foundation for *Star Trek* to follow.

As the first *Star Trek* episode to have the main star directing himself in a significant manner, "Far Beyond the Stars" sees Avery Brooks pull double duty, overseeing a Sisko story that requires completely new sets, new characters, new costumes, and a powerful performance from himself. Like "Our Man Bashir," it's an incredible amount of work for just one episode, but Brooks pulls it together and makes it all worthwhile, thanks to his work both in front of and behind the camera, with a big assist from Dennis McCarthy, who gives the episode the perfect period score.

The key to his character is the characterization, because the plot isn't ready-made for sympathy. "Benny," Sisko's alter-ego in the side-universe, doesn't have a son or daughter who's dying, he's not going to jail for a crime he didn't commit, and there's no real threat to his safety so long as he keeps his head down. Because the writers chose the 1950s rather than the 1960s, it's easy to dismiss his problems as unimportant and handwave them away by saying there are many worse injustices going on even in today's world. But his disappointments and successes are important to us because they're important to *him*. It's the reason *Star Trek*—and all fictional stories—work at all. We cry for Beth in *Little Women* not because we believe the story is real, but because we care for the characters, even if they only exist only in our heads.

176

In this episode, Benny creates characters of his own, turning his coworkers into the *DS9* characters, and what's interesting is how the whole idea works "backwards" so to speak. Benny casts his boss, Pabst, who tries to conform with society, as a shape-shifter who works for whoever is running the space station. He turns Herb, who is constantly bickering with Pabst, into an alien bartender who argues with the shape-shifter. Albert, who loves robots, becomes the station's engineer. In a bit of fantasy, Benny recasts Jimmy, who can never seem to find the right path, as his son Jake, whom Benny is able to mentor and turn into a responsible member of society. Jake even becomes a writer like Benny. His girlfriend Cassie gets a ship and an adventure of her own. Willie, the handsome star baseball player who is constantly hitting on her, is turned into an ugly warrior. Yet all the characters have something admirable about them, and there's something touching about how Benny creates heroes out of ordinary people and turns himself into their captain.

As Benny fights the intolerant to get his stories published, *Star Trek* fans are reminded of Roddenberry's struggles in the 1960s, when NBC and its sponsors demanded the removal of Mr. Spock, female officers, and blacks from *TOS*. It's ironic that the same arguments that took place behind the scenes during *Star Trek's* formative years are now inside an episode set in the same fictional universe Roddenberry and those executives fought about. And in a stroke of genius, the episode's writers make the episode's true antagonist someone who doesn't even appear. Benny's dreams are ultimately crushed by an uncaring businessman sitting offscreen behind a desk.

The only drawback to the story is that we know from the beginning that it's all a dream and that there will be no tangible consequences to what's going on. The episode even acknowledges the issue with a line from Herb inside the episode, but that doesn't solve the problem. The dream is, however, a shrewd way to use the Prophets. Rather than having them be an external force as in "Sacrifice of Angels," here they are an internal source of struggle and strength within Sisko, like a true religion. They reach into mankind's own history to interact with him in a way he can understand and help sort through his feelings through an allegory of his own world's creation. It's a profound way of communicating that makes for exciting television.

DS9 returns to these ideas in Season Seven's "Shadows and Symbols."

"Far Beyond the Stars" was nominated for Emmys for art direction, costume design, and hairstyling.

Did you know? This episode includes some interesting artwork. The cover of an issue of *Incredible Tales* depicts the surface of Delta Vega as seen in *TOS's* "Where No Man Has Gone Before." The cover for a *Galaxy* magazine features a matte painting of Starbase 11 as seen in *TOS's* "Court Martial." The cover for *Astounding Science Fiction*, read by K.C. Hunter, features the matte painting of Eminiar VII from *TOS's* "A Taste of Armageddon."

"One Little Ship": D+

When the Defiant is taken over by the Jem'Hadar, the runabout and its crew, shrunk to the size of toys thanks to a spatial anomaly, must save the day.

Air date: February 16, 1998
Written by David Weddle & Bradley Thompson
Directed by Allan Kroeker
TV rating: 5.1

"This is the story of a little ship that took a little trip." —Worf

This "Honey, I shrunk the runabout" story, reminiscent of *TNG's* "Rascals," is basically an hour of stalling while the titular vessel and its crew flies around inside the Defiant trying to save the others from the occupying force. There's also a mini-story— pardon the pun—where O'Brien and Bashir team up to rework a circuit relay, *Land of the Giants*-style, from the inside. It's all harmless fun, and it's clear that even the writers don't take the miniature gimmick too seriously, but it's probably not the best use of the concept. (It would be more interesting, and easier from a scientific accuracy standpoint, to have the Defiant captured by an enormous ship, allowing for the same visuals but avoiding issues of miniaturization.)

The Jem'Hadar themselves, however, are well handled by the writers, with an internal conflict introduced. We learn there are "Alpha" Jem'Hadar and "Gamma" Jem'Hadar who have issues with each other. But despite Weddle and Thompson hitting us over the head with a sledgehammer to get this point across, the whole idea is dropped after this episode.

"One Little Ship" was nominated for an Emmy for visual effects.

Did you know? Tongue firmly in cheek, Ira Steven Behr makes no apologies for green-lighting this episode. "How many shows can do a salute to *Land of the Giants*, to *The Incredible Shrinking Man*? We had to do it! We owed it to all the schlock science fiction that had come before us. If we hadn't done it, it would have been a crime."

Did you also know? Ron Moore found it disappointing that the differing breeds of Jem'Hadar are never mentioned again. "We dropped the ball on that one. It sounded like a cool idea at the time and we kept telling each other that we'd follow it up eventually, but it just kinda got away from us."

178

"Honor Among Thieves": B–

O'Brien, working undercover for Starfleet Intelligence, befriends a man he will have to betray.

Air date: February 23, 1998
Teleplay by René Echevarria
Story by Philip Kim
Directed by Allan Eastman
TV rating: 4.6

"If they find out who you are, they'll kill you." —Chadwick

DS9's version of *Donnie Brasco* (1997) is the age-old story about the spy who begins to sympathize with those he or she is fooling. In this case, it's O'Brien infiltrating an organized crime unit, which turns into a two-man show as he deals with its leader, Bilby. Anytime the two interact, there's instant suspense and intrigue because we know if O'Brien slips and says the wrong thing, it could cost him his life. Echevarria, knowing just how to play the game, keeps the dialogue sharp and unpredictable to keep us on the edge of our seats, throwing in a few twists and turns in the plot to fill out the hour. And while some of his writing is forced—since it's unlikely anyone as low as Bilby would be trusted to carry out a mission with the fate of the Quadrant hanging in the balance or that anyone as high as the Vorta would explain the master plan to those on the bottom rung—the success or failure of the episode is really dependent upon the actors. Thankfully, Colm Meaney is joined by Nick Tate, who does a fine job of bringing Bilby to life by creating a three-dimensional portrait of a man who values family, loyalty, and respect. It's easy to see how O'Brien could sympathize with him, turning the hour into a poignant character study that's entertaining enough to spawn a sequel of sorts in Season Seven's "Prodigal Daughter." And hey, it's better than doing an episode about Dax and Worf bickering over where to spend their honeymoon.

Did you know? For the role of Bilby, Tate, who had previously guest starred in *TNG's* "Final Mission," was initially passed over in favor of Charles Hallahan, an actor best known for playing police captain Charlie Devane on NBC's *Hunter*. But Hallahan died of a heart attack/car accident shortly before shooting was to commence, and Tate was given the part.

179

"Change of Heart": C

Dax and Worf bicker over where to spend their honeymoon, finally settling on a dangerous trip through a jungle to rescue a Cardassian defector.

Air date: March 2, 1998
Written by Ronald D. Moore
Directed by David Livingston
TV rating: 5.5

"How are you enjoying your honeymoon? Are you suffering enough?" —Dax

As *Star Trek* moved from episodic adventures to more serialized stories, it's only natural that the show's relationships would move more to the forefront. There's a reason soap operas were able to build themselves on couples whereas primetime television was historically built on situations. Romantic relationships on television are only interesting when the couple has time to learn and grow, taking the audience along for the ride. But with the advent of VCRs allowing fans to catch up on missed episodes, primetime TV became more confident in moving relationships forward , and soon after, the internet became popular, giving fans a way to discuss and argue about who should be with whom.

For *Star Trek*, this was a game changer. Sure, *TOS* and *TNG* tease relationships between regulars such as Kirk and Rand, Troi and Riker, Picard and Dr. Crusher, and Worf and Troi. But the pairings skirt the edge of the stories and never really develop into anything significant. With serialized television and the internet, *Star Trek* could be less ambiguous and more ambitious with relationships like Dax and Worf, complete with a marriage and a honeymoon.

Yet as a sequel to "You Are Cordially Invited," "Change of Heart" is a strange post-wedding episode that doesn't quite work. With its long trek in the jungle, seemingly taking advantage of several days on location, but really shot on an impressively dressed stage set, the A story with Worf and Dax looks more like a *TNG* episode than the darker *DS9* and offers potential as a dramatic thriller. But the plot stagnates and never quite gets there. Meanwhile, a station based B story about O'Brien and Bashir plotting to end Quark's tongo winning streak peters out about halfway through. In fact, all the important plot points of the episode could be covered in about a quarter of the time.

The real point of it all, of course, is to allow Worf and Jadzia's relationship to develop by giving the two a struggle and giving Worf a choice between his duty and his wife. But this doesn't come together in a way that's must-see-TV. *Star Trek* is just getting its feet wet with a serious relationship here, and Ron Moore is probably not the best writer to blaze the path. (You want Klingons battling? Moore is your guy. You want Klingons kissing? Maybe try Echevarria.) Then again, at least Worf and Jadzia don't turn into lizards and have babies.

Did you know? During shooting of this episode, the general consensus among the crew was that the greens department did *too* good a job in constructing the oppressive jungle. According to art director Randy McIlvain, "We had designed small platforms to put all these trees on, so that the filmmakers could move the platforms out and get into the jungle area to shoot. But they added more and more plants, until we couldn't move the platforms!"

"Wrongs Darker Than Death or Night": B

After Dukat tells Kira that her mother was once his lover, Kira travels back in time learn the truth.

Air date: March 30, 1998
Written by Ira Steven Behr & Hans Beimler
Directed by Jonathan West
TV rating: 4.6

"Let me get this straight. You want to travel back in time to see if Gul Dukat and your mother were lovers?" —Sisko

Taking its title from Percy Bysshe Shelley's 1820 lyrical drama *Prometheus Unbound*, "Wrongs" cleverly uses the pre-established Orb of Time to allow Kira to witness firsthand a tragic but important part of her mother's past.

Doing this sort of story in Season Six is a bold choice. Ideally, the story would appear earlier in the run to make the plot seem less contrived. After all, why would Dukat wait until this point to say, "Oh, by the way, Nerys, I used to be close to your mother."? Dukat and the Major have even been on tandem missions together, allowing them to grow closer, at least in a way. But perhaps Dukat doesn't want to tell Kira until now because he wanted to win her over on his own merits. When he realizes this is no longer a possibility, and his mental state is breaking down, he finally lays the card down in retribution. It's fitting for the character, and the revelation does fit in well with Kira's established history, making it seem like the final clue falling into place to make sense of Dukat's relationship with the younger Kira.

Leslie Hope guest stars as Kira's mom, though she's upstaged by Marc Alaimo (Dukat), David Bowe (a Bajoran collaborator in charge of the women), Wayne Grace (a Cardassian Legate with a playful taste for the ladies), Tim de Zarn (a resistance organizer), and possibly the third Cardassian from the left. Actually, she plays her part just fine. But with the story taking place in the past, most of the regulars aren't present, so director Jonathan West ("Trials and Tribble-ations") has to make up for it by getting flamboyant performances from several of the guest stars instead. (And really, who doesn't Alaimo try to upstage anyway?) In the end, the episode is stronger for its assortment of unique actors, and when it comes down to it, the episode isn't really about Kira's mother anyway. It's about Kira herself and her hopeless attempt to process the information she's getting. It's a bit like what Marty goes through in *Back to the Future*, a film that Bob Gale conceived after flipping through his father's old high school yearbook and wondering what it would be like to have gone to school with his dad— but Kira's experience isn't quite so pleasant.

Did you know? Leslie Hope would go on to play Jack Bauer's wife, Teri, during the first season of *24*.

"Inquisition": C+

Starfleet accuses Dr. Bashir of being a Dominion spy.

Air date: April 6, 1998
Written by Bradley Thompson & David Weddle
Directed by Michael Dorn
TV rating: 4.7

"I can assure you, Doctor, this is no game." —Sloan

Director Michael Dorn cuts a quick pace to build the tension in this Bashir episode that initially seems a lot like *TNG's* "The Drumhead" —a witch hunt filled with paranoid hearings that mines past episodes in search of evidence of wrongdoing—before turning into something more akin to *TNG's* "Future Imperfect."

Alexander Siddig, avoiding the temptation of overacting, plays it well, showing frustration but never allowing Bashir to lose his head. He's joined by guest star William Sadler, who gives a memorable performance as Sloan, a mysterious disciple of Joseph McCarthy who tries to corner his opponent with words. Meanwhile, just as Picard is pulled into the fray in "The Drumhead," a frustrated Sisko comes to the aid of Bashir, allowing Brooks to deliver some passionate arguments, which is right up his alley. But as events and characterizations get more and more preposterous, it becomes evident that all is not as it seems, with Sloan turning out to be more Colonel Jessup than McCarthy, all but saying, "Son, we live in a world that has walls, and my existence, while grotesque and incomprehensible to you, saves lives!"

In the end, we're teased with the promise of a sequel, which happens later in the season with "Inter Arma Enim Silent Leges." Meanwhile, the mysterious Section 31, introduced here, becomes a somewhat recurring part of *Star Trek* from here on out.

Did you know? Michael Dorn had to direct much of this episode in his Worf make-up.

"In the Pale Moonlight": A+

Sisko enlists Garak's help to persuade the Romulans to help the Federation in the war against the Dominion.

Air date: April 13, 1998
Teleplay by Michael Taylor
Story by Peter Allan Fields
Directed by Victor Lobl
TV rating: 4.8

"I'm already involved in a very messy, very bloody business, and the only way I can see to end it is to bring the Romulans into the war. I am prepared to do whatever it takes to accomplish that goal." —Sisko

A famous and memorable episode, "Moonlight" takes Sisko where no *Star Trek* leading man has gone before, ultimately leaving *Star Trek's* established ideals behind. Teaming up with Garak, circumstances lead Sisko down a path where each questionable decision he makes digs himself into a deeper hole until he's forced to come out the opposite end. And Avery Brooks uses the opportunity to give one of his finest performances of the series.

The savvy script, actually written by Ron Moore and based on a draft by Michael Taylor, is another offering with many things happening offscreen, making the story seem bigger than what was actually shot and simultaneously making an inexpensive show seem more luxurious than it really is. Add to this that some of these reports are coming from Garak, and the plot becomes even more complex. Can we really believe his claims, or is Garak making some of them up to get Sisko to go along with his plan? Heck, knowing Garak, he might not even have the friends on Cardassia he claims to at the beginning and is simply manipulating Sisko from the outset.

Along with the creation of Section 31 for the previous episode, it's led to a lot of discussion about where the idea of "the ends justifying the means" fits into *Star Trek's* idealistic universe and what Gene Roddenberry would think of it. But such arguments miss the real point. The episode doesn't defend immoral decisions "for the greater good." It doesn't try to say the rules of a dystopian universe are different from the rules of utopia. What it does is explore these ideas to challenge the preconceived beliefs of Sisko and the audience before leaving the ultimate judgment of Sisko and his decisions up to the viewer. It's not about what Gene thinks of it, it's about what we think.

It's noteworthy that the episode was originally conceived as a Jake episode, with the framing device being about his attempts to discover what his father and Garak are up to. Switching the frame to an insider's perspective serves the story better, turning a mystery episode into a more personal "What am I doing?" episode that forces Sisko to deal with the consequences of his decisions on camera. At the same time, this doesn't negate the Jake story idea.

Having the young man discover a clue that leads him to investigate what happened in "Moonlight" would make for a really fun sequel—more fun, in fact, than the original Jake idea, because we would already know exactly what he's stumbled onto and know why his father wants to stonewall the investigation. As it happens, however, *DS9* does not pursue this story, leaving a good idea out there for a *Star Trek* novel.

In the end, "Moonlight" represents one of the finest hours of *DS9*, being a pivotal part of the war arc that spans Season Six while also remaining an episode that can be enjoyed on its own, requiring no other episodes to understand and appreciate the story. As a top notch offering, it's no faaake.

Did you know? Guest star Stephen McHattie's delivery of a line in this episode is so memorable, it's often shared on social media to dispel fake news.

"His Way": B−

Odo consults Vic Fontaine, a holographic lounge singer, about his relationship with Kira.

Air date: April 20, 1998
Written by Ira Steven Behr & Hans Beimler
Directed by Allan Kroeker
TV rating: 4.3

"Look, pally, you want to win the girl, we've got to thaw you out a little."
—Fontaine

Late in the series, *DS9* fearlessly introduces yet another recurring character in this Odo episode with a title inspired by a famous Frank Sinatra song. James Darren, an old friend of Sinatra's, steps into the shoes of Vic Fontaine, a self-aware holographic lounge singer with an intuitive understanding of relationships. Like Joe Piscopo teaching Data about comedy in *TNG's* "Outrageous Okona," Fontaine takes Odo under his wing and shows him how to cut loose and win Kira's heart. Auberjonois hams it up, and Visitor nearly steals the show performing a sexy song, creating the light-hearted story needed to follow up the drama of "Inquisition" and "Moonlight." The result is not only one of *DS9's* better romantic comedies, but the only *Star Trek* episode to ever get an Emmy nomination for Outstanding Music Direction.

Darren himself, playing Fontaine after Rene Goulet, Tom Jones, Jerry Vale, and Frank Sinatra Jr. declined the part, proves a breath of fresh air in the series and returns for seven more episodes, starting with the Season Six finale, "Tears of the Prophets."

Did you know? "My Way," with music borrowed from "Comme d'habitude," a popular French song in the late 1960s, was written by Paul Anka for Frank Sinatra. Anka, a successful performer in his own right, discovered that putting himself in Sinatra's mindset for the song was liberating. "I used words I would never use, like 'I ate it up and spit it out,'" he says. "But that's the way Frank talked." After finishing up the song in one night, Anka called Sinatra and said he had something special for him. "When my record company caught wind of that," Anka recalls, "they wanted to kill me," (Anka was under contract with RCA Victor. Sinatra had his own label, Reprise Records.) Nonetheless, Sinatra recorded the song in late 1968 and released it in 1969, making Anka, Sinatra, and Sinatra's record label lots of money. (Anka did record his own version shortly thereafter, making his own record company some money.) "My Way" went on to become Sinatra's signature song, with many people falsely assuming he wrote it himself…exactly as Anka intended.

"The Reckoning": D+

Sisko studies an ancient Bajoran tablet that declares a time of Reckoning when the future of Bajor will be decided.

Air date: April 27, 1998
Teleplay by David Weddle & Bradley Thompson
Story by Harry M. Werksman & Gabrielle Stanton
Directed by Jesus Salvador Trevino
TV rating: 4.2

"During the Reckoning, the Bajorans will either suffer horribly or…eat fruit."
—Dax, trying to translate the ancient writing on the tablet

Throwing a bit of Kai Winn into a Sisko story, this loose follow-up to "The Assignment" and "Rapture" has a lot of talk for the first three quarters before a comic book ending that pits good versus evil. What makes it unique, however, is that instead of Sisko trying to do the right thing while Winn invokes the Prophets to further her agenda, the formula is reversed, with Sisko coming off as kind of a jerk if you look at it from Winn's perspective. (Actually, it's sort of funny to see Sisko explain that the Prophets want him to do the things he does while Winn throws a fit in protest.)

It all leads to a "main character must die" tease that's reminiscent of "Amok Time" but which is visually more along the lines of *Ghostbusters*. In the end, the dilemma is resolved by one character's surprising decision, though the story suffers from not having an explanation for it, leaving fans to argue over why the decision was made.

Still, the episode is fun for what it is and serves as a turning point for Kai Winn, sending her down the path she will continue on until the series finale. Winn returns in Season Seven's "'Til Death Do Us Part."

Did you know? Despite the O'Briens being the focal point of "The Assignment," they don't appear in "The Reckoning."

187

"Valiant": C–

Fleeing a Jem'Hadar attack in space, Jake and Nog are rescued by a ship manned by cadets.

Air date: May 5, 1998
Written by Ronald D. Moore
Directed by Michael Vejar
TV rating: 4.6

"We're Red Squad and we can do anything!" —Captain Watters

This off-station Jake and Nog piece uses the Defiant sets to represent a sistership, the Valiant, and introduces us to a young, eager crew that lacks the experience we're used to seeing on *Star Trek*.

The idea of a cadet crew isn't new to the franchise. It's part of *Star Trek II: The Wrath of Khan* and was even considered for the show that became *TNG* before Roddenberry insisted on a more seasoned cast. (It was also rumored to be the premise of *VOY*, with some fans calling it *Star Trek 90210* before the true details of the show were released.) It's a fun area of turf for Ron Moore to explore, since he, like Nog, was an officer in his youth before, like Jake, he decided he wanted to be a writer instead. The background allows him to effectively write both characters, using them to describe the opposing viewpoints of their situation.

Unfortunately, Moore makes things a little too black and white, painting the crew of the Valiant a little too harshly as arrogant fanatics as opposed to intelligent, capable cadets while Jake, instead of presenting one of several compelling arguments why the crew is headed down the wrong path, plays the "my dad is Captain Sisko" card instead, a ploy doomed to fail. (Perhaps this is why Lofton mails in his performance while Eisenberg gives a little more effort.) It all leads to a predictable second half, with the episode's *Lord of the Flies* message about mindless ambition coming through a little too loudly before a convenient climax.

Did you know? Originally, Ron Moore, who wrote the episode that introduced the Defiant ("The Search, Part I"), wanted to call *DS9*'s ship the Valiant as an homage to a ship mentioned in *TOS*'s "Where No Man Has Gone Before." The producers, however, asked him to change the name to something else so it wouldn't be confused with Voyager. He then chose the name Defiant as an homage to *TOS*'s "The Tholian Web" and waited for another opportunity to introduce the Valiant as a sister-ship.

"Profit and Lace": D

Quark becomes a woman to stop Brunt from becoming the next Grand Nagus.

Air date: May 11, 1998
Written by Ira Steven Behr & Hans Beimler
Directed by Alexander Siddig
TV rating: 4.2

"Boys, together we're going to re-conquer an empire or die in the attempt."
—Zek

It's another Ferengi farce with *DS9's* Ferengis joined by ex-Grand Nagus Zek, Quark's mom, and Acting Grand Nagus Brunt in a sequel to Season Five's "Ferengi Love Songs." Using the multiple characters, director Alexander Siddig cuts a swift pace with snappy dialogue and plot points thrown out fast and furious. It all leads to Quark in drag, which, as it happens, was the "high concept" that led to this episode.

While a harmless hour, there's not much new here, with the episode coming together like a stitched-up version of "the Ferengi's greatest hits." You get Quark bickering with his mom, Rom being a lovable idiot, Zek yelling in his high-pitched voice, and Brunt...well, being Brunt. Perhaps worst of all, the comedy is anchored by the misguided 20th century notions that sexual harassment is funny, a man dressed as a woman is funnier, and sexual harassment of a man playing a woman is the most hilarious thing of all. We expect more from *Star Trek* and *DS9* by this point in the series, and it all feels like a step back.

Did you know? Before shooting this episode, Armin Shimerman watched *Some Like It Hot* (1959) and *Tootsie* (1982) to study men acting as women.

189

"Time's Orphan": F

After an accident sends Molly O'Brien back in time to live on an uninhabited world, she's beamed back to the present at eighteen years old with no immediate recollection of her family.

Air date: May 18, 1998
Teleplay by Bradley Thompson & David Weddle
Story by Joe Menosky
Directed by Allan Kroeker
TV rating: 4.6

"Oh, bollocks!" —Chief O'Brien

Poor Rosalind Chao (Keiko) returns just in time for this lemon based on a failed story pitch meant for Worf's son that was revived to help fill out Season Six. Give the actors credit. Chao, Meaney, and guest star Michelle Krusiec, playing an 18-year-old Molly, pour themselves into this O'Brien family portrait. But the fundamental problem is that no matter how hard the writers try to weave Chief O'Brien and his wife into the narrative, the focal point of the plot is Molly, and her character hasn't been developed enough for us to be as interested in her issues as, say, Commander Riker in "Future Imperfect" or Jake Sisko in "The Visitor." It doesn't help that her story doesn't make much sense either, with Menosky doing his usual outside-the-box approach. (It would have been better to borrow from *The Searchers* and have Molly raised by another culture for ten years only for her to come back with different ideas and values.)

The B story, added after it was discovered the episode was running short, features Worf looking after Yoshi, the O'Briens' son, which is supposed to be funny in a *Kindergarten Cop* way but falls flat itself.

Are there worse *Star Trek* episodes? Probably. But they aren't much worse.

Did you know? While the crew was shooting a picnic scene on location at Malibu Creek State Park, a rattlesnake began approaching the actors. Producer Steve Oster calmly asked them to vacate the area, and the snake proceeded through the shot.

"The Sound of Her Voice": C

The crew of the Defiant gets to know a woman through her voice as they race to rescue her from the inhospitable planet she's stranded on.

Air date: June 8, 1998
Teleplay by Ronald D. Moore
Story by Pam Pietroforte
Directed by Winrich Kolbe
TV rating: 4.1

"Chief, I want you to establish a two-way comlink with this woman and when you do, tell her her heroes are on the way." —Sisko

With a premise and payoff that would have been right at home in the 1980s *Twilight Zone* series, *DS9* gives us its most talky episode yet, with guest star Debra Wilson seeming more like the host of a talk radio program than a Starfleet captain as her character fills the hour by yakking with Sisko, O'Brien, and Bashir, giving them some good advice for their problems. It makes for a mellow penultimate season offering but allows for some good character development if you can get through the lengthy dialogue. Unfortunately, all the stalling makes the end seem more like a cheat than the catalyst for the premise. What the writers needed to do was to drop the threat of carbon dioxide poisoning, used to create a race against time, and have the Defiant reach her planet in the middle of the episode, which tightens up the discussions between her and the crew, doesn't allow the crew to look up who she is, and turns the second half into a planet-based search. In such a scenario, as the Defiant approaches her planet and crosses an anomaly, her voice suddenly cuts out, and the crew spends most of the remaining time trying to locate her, discovering clues along the way that finally let everyone put the pieces together to figure out the twist. Afterwards, the crew flies back to the other side of the anomaly expecting to regain communication with her on the other side...only to discover that the Defiant has altered the harmonic resonance of the anomaly, making the reestablishment of communication impossible. The crew suddenly realizes it's out of options, and everyone knows they'll never hear from her again. By making the episode more about the mystery than the woman, the payoff becomes more intriguing.

The station-based B story, on the other hand, is perfectly acceptable as is, if a bit vanilla, giving us Quark versus Odo in a sitcom-like battle of wits as they each try to stay one step ahead of the other, with Jake serving as Quark's confidant. Jake adds nothing, but Quark versus Odo is always good filler.

Did you know? Just a few months before this episode aired, Debra Wilson played Uhura in a sketch for *MadTV* and played a role in the "Klingon Encounter" interactive ride/movie program at *Star Trek: The Experience* in Las Vegas.

"Tears of the Prophets" (1): B

Sisko leads an invasion fleet into Cardassian territory. (Season finale)

Air date: June 15, 1998
Written by Ira Steven Behr & Hans Beimler
Directed by Allan Kroeker
TV rating: 4.1

"The Prophets don't see me as a Starfleet captain. They see me as their Emissary." —Sisko

Gathering up all the major story threads from Season Six, this season finale ties them together in an episode with a little bit of everything—the war, the Prophets, the Pah-wraiths, even Vic Fontaine—as it moves from character to character in a story that's essentially about choices and loss. In fact, if the episode can be faulted, it can be argued that it includes too many characters, with some, like Jake and Garak, tossed into the script without contributing anything significant to the story at large, and others, such as Dukat, becoming overly simplified due to a lack of time.

The title itself is derived from the pilot, where Kai Opaka introduces an Orb as the "tear of the Prophets." And like the pilot, Sisko is the central figure, summoning his inner Obi-Wan Kenobi to feel a great disturbance in the force when the episode's most memorable moment happens. In fact, as the episode comes to its conclusion, Sisko finds himself in a completely different mindset than we've ever seen from one of our beloved *Star Trek* captains before, and we're left to ponder all the loose ends, with "Tears" offering questions but no answers. After many filler episodes in the latter half of Season Six, this one begins to reshape the game and leaves us to wonder just what everything will resolve into for the final season of the series.

Did you know? The day after finishing her scenes for "Tears of the Prophets," Terry Farrell went around the corner to audition for *Becker*, another Paramount production. She was ultimately successful, landing the part of Reggie, the owner of a greasy spoon diner frequented by the title character.

The Sixth Season in Review

DS9 opens Season Six with an ambitious six-episode continuous war story before presenting the remainder of the season in a more episodic way, flipping back and forth between dark, serious episodes and comedic filler with mixed results. Yet through it all, there's a serial mentality that includes a wedding, a reckoning, and a death. Just as importantly, if less noticeable in the short term, are subtle character shifts: Bashir stops babbling, Garak becomes less ambiguous, and Sisko becomes more than just a token Emissary.

Meanwhile, the writers, including new story editors Bradley Thompson and David Weddle (replacing the departed Robert Hewitt Wolfe), embrace *DS9's* reputation as the most character-rich show in *Trek* history, celebrating the secondary characters with a Morn episode, a Ferengi episode, a Jake and Nog episode, and episodes that introduce Admiral Ross and Vic Fontaine. Even Ziyal and Alexander get their own episode before subsequently making their final appearances. The regulars, of course, need not fear being forgotten, with great episodes like "Behind the Lines" and "Favor the Bold." But moreover, Season Six is remembered most for "Far Beyond the Stars" and "In the Pale Moonlight," two of the most unique, famous, and appreciated *Star Trek* episodes of all time that, together, went on to earn six Emmy nominations.

Behind the scenes, Hans Biemler, a former story editor for *TNG* who contributed to *DS9's* "The Sword of Kahless" and "Trials and Tribble-ations," joins the show fulltime as supervising producer and becomes Ira Behr's writing partner, with the two penning nine of the season's scripts. But despite the writing team's new blood, the penultimate season takes *DS9* back to its roots, bringing back the Prophets to point the show toward its final destination.

Marc Alaimo, Armin Shimerman, and Colm Meaney (photo by Beth Madison)

193

Season Seven

Production Order
(with air date order in parentheses)

1. "Image in the Sand" (1st)
2. "Shadows and Symbols" (2nd)
3. "Afterimage" (3rd)
4. "Take Me Out to the Holosuite" (4th)
5. "Chrysalis" (5th)
6. "Treachery, Faith and the Great River" (6th)
7. "Once More Unto the Breach" (7th)
8. "The Siege of AR-558" (8th)
9. "Covenant" (9th)
10. "It's Only a Paper Moon" (10th)
11. "Prodigal Daughter" (11th)
12. "The Emperor's New Cloak" (12th)
13. "Field of Fire" (13th)
14. "Chimera" (14th)
15. "Inter Arma Enim Silent Leges" (16th)
16: "Badda-Bing, Badda-Bang" (15th)
17: "Penumbra" (17th)
18. "'Til Death Do Us Part" (18th)
19. "Strange Bedfellows" (19th)
20: "The Changing Face of Evil" (20th)
21. "When it Rains…" (21st)
22. "Tacking into the Wind" (22nd)
23: "Extreme Measures" (23rd)
24. "The Dogs of War" (24th)
25. "What You Leave Behind" (25th)

The Seventh Season Cast

Captain Sisko: Avery Brooks
Colonel Kira: Nana Visitor
Odo: René Auberjonois
Chief O'Brien: Colm Meaney
Dr. Bashir: Alexander Siddig
Jake Sisko: Cirroc Lofton
Quark: Armin Shimerman
Worf: Michael Dorn
Dax: Nicole de Boer

Notable Guest Stars

Jeffrey Combs
Casey Biggs
Barry Jenner
J.G./ Garman Hertzler
Aron Eisenberg
James Darren
Brock Peters
Andrew Robinson
Chase Masterson
Penny Johnson
Max Grodénchik
Faith C. Salie
Salome Jens
Bill Mumy
James Darren
Marc Alaimo
Norman Parker
Leigh Taylor-Young
Wallace Shawn
William Sadler
Louise Fletcher
Vaughn Armstrong

"Image in the Sand" (2): B+

Sisko attempts to regain contact with the Prophets.

Air date: September 28, 1998
Written by Ira Steven Behr & Hans Beimler
Directed by Les Landau
TV rating: 4.4

"I came back here to clear my head. To try to figure out what to do next. Maybe learning the truth about my mother is the first step of this journey." —Sisko

"Image," featuring an eight-minute introduction before the opening credits, is an introspective, character-based episode with four separate storylines and no resolution.

    The centerpiece, naturally, is the show's leading man, with Avery Brooks reprising Sisko as the same man we saw at the close of Season Six: a lost soul who has come home in search of a direction. With a little help from the Prophets and his family, two aspects of his life now becoming intertwined, he finds one. The idea behind this direction is bold but makes quite a bit of sense. With the Prophets existing outside of time, Sisko's connection to them should not be confined to the present but should also include his past and his future. In the short-term, by crafting this dynamic in an abstract way, the writers create mystery and intrigue. In the long-term, they subconsciously make the entire tapestry of his life more understandable and his story more powerful. It's heady stuff, but it comes across well here and in the future, with Brooks shelving his usual dramatic acting and internalizing just about everything instead.

196

Meanwhile, a station-based B story features Kira, now a colonel, being forced to work with a Romulan. The worst part for the colonel? The Romulan is actually reasonable and polite. Eventually, however, the Romulan turns out to be more "Romulan" and Visitor gets to play to her strengths, portraying Kira as the same opinionated officer unwilling to be intimidated by the higher-ups as she did way back in "Emissary."

Then there's a station-based C story where Worf's friends try to help him with his depression. This includes an appearance from holographic lounge singer Vic Fontaine that's gratuitously shoehorned in, with Fontaine singing "Jadzia's favorite song" for Worf before the Klingon smashes the holographic furniture. This might mean something to fans of the show if we'd ever actually heard Fontaine sing it to her. As is, it would make more sense (and be shorter) if Worf were to catch sight of a Tongo game at Quark's and break the bar in half instead. But the writers probably figure that with a new character like Fontaine, it's important to keep him involved to continue to build his part in the show.

There's also a D story on Cardassia with Weyoun and Damar assessing the situation, and we even get the introduction of a new character, a curious addition that doesn't have any connection to the other events of the episode, making it a pleasant surprise, as well as a poignant, if underplayed, moment.

The interesting thing to think about in real world terms is that all these stories were probably shot right next to each other, but *Star Trek* has always been good at establishing different looks and feels from the same stages. It has to. It supposedly takes place all over the universe but has always shot its television in limited locations in California. This episode demonstrates just how well *Deep Space Nine* can do it. We have the station, New Orleans, a holographic Las Vegas, and Cardassia all shot on adjacent stages, and they're all believable locations that seem light-years away from each other. It's the universe on a budget!

Did you know? While Damar, as illustrated in this episode, enjoys his drink of choice, Kanar, the actor who played him did not. To create the Cardassian liquor, the property master used Karo, a brand of sweetener used for cooking, or pancake syrup. Neither were enjoyable for Casey Biggs, who had to down glass after glass while shooting multiple takes for each scene.

"Shadows and Symbols" (3): B

Sisko searches for the mysterious Orb of the Emissary.

Air date: October 5, 1998
Written by Ira Steven Behr & Hans Beimler
Directed by Allan Kroeker
TV rating: 4.2

"Ben, you came here to find the Prophets, remember?" —Dax

Tying up the plot threads introduced in "Image in the Sand," this episode is a satisfactory conclusion that takes the series back to homebase while simultaneously promising more intrigue to come.

Tapping into "Far Beyond the Stars," the A story with the Siskos and Dax takes advantage of desert location shooting for a *Raiders of the Lost Ark*-like plot. As the plot moves along and becomes more surreal, it becomes more delicious, and a conclusion with some long-awaited answers pays it off well. Along the way, Nicole de Boer begins developing the new Dax, teaming up with the writers in an attempt to flesh out the character as quickly as possible. Fortunately, the character allows them to combine old and new elements, simultaneously giving the actress a foundation while leaving room for experimentation. And giving her an A story to allow Ezri to build some chemistry with Sisko before throwing the character into the mix with the rest of the regulars is a smart move.

The B story with Worf and his friends trying to win Jadzia a spot in Sto-vo-kor is just a paint-by-numbers mission made up of elements we've seen before, but it gets away with it by doing it well and having some killer visual effects in the payoff. Meanwhile, a C story holds its own as Kira, backed by Odo, engages the Romulans in a Cuban Missile Crisis-like bluff.

Finding just the right balance between the three plotlines, the episode doesn't rush a moment or shortchange any of the featured players. You could argue that Brock Peters, in his final appearance as Joseph Sisko, is extraneous to the story. However, Peters is such a great actor, it's wonderful to see him in any capacity, and at least the writers don't gratuitously give him something important to do to justify his appearance.

All that said, it is a bit disappointing that the Dominion War has shifted from a war between the Federation and the Dominion to a contest between the Prophets and the Pah-wraiths. Sisko, Admiral Ross, Damar, Weyoun and the Changeling leader are great characters, and we enjoy seeing their struggles, whereas the wormhole aliens and their adversaries are abstract concepts that come across in a less understandable and identifiable way.

Did you know? If you watch Season Seven closely, you'll notice that de Boer will sometimes clasp her hands behind her back to tie her character into what Terry Farrell previously established.

"Afterimage": C

Ezri Dax has trouble adjusting to life on Deep Space Nine.

Air date: October 12, 1998
Written by René Echevarria
Directed by Les Landau
TV rating: 4.3

"Look at you. You're pathetic. A confused child trying to live up to a legacy left by her predecessors. You're not worthy of the name 'Dax.' I knew Jadzia. She was vital, alive. She owned herself, and you…you don't even know who you are. How dare you presume to help me? You can't even help yourself. Now, get out of here before I say something unkind." —Garak

The first Ezri Dax-centric episode begins awkwardly (as it should) before finding its footing as a Dax/Garak story. Stepping into a beloved role and making it her own for a single season is a thankless task for Nicole de Boer, but it opens many doors for the writers, with lots of issues that need to be addressed. Foremost? Dax's relationship with Worf, who gets the B story. As Bashir and Quark get to know the new Dax better, the hopelessly confused Klingon takes offense. Even without the other guys in the picture, he can't accept her. ("How can I honor the memory of the woman I loved when she is not really dead?") Giving Dax and Worf their own separate stories to deal with the issue is a productive formula and a clever exploration of a science fiction idea that other television shows can't do.

It is, of course, Dax who gets the lion's share of the episode, with the writers returning to the concept of a counselor for the crew. It's a good idea that helps differentiate her from Jadzia, and Deanna Troi need not fear the competition. Ezri is the opposite of Starfleet's best and brightest, having a naive immaturity more often seen on teen shows than *Star Trek*. And while this can be uncomfortable to watch, it also makes for some interesting drama.

Unfortunately, writer Echevarria does her no favors with lines that sound like someone with no training trying to impersonate a therapist. It also makes Sisko look especially ignorant as well, since his continual assertion that she should skip the rest of her training seems, in light of her job performance, like an insult to therapists who've actually taken the pains to learn what they're doing. A significant part of the problem is the oversimplification of her dialogue, a problem that undermines the episode as a whole.

Be that as it may, even with a predictable formula that includes triumphs and setbacks just when a veteran TV viewer would expect them, "Afterimage" is an acceptable hour of entertainment. The point of the story, after all, isn't to surprise or amaze but to simply integrate Dax into the show—and on this count, the episode succeeds.

Did you know? With the dangerous away missions, the phaser fights, and the time travel headaches, being a Starfleet officer can be a difficult job. But maybe worst of all are mere words. Even the actors playing the characters probably felt a little taken aback during shoots as Patrick Stewart or Natalija Nogulich dressed them down. (Heck, I feel a little uncomfortable *watching*. If I were in these actors' shoes, I'd need a hug and some counseling from Marina Sirtis after the take, although she'd probably remind me she's not really a licensed therapist.) Here are some of the most dramatic tongue lashings in the history of *Star Trek*.

• Picard to Wesley (*TNG*, "The First Duty")
• Admiral Nechayev to Picard (*TNG*, "I Borg")
• Picard to Seta (*TNG*, "Lower Decks")
• Garak to Dax (*DS9*, "Afterimage")
• Janeway to Torres (*VOY*, "Prime Factors")
• Janeway to Neelix (*VOY*, "Fair Trade")

"Take Me Out to the Holosuite": C

A group of Vulcans challenge the Deep Space Nine gang to a game of baseball.

Air date: October 19, 1998
Written by Ronald D. Moore
Directed by Chip Chalmers
TV rating: 4.7

"When their captain challenged us to a contest of courage, teamwork, and sacrifice, I accepted on your behalf." —Sisko

Well, it was bound to happen: after all the baseball metaphors throughout *DS9's* first six seasons, the show finally gives us the game itself in this ensemble episode. It's a standalone piece of fluff in the spirit of *The Bad News Bears* that's probably the least claustrophobic episode in *Star Trek's* history. Shot on location at Loyola Marymount University's baseball field, "Take Me Out," spends the first half moving its characters into the positions they need to be in while setting up the big game. The opponents? Vulcans so smug, you'd swear they're from *ENT*. When the big contest finally occurs, it unfolds like a cheesy sports movie, complete with a hundred extras in the stands.

This one is never going to be remembered as one of *DS9's* signature pieces, but it moves along nicely and has some genuinely funny moments.

Did you know? The song "Take Me Out to the Ball Game" was composed and written by Albert Von Tilzer and Jack Norworth in 1908. While it was an instant hit on the Vaudeville circuit, it wasn't until the 1930s that the song worked its way into baseball stadiums. As for Tilzer and Norworth, they didn't attend their first baseball games until 1928 and 1940, respectively!

"Chrysalis": C–

The genetically-engineered Jack-pack returns to the station to ask Bashir to help one of their own.

Air date: October 26, 1998
Written by René Echevarria
Directed by Jonathan West
TV rating: 4.3

"So what's a genetically enhanced girl supposed to do when she wakes up from a long sleep? Point to one of those specks of light out there, pack a bag, and go make a life for herself?" —Sarina

This Bashir episode, a sequel to Season Six's "Statistical Improbabilities," is a character-based story reminiscent of "Flowers for Algernon" that's predictable but sweet. Jack and his pals return in a hilarious scene that shows how easy it is to impersonate an admiral before the focus of the episode shifts to the relationship between Bashir and Sarina, with the latter reprised by Faith C. Salie as her character finally comes out of her shell. Sarina's innocence is refreshing and her rebirth leaves a lot of territory for the writers to explore. How will she integrate into society? How will she adapt to social situations? How will she deal with people who lie, cheat, and bully? Will Counselor Dax be able to help her? The writers, however, choose not to dig very deep and keep the story somewhat simple, uneventful, and forgettable. It's a bit of a shame, because the actress, despite debuting in "Statistical Improbabilities" as little more than an extra, seems capable of being much more than a plot device for a lonely Dr. Bashir.

Did you know? Faith C. Salie, who had no lines in "Statistical Improbabilities," had to re-audition for Sarina, who speaks, sings, and drives the story forward in "Chrysalis."

"Treachery, Faith and the Great River": B

Odo finds himself caught in the middle of two Weyouns.

Teleplay by David Weddle & Bradley Thompson
Story by Philip Kim
Directed by Steve Posey
TV rating: 4.8

"I don't think the universe is ready for two Weyouns." —Odo

This variation of the "evil twin" idea features two new Weyoun clones, both played by Jeffrey Combs, with one being evil and the other being good, making the latter a dangerous rebel in the eyes of the Dominion.

Good-Weyoun gets the A story with Odo, a variation of the old "sheriff taking the prisoner from point A to point B" tale, which, as usual, allows for a lot of conversation. Auberjonois and Combs work well together, and after some character-building banter, the writers give them something of particular interest to talk about that will factor into the future of the season. There is also a nice effects sequence with their shuttle that's reminiscent of the Millennium Falcon's trip through the asteroid belt in *The Empire Strikes Back*.

Meanwhile, evil-Weyoun works with Damar to stop Odo from reaching the Federation with his prisoner. Combs and Biggs are also particularly good together, better than Combs and Alaimo, which is probably the reason why the writers have Damar displace his former superior. Biggs has an at ease style that works well with Combs's paranoid persona. As the two interact, Damar introduces Weyoun to a form of trickery new to the Dominion, and it's fun to see Weyoun head down the slippery slope and wonder where he'll land.

The C story is a comedy runner with Nog and Chief O'Brien that's really just a redo of Nog's scavenger hunts in "Progress" and "In the Cards." Despite that, the story works fine because it's mostly about O'Brien's reactions to Nog's offscreen actions, with Colm Meaney delivering just the right facial expressions, and it's short enough to avoid overstaying its welcome.

All three stories are nicely interwoven, giving the episode a nice balance between the comedy and drama. As they build toward their resolutions, savvy viewers will probably guess how they will all end, but that's because there's only one way each *can* end. Nonetheless, it all makes for a fun hour of television.

Did you know? Jeffrey Combs is a sought after voice actor for animated shows and has contributed to *Justice League*, *The New Batman Adventures*, *Transformers: Prime*, *Avengers: World's Mightiest Heroes*, *Thundercats*, and *Teenage Mutant Ninja Turtles*.

"Once More Unto the Breach": B

An old Klingon warrior finds his efforts to play a part in the Dominion war stymied by General Martok.

Air date: November 9, 1998
Written by Ronald D. Moore
Directed by Allan Kroeker
TV rating: 4.5

"Know this Worf: Kor is your responsibility. I want nothing to do with him."
—Martok

This episode featuring Worf and Martok is most notable for the final appearance of Kor (John Colicos), *Star Trek's* first Klingon of note. With most of the story taking place aboard a Bird-of-Prey, the substance of "Once More" is hardly anything new for Moore and the Klingon culture. We get the petty bickering, mess hall insults, a battle, and the required variation of "a good day to die." But while working his way through all the old clichés, Moore develops a plot that's a thing of beauty, and the actors help him out with some great performances.

Like "Soldiers of the Empire," the point of the story is to set up an underdog for an elusive victory. But this time it's more personal because it's not about a ship, it's about Kor. John Colicos, in his third *DS9* episode, does a magnificent job of giving his character, the famous *Dahar* Master, a fitting end before his own passing in March of 2000. Meanwhile, J.G. Hertzler nearly steals the show, playing Martok with such gravitas you'd swear he's the Klingon who once went toe to toe with Captain Kirk. Like in "Soldiers," Martok serves as a bit of an antagonist, but whereas his motivation there is unclear, here he gets a well written backstory that allows us to understand where he's coming from.

But it's Neil Vipond as Derok, Martok's servant, who proves the biggest surprise. Vipond doesn't have a lot of screen-time early, so it's easy to dismiss him as unimportant. But he does the most with the least, setting up his importance later with a subtlety that's easy to miss the first time around.

Throw in Michael Dorn, who brings his eleven years of experience as Worf to the table, and you get a Klingon episode that, in the spirit of *Henry V*, goes once more unto the breach and savors the fruits of victory.

The Kor Episodes:

- "Errand of Mercy" (*TOS*)
- "The Time Trap" (*TAS*)
- "Blood Oath" (*DS9*)
- "The Sword of Kahless" (*DS9*)
- "Once More Unto the Breach" (*DS9*)

205

Did you know? Before he was president, Teddy Roosevelt was a war hero, leading his band of "Rough Riders" into battle during the Spanish-American War for which he eventually earned the Medal of Honor. After he was president, he continued to show his toughness, once speaking for nearly an hour in Milwaukee, Wisconsin immediately after an assassination attempt that left a bullet in his body for the remainder of his life. But by 1917, a 58-year-old Roosevelt was out of the public eye and upset about a situation he was missing out on: World War I. Had the war happened ten years earlier, it would have been under his watch, giving him the possibility of a crowning achievement. Instead, his former political adversary, Woodrow Wilson, was guiding the U.S. into the war while Roosevelt sat on the sidelines. Not content with such a position, the former Commander in Chief met with Wilson personally to request a return to the Army as a division commander. "I told Wilson that I would die on the field of battle," Roosevelt said later, "that I would never return if only he would let me go!" Wilson, however, refused the request, later writing, "I really think the best way to treat Mr. Roosevelt is to take no notice of him. That breaks his heart and is the best punishment that can be administered."

Teddy Roosevelt in 1898 (public domain photo)

206

"The Siege of AR-558": B

Sisko must help Starfleet defend subspace relay AR-558 from a Dominion attack.

Air date: November 16, 1998
Written by Ira Steven Behr & Hans Beimler
Directed by Winrich Kolbe
TV rating: 4.5

"There's only one order, Lieutenant. We hold." —Sisko

In the spirit of *Zulu* (1964), *Platoon* (1986), and *Saving Private Ryan* (1998), *DS9* presents this ground-based battle story featuring Sisko, Bashir, Dax, Nog, and Quark. Similar to "Nor the Battle to the Strong" (and, like that, taking place largely in the cave set), it's gritty, depressing, and sometimes doesn't make a lot of sense. In other words, it's a lot like war.

Directed by Vietnam veteran Winrich Kolbe, the story takes place on a small planet where a demoralized group is defending a MacGuffin. By necessity, Sisko takes over as military leader, often voicing his thoughts to Quark who has tagged along to please the Nagus (and because the writers want him there as a civilian surrogate). Nog, Bashir, and Dax, also chosen by the writers because of their lack of battle experience, find themselves in the midst of the chaos as well, and as the story moves along, the regulars become entangled with several guest stars. Bill Mumy, best known for playing Will Robinson on *Lost in Space* and Lennier on *Babylon 5*, guest stars as Kellin, a good natured crewman, Patrick Kilpatrick plays Reese, a tough guy, and Raymond Cruz plays Vargas, an officer suffering deep psychological trauma. They're all one time appearances, but it's clear these aren't people who will suddenly be okay at the end of the hour, and these aren't situations that will suddenly be forgotten next week. While *DS9* will move on to tell other stories, the trauma of what is essentially a mini war movie is something that lives on far past its screen-time. It's the sort of *Star Trek* episode only *DS9* could do, because of all the captains, only Sisko would get his hands so dirty.

Scored by Paul Baillargeon, the music enhances the episode in the same way *Adagio for Strings* colors *Platoon*, a melancholy overlay that augments the action through its disconnection. It's a fitting choice, because the episode is not intended to be enjoyable. In the end, the various elements come together to create what the writers are really shooting for: poignancy.

Two episodes after this, *DS9* follows it up with a station-based sequel devoted to Nog's recovery in "It's Only a Paper Moon".

Did you know? According to those involved, "The Siege of AR-558" generated more backstage controversy than any other *DS9* show. "A lot of people didn't want us to do that episode," Ira Steven Behr says, "and a lot of people were unhappy it was being developed. But I felt we needed to do it."

"Covenant": C+

Kira is abducted by a Bajoran cult led by Dukat.

Air date: November 23, 1998
Written by René Echevarria
Directed by John Kretchmer
TV rating: 4.4

"You believe the Prophets are the true Gods of Bajor. I believe the Pah-wraiths are. Let's just leave it at that." —Vedek Fala

Dukat is back for another Kira episode about the two at odds. Turns out that the Cardassian has done a pretty good job of making a copy of all he's lost. Taking over Deep Space Nine's abandoned sister-station, Empok Nor, he's become the head of a cult of Bajorans that worships the evil Pah-wraiths. In a way, it's better than his old gig. The Bajorans love him, and he has no superiors. The only thing missing from his fantasy life is Kira, whom he fetches (or abducts, depending upon your choice of words) to begin the episode. And with that, we're off and running.

As in his teleplay for *TNG's* "Birthright Part II," René Echevarria sketches out the characters and layers them into the battle of wills between the protagonist and cult leader. But whereas "Birthright" is more or less a prison escape story, this episode draws inspiration from the Heaven's Gate cult, with Kira seeing the group descending into madness but being powerless to stop it.

Marc Alaimo, of course, chews the scenery as Dukat, but it's Norman Parker with an outstanding performance as a Bajoran religious leader, Fala, who really anchors the episode.

Unfortunately, Echevarria's exploration of cult life and death must fit inside the hour with time for commercials, limiting his plot points and forcing a quick conclusion. But even if the ideas are oversimplified, the issues that are addressed make for interesting television.

Did you know? The members of the Heaven's Gate cult wore *Star Trek*-inspired "away team" patches when they committed mass suicide in March 1997 in their attempt to transport aboard an alien spacecraft they believed was following a comet.

"It's Only a Paper Moon": C+

After being injured in battle, Nog seeks shelter inside Vic Fontaine's fictional holosuite program.

Air date: December 28, 1998
Teleplay by Ronald D. Moore
Story by David Mack & John J. Ordover
Directed by Anson Williams
TV rating: 4.3

"Can I stay with you?" —Nog

With a title referring to an old jazz standard about a fake backdrop, this Nog and Vic Fontaine episode is a follow-up to "The Siege of AR-558," with Nog's mental recovery lagging behind his physical recovery while he takes refuge in Fontaine's fictitious holosuite world.

It's a fun use of Fontaine, the holographic lounge singer, giving the guy his own little story about what's it's like to finally live a full life as opposed to having his world turned on and off each day, something more fully explored with the Doctor on *VOY*. But the main thrust of the episode lies with Nog, allowing Aron Eisenberg to carry the show with a story that *Star Trek* hasn't really done before. The idea of post-traumatic stress disorder immediately brings the military to mind, but physical stress can cause mental stress in all walks of life and is something even civilians identify with. When someone becomes ill or injured and can't work, or a student misses significant time at school, or someone suffers a great loss, it's not always easy to jump back on the horse and carry on, even with no threat to life. An injury, absence, or traumatic event can crush the spirit, and emotional recovery can be as painful as physical therapy. Feelings of inadequacy and anger surface, and facing everyday life once again becomes a daunting task. Fictional universes are a tempting escape because they offer a place of interest that's disconnected from the real world, with no reminders of real problems or tragedies past and present. So people lose themselves in worlds online, or in music and books, or even films and television shows. And yes, there's more than a bit of irony for just this sort of entertainment providing a forum to explore the issue. This sort of escapism is even more extreme than Barclay's "Walter Mitty" fantasies because instead of being an occasional diversion or being woven from reality, it's a complete bail-out, with all connections to the real world and consequences to actions cast away.

Aron Eisenberg handles it all like a pro, and James Darren works well with him, but it's Nicole de Boer who sneaks in the back door and gives the episode a lift as Counselor Ezri Dax. Unlike "Afterimage," where Garak's problem seems manufactured by the writers for her benefit, Nog's problem brings Dax into the fold organically and even opens the door for her to counsel Fontaine, albeit more

209

subtly, which is all the better. And this time, with apologies to Echevarria, the writer gets his dialogue right and creates a believable therapist as a result.

All that said, while this is Aron Eisenberg's magnum opus, it is just an hour of Nog moping and "Moon" isn't going to crack any top ten lists.

Did you know? Yip Harburg, Billy Rose, and Harold Arlen wrote and composed "It's Only a Paper Moon" for an unsuccessful Broadway play in 1932. Later in the decade, Harburg and Arlen wrote and composed the music for *The Wizard of Oz* (1939).

It's Only a Paper Moon

Lyric by Billy Rose and E.Y. "Yip" Harburg
Music by Harold Arlen

"Prodigal Daughter": D+

Dax returns home to ask for her family's help when Chief O'Brien becomes entangled with the Orion Syndicate in their area.

Air date: January 4, 1999
Written by Bradley Thompson & David Weddle
Directed by Victor Lobl
TV rating: 4.3

"You have to face the possibility that somebody in your family may have been involved." —O'Brien

This Ezri family character study tucks in a follow-up to Season Six's "Honor Among Thieves," with Ezri Dax and O'Brien visiting Ezri's home planet. Most of the story revolves around Ezri and her family, playing out like a soap opera, with internal friction as self righteous characters give each other speeches. The plot itself becomes almost secondary, and it's certainly not necessary to know anything about "Honor Among Thieves" to understand it.

Leigh Taylor-Young heads the fine guest cast, playing Ezri's mother, and she establishes from the outset that her character needs to be in control of everything. That includes Ezri's younger brother, Norvo, played by Kevin Rahm, who is constantly made to feel inadequate and doesn't know how to achieve his dreams. It also includes, to a lesser extent, Ezri's older brother, Janel, who shows more promise running the family business. But when O'Brien makes it clear that someone is hiding something, the episode turns into a "whodunnit."

Fleshing out an entire ensemble of supporting players for one mystery episode is always a difficult task, and the episode struggles as a result. (Most fans see it less as a whodunnit and more as a "who cares?") What the writers should have done was beef up O'Brien's part with the Orion Syndicate and turn the whole thing into a two-parter. But the truth is Thompson, Weddle, and an uncredited Ron Moore were just trying to plug a hole in the season and get something watchable on the air. In fact, they had to rush their script to have it ready in time for shooting, leading to one of the weaker episodes of Season Seven.

"Prodigal Daughter" was, however, nominated for an Emmy for art direction.

Did you know? Leigh Taylor-Young is the older sister of Dey Young, the guest star who plays the subject of *DS9's* "A Simple Investigation."

"The Emperor's New Cloak": D+

When the Grand Nagus is abducted in the mirror universe, Quark and Rom attempt a rescue operation.

Air date: February 1, 1999
Written by Ira Steven Behr & Hans Beimler
Directed by LeVar Burton
TV rating: 4.6

"You're probably wondering how I got here. Well, you're going to have to keep on wondering, because I don't have time to tell you. You see, I'm in a bit of trouble. I'm being held prisoner by the Alliance, and I'm going to need you to help me regain my freedom." —the Grand Nagus

It's once more unto the mirror universe with this Ferengi comedy featuring Quark and Rom. And I might as well throw out my grading system and insightful analysis because it's clear from the outset that the plot, such as there is, is simply there to serve as an excuse for the cast to cut loose and have some fun. (And if it gets Nicole de Boer into a leather costume, so much the better.)

With Vic Fontaine, Brunt, Garak, and most of the regulars getting their moments to play against the usual expectations, the story emphasizes the comedy of its preposterous nature, completely self-aware that this parallel universe makes no sense. (In fact, the episode even uses a cloaking device as a MacGuffin under the theory that the mirror universe doesn't have the technology, despite previous episodes establishing that it does.)

No matter. It's all in good fun, and director Burton, in his second episode in a row with mirror universe characters, ensures that no moment is played too seriously, even if it is a bit of a shame that the show has increasingly used this setting as a backdrop for silliness.

The mirror universe comes back into play in a more serious way with *ENT's* two-parter "In a Mirror, Darkly" and later in multiple episodes of *DSC*. As for "The Emperor's New Cloak," it's the last *DS9* episode to visit this alternate reality and is dedicated to the memory of Jerome Bixby, the writer of *TOS's* "Mirror, Mirror," who died in April 1998.

Did you know? As an inside joke, the *DS9* writers kill off one mirror universe Ferengi in each visit.

"Field of Fire": F

After several crew members are murdered, Dax summons the memories and personality of a past host to help her find the culprit.

Air date: February 8, 1999
Written by Robert Hewitt Wolfe
Directed by Tony Dow
TV rating: 4.1

"You want to find out who killed Ilario, don't you? Then what are you waiting for? Perform the Rite of Emergence and just ask for my help, and then we can get to work." —Joran

This Dax episode, written by the former writing partner of Ira Steven Behr, is a dark murder-mystery with an emphasis on Joran, a former host of the Dax symbiont introduced in Season Three's "Equilibrium."

Its premise, somewhat in the spirit of Showtime's *Dexter* series, is that no one can understand a serial killer like a serial killer, forcing Dax to summon a part of her she generally buries. It's quite a recharacterization of Joran, who in "Equilibrium" is presented as a troubled musician with a violent temper who killed someone out of anger. Here he's played by a new actor, Leigh J. McCloskey, and is presented as a thrill-seeking murderer who wants to manipulate sweet Ezri into killing strangers for sport.

The investigation itself plays out slowly to build the suspense, though Wolfe cleverly layers it with an interesting new weapon concept that allows the director to create some new X-ray-like visuals. (I'm not sure why, however, Odo needs to wear goggles to see a demonstration of this weapon, considering the shape-shifter doesn't even have real eyes!) Unfortunately, as the story moves along, the script struggles to find its footing. The biggest issue is that Joran proves to be an extraneous character, and it doesn't help that a key plot point involves Dax (and Wolfe) insulting a whole planet, insisting that anyone who doesn't like seeing people smile *must* be from Vulcan.

It's all a rather dreary mess that director Tony Dow and actress Nicole de Boer can't save.

Did you know? Tony Dow is best known as the actor who played Wally, the older brother of the Beaver, on *Leave it to Beaver* (1957–1963).

213

"Chimera": C

Odo meets a Changeling who was sent out to explore the galaxy.

Air date: February 15, 1999
Written by René Echevarria
Directed by Steve Posey
TV rating: 4.3

"You're wasting your time trying to be a humanoid. You're limiting yourself. Let's leave here, Odo. Let's find the others." —Laas

This quiet, character-based Odo episode uses a long-lost Changeling as a figurative mirror for Odo to look into and reflect upon himself. Unfortunately, in a non-figurative sense, the new Changeling is a real jerk. As Odo begins soul-searching, he once again begins to waffle about what he really wants, which is the real point of the story. (It is a bit odd to see Odo go on about Changelings getting no respect, when he's always been given respect by both sets of humanoids he's worked for on the station, but whatever.) In fact, Odo could really use a counselor here, and yet it's one of the few episodes without Dax!

Guest star "Garman Hertzler" (J.G. Hertzler) is fine as Odo's new pal, using a completely different voice than his usual General Martok gravel, but it's the two Renés, Auberjonois and Echevarria, who make this one work by pointing Odo in the direction he needs to go to finish the series.

Did you know? In Greek mythology, the Chimera is a three-headed fire-breathing monster that's part lion, part goat, and part snake. In modern times, the term has come to describe any mythical or fictional beast with parts taken from different animals.

(Photo by Francesco Bini)

214

"Badda-Bing, Badda-Bang": B

When holographic mobsters assume control of Vic Fontaine's lounge, the DS9 gang plot to run Fontaine's rival out of business and restore the program to normal.

Air date: February 22, 1999
Written by Ira Steven Behr & Hans Beimler
Directed by Mike Vejar
TV rating: 4.1

"I just talked to Felix. I know what's been affecting Vic's program. It's a jack in the box." —Bashir

Star Trek does *Ocean's Eleven* in this ensemble caper episode that gives the *DS9* cast another chance to cut loose and have some fun in a holosuite.

With a flimsy premise that's another variation of the old malfunctioning holodeck idea, even the writers know the audience is going to have to suspend belief more than usual. Thankfully, Behr and Beimler are shrewd enough to establish that only a holographic character is at risk, which is easier to swallow than a real person—though the episode's promotional spot is artfully edited to make it seem like everyone is in danger. But like "Our Man Bashir" and "Take Me Out to the Holosuite," the plot itself is secondary. What this one is really about is a chance to get the cast into some new clothes and to do something left of center.

Veteran character actor Robert Miano guest stars as Frankie Eyes, the episode's heavy, which would seem like an opportunity for hamminess, though Miano, apparently taking this a little too seriously, plays it straight. With Mike Starr as his right-hand man, Cicci, and 89-year-old Marc Lawrence as his boss, Mr. Zeemo, however, there are plenty of scene stealing performances nonetheless. (In fact, the replacement accountant, played by the familiar "Bobby Reilly", is pretty good in his own right.)

But perhaps the most notable character in the whole deal is Sisko. Used initially as an audience surrogate for those who dislike Vic Fontaine, he's ultimately won over and steals the show at the end with a special duet stuck in by the writers to show off his musical talent and send a message to the fans that the best is still to come. It's all tied together by Jay Chattaway's score, a throwback to the 60s with classics like "Night Train" thrown in to perfectly match the old-style cinematography employed by Jonathan West.

All in all, it's not something *DS9* would want to do every week, especially since it's one of the most expensive episodes of the season, but for a breather before the upcoming war issues, it's a lot of fun.

"Badda-Bing" was nominated for an Emmy for hairstyling.

215

Did you know? The writers were well aware that *DS9's* representation of 1960s Las Vegas was not 100% accurate. To acknowledge this, the episode includes a conversation about it between Sisko and his girlfriend, Kasidy Yates:

SISKO
In 1962, black people weren't very welcome there. Oh, sure, they could be performers or janitors, but customers? Never.

YATES
Maybe that's the way it was in the real Vegas, but that is not the way it is at Vic's. I have never felt uncomfortable there and neither has Jake.

SISKO
Don't you see? That's the lie. In 1962, the Civil Rights movement was still in its infancy. It wasn't an easy time for our people, and I'm not going to pretend that it was.

YATES
Baby, I know that Vic's isn't a totally accurate representation of the way things were, but it isn't meant to be. It shows us the way things could have been. The way they should've been.

"Inter Arma Enim Silent Leges": B–

Attending a medical conference on Romulus, Dr. Bashir becomes embroiled in an elaborate scheme devised by the mysterious Section 31.

Air date: March 1, 1999
Written by Ronald D. Moore
Directed by David Livingston
TV rating: 4.1

"Let's make a deal, Doctor; I'll spare you the 'end justifies the means' speech, and you spare me the 'we must do what's right' speech. You and I are not going to see eye to eye on this subject, so I suggest we stop discussing it. This mission is reconnaissance." —Sloan

With a title that's Latin for "in the presence of arms, the laws grow silent," this Bashir spy episode is a loose sequel to Season Six's "Inquisition" that brings back special guest star William Sadler as Agent Sloan from the mysterious Section 31. In a way, it's vintage Ron Moore, with a storyline that's meticulously laid out and sci-fi that's made understandable and relatable. In another way, it feels like Chris Carter's *The X-Files*, insinuating a lot going on offstage and playing up the paranoia. Either way, it feels like we're in the hands of a good storyteller who knows what's he's doing.

Like Thompson and Weddle's "Inquisition," Moore is sure to give Sadler a meaty part, finding a way for Sloan to accompany Bashir on the mission. He also uses Barry Jenner well as Admiral Ross, giving him his first one-on-one scenes with Alexander Siddig. Meanwhile, Adrienne Barbeau replaces Megan Cole as Romulan Senator Cretak, redefining the part to present the character in a more sympathetic light. With new characters introduced—most notably, Romulan Senator Koval, generically played by John Fleck—and much of the episode taking place on Romulus, there's always a sense of tension in the air, with the multitude of characters scheming behind the scenes leaving Bashir unsure of whom to trust. And as the plot spirals out of control and gets really crazy, it's tempting to believe it's all another elaborate mindgame by Section 31. To the episode's credit, however, it doesn't take the easy way out and delivers a satisfying conclusion instead.

Supervising Producer David Livingston, directing his last of seventeen *DS9* episodes, does a great job of fleshing it all out, borrowing *VOY's* sets as a stand-in for her sister-ship, the Bellerophon.

As with "Inquisition," the end result proves entertaining enough to warrant a sequel. And sure enough, William Sadler returns to reprise Sloan for the final time in "Extreme Measures." Truth be told, however, "Inter Arma" is probably his best episode.

217

Did you know? As of this writing, there are nine *Star Trek* episodes with Latin titles. They are:

- *DS9's* "Dramatis Personae"
- *TNG's* "Sub Rosa"
- *VOY's* "Ex Post Facto"
- *VOY's* "Non Sequitur"
- *VOY's* "Alter-Ego"
- *DS9's* "Inter Arma Enim Silent Leges"
- *ENT's* "Terra Nova"
- *ENT's* "Vox Sola"
- *DSC's* "Si Vis Pacem, Para Bellum"

"Penumbra" (1): D+

When Worf goes missing, Dax takes matters into her own hands.

Air date: April 5, 1999
Written by René Echevarria
Directed by Steve Posey
TV rating: 4.4

"I talked to Benjamin this morning. He said that according to the Koraga's crew, Worf was the last one to leave the bridge. No one knows if he made it to the escape pod." —Dax

DS9 starts up what it calls "the final chapter," a nine-part finale, with this Dax/Worf romance episode that's great for fans of the Dax/Worf relationship but a bit of a snoozer for everyone else.

Dax and Worf get the A story, but it seems more like a Jadzia thing than anything else. It's an "Out of the frying pan, into the fire" adventure away from the station, giving the Dax and Worf a chance to bicker and quarrel before getting physical. Joining the series so late, it's a challenge for Nicole de Boer to establish Ezri Dax as a beloved character even with the best of scripts, but having to deal with old Jadzia stuff doesn't even give her a chance. Unfortunately, Michael Dorn is dealing with the opposite end of the spectrum. He's played Worf in so many *Star Trek* episodes that it seems as though the writers have run out ideas for him, and they're trying to return to the well once or twice too often.

The station-based B story, on the other hand, shows more promise, though it's more abstract. Sisko and Kasidy Yates talk about getting married, but Sisko's status as Emissary complicates the situation. It's a lot of fun to see Sisko get so excited about his future beyond Deep Space Nine, and there's something exciting about knowing that some interesting things are going to happen in the future no matter how it all turns out.

There's also some exposition from Cardassia, where the Dominion, Damar, and Dukat begin to set some new schemes in motion.

As the opener of a multi-part finale, it's easy to give the episode a pass. It's not meant to pay anything off. It's meant to set stories in motion. But with old Jadzia/Worf issues forming its spine, as an episode on its own, it's underwhelming.

Did you know? Michael Dorn holds the record for most *Star Trek* appearances in history, appearing in 174 episodes of *TNG*, 98 episodes of *DS9*, and five movies.

"'Til Death Do Us Part" (2): D

Sisko struggles with the decision of whether or not to marry Kasidy Yates.

Air date: April 12, 1999
Written by David Weddle & Bradley Thompson
Directed by Winrich Kolbe
TV rating: 4.1

"If you do this, you will know only sorrow." —the Prophets

Providing the characters with an episode to discuss their issues with each other and come to decisions, "'Til Death" doesn't do much to advance the storylines established in the previous episode but lays more of a foundation for what's to come.

Sisko gets the weightiest matter, with his heart telling him to marry Yates and the Prophets saying otherwise. The subject matter plays straight into Brooks's wheelhouse, with Sisko having an internal struggle, unsure of what the right choice is to make…or if there even is one.

Meanwhile, Worf and Dax spend the episode in a Breen holding cell, giving them plenty of opportunity to continue their bickering in a repetitive plotline that just goes in circles. The idea works for *Waiting for Godot* because the circular nature of the play includes subtle variations to sustain interest. Here, however, it's just a stall that draws attention to the fact that these two characters have no chemistry together.

As this is going on, the Dominion continues to plot, giving Jeffrey Combs another opportunity to steal a scene. But the most interesting—and perverse—plotline, sees Dukat, disguised as a Bajoran, courting Kai Winn and winning her heart through falsehoods. Proving the *DS9* writers are a sick, twisted bunch—in a good way—the sequence of scenes between the two just gets creepier and creepier as it moves along. Still, *DS9* gets ahead of itself with this particular thread, with the writers later admitting that they started up this relationship too soon, leading to some stalling in later episodes. Looking back, "Penumbra" and "'Til Death" would be better if they were combined into one fast-paced Sisko episode, with the Dukat/Winn situation postponed for later. As is, "'Til Death" is sort of like sitting in a waiting room.

Did you notice? In this episode, Winn says the Prophets have never spoken to her. Yet in her first appearance on the show in the episode "In the Hands of the Prophets," she claims the Prophets have spoken to her through the Orbs. Could it be that she started her *DS9* odyssey with a lie? Where's Bajor's PolitiFact when you need it?

"Strange Bedfellows" (3): B–

While the Dominion and the Breen negotiate an alliance, Dax and Worf are sentenced to death.

Air date: April 19, 1999
Written by Ronald D. Moore
Directed by René Auberjonois
TV rating: 4.2

"The alliance between the Breen Confederacy and the Dominion will end the destructive war that has torn this quadrant apart. With the Breen at our side, the Federation will not be able to stand against us." —Changeling leader

With a focus on the antagonists, the third piece of the nine-part "final chapter" is an exciting look at one character turning to the "dark side," another experiencing a rebirth, and another experiencing a quick death.

In the roles of Anakin Skywalker and Chancellor Palpatine we have Kai Winn and Dukat, with Winn struggling to reject the power evil offers. With Marc Alaimo's consistently strong performances, it would be easy for the writers to turn this into a Dukat moment, where the Cardassian wins her heart just as easily as he wins his followers in "Covenant." But instead, Ron Moore wisely uses Dukat as a mere supporting player and sets the episode on Louise Fletcher's shoulders, giving Winn an internal struggle which ties together all the sympathetic and not so sympathetic things we've learned about her over the years.

At the same time, writers Ira Steven Behr, Hans Beimler, and René Echevarria, who were forced to finish the script after Moore's wife unexpectedly went into labor, effectively mine the history between Weyoun and Damar from previous seasons, giving the two some terrific scenes to drive the other half of the plot. There's also the climax of the Worf/Dax storyline that begins as a comedy runner before finally getting the point.

With several episodes left in the saga, what we have here, of course, is mostly exposition for future episodes, and the writers don't really need a full episode to show us how all these characters, most notably Winn and Damar, have arrived at their decisions. But in this case, there is something special about seeing the decisions drawn out, and it's nice to gain insight into their thought processes.

For René Auberjonois, helming his eighth and final *Star Trek* episode, it's a worthy finish to his time in the director's chair.

Did you know? After going into labor a month early, Ron Moore's wife, Terry, gave birth to the couple's first daughter, Robin.

"The Changing Face of Evil" (4): B+

As the Breen ally with the Dominion and attack the Federation, Kai Winn begins to read forbidden texts about the Pah-wraiths.

Air date: April 26, 1999
Written by Ira Steven Behr & Hans Beimler
Directed by Mike Vejar
TV rating: 4.5

"Abandon ship. You heard me. Everyone get to the escape pods now!" —Sisko

Living up to its title, the fourth part of "the final chapter" is a game-changer that puts a cap of sorts on the first block of episodes while leaving a cliffhanger for the remaining episodes to follow up upon.

Full of bold strokes and political intrigue, "Changing Face" finally brings several plot lines to their breaking points, balancing its big war story with small, personal moments. There's an exciting battle with unexpected consequences stuck right in the middle, along with fast-paced scenes that give each character (not named Jake) at least one moment to shine. But the real substance of the episode lies with Kai Winn and Dukat on Bajor and Damar and Weyoun on Cardassia. The previous episode shows us Winn and Damar coming to decisions. This one shows us the consequences. The beauty of it lies in the reactions, whether it be Winn coming to terms with herself, or Weyoun coming to terms with the new Damar. (Jeffrey Combs's icy look is priceless.)

Being stuck in the middle of a giant multi-parter, "Changing Face" is easy to overlook when reflecting upon the season and the series as a whole, but it's some of *DS9's* best work and gives "the final chapter" the kick in the pants it needs.

Did you know? Gul Rusot, a Cardassian commander introduced in this episode, is played by John Vickery, the same actor who plays Deanna Troi's Betazoid counterpart in *TNG's* "Night Terrors." He would go on to play a Klingon in *ENT's* Season Two episode "Judgment."

"When it Rains..." (5): C+

Deep Space Nine prepares for the final stage of the war.

Air date: May 3, 1999
Teleplay by René Echevarria
Story by René Echevarria & Spike Steingasser
Directed by Michael Dorn
TV rating: 4.3

"You're going to have to put your personal feelings aside. Now, whether you like Damar or not is irrelevant. We need him. The Dominion knows they have to stop his rebellion before it spreads, and it's up to you to see that they don't."
—Sisko

Starting up the second half of *DS9's* nine-part finale, "When it Rains" introduces several new plot lines, moving from story to story until it ends so abruptly, the credits hit like a cold bucket of water.

Balancing the predictable with unpredictable, writer René Echevarria and director Michael Dorn team up to cut a quick pace from the get-go and throw everything but the kitchen sink at viewers. Gowron returns to replace Martok, Bashir must deal with a bureaucratic runaround, Kira and Garak are forced to help Damar, and Dukat finally goes too far and gets a lecture from Kai Winn about humility, which is sort of like Quark giving a sermon on the evils of greed. They're all such diverse ideas, and they're all thrown out so quickly, there's no time for the viewer to stop and process it all until the episode is suddenly over.

What to make of it all? Well, it's like a *DS9* sampler, with a taste of upcoming *DS9* episodes thrown together before the subsequent episodes share the proper servings. Yet as an episode itself, it works splendidly, perhaps even better in some ways than the episodes it sets up.

Did you know? This episode introduces a Cardassian, Seskal, played by Vaughn Armstrong. One of *Star Trek's* most versatile actors, the native Californian's other *Star Trek* roles include a Klingon (*TNG's* "Heart of Glory"), another Cardassian (*DS9's* "Past Prologue"), a Vulcan (*VOY's* "Eye of the Needle"), a Borg (*VOY's* "Survival Instinct"), a Vidiian (*VOY's* "Fury"), a Hirogen (*VOY's* "Flesh and Blood"), another Klingon (*VOY's* "End Game"), a human vice admiral (seven episodes of *ENT*), yet another Klingon (*ENT's* "Sleeping Dogs"), and a Kreetassan (*ENT's* "Vox Solo" and "A Night In Sickbay"). After the conclusion of *DS9*, *VOY*, and *ENT*, he formed a singing group with Casey Biggs called The Enterprise Blues Band. Their song lyrics include, "I gotta Cardassian neck, what the heck. I'm wearing Klingon shoes, I got the blues."

"Tacking Into the Wind" (6): C

While Kira and the Cardassians plot to steal a Breen weapon, Gowron engages in reckless attacks against the Dominion.

Air date: May 10, 1999
Written by Ronald D. Moore
Directed by Mike Vejar
TV rating: 4.4

"We're all in this together. By helping Starfleet, we're helping ourselves."
—Damar

With a Deep Space Nine/Cardassian alliance as one story and some Klingon political intrigue as another, "Tacking" is a fast moving, somewhat satisfying episode with some resolutions to "When it Rains" while also teasing what's coming next.

The A story is really a character-based caper plot with Kira and Damar leading a risky undercover heist. It's a fun away mission that tucks in some touching moments between Odo and Kira, but it's undermined by a conclusion that's as predictable as the end of an episode of *Gilligan's Island*. (Personally, I wish I could see Weyoun, with the Changeling leader prodding him on, chasing Damar around the galaxy.) Damar himself, thanks in large part to Casey Biggs, is one of the show's great secondary character successes, but after what the Cardassian does to Ziyal early in Season Six, it's difficult to entertain the notion of the character's redemption. Looking back, it would have been better had the writers not given him this baggage.

Meanwhile, we have Ron Moore once again writing Klingon stuff for Worf and Gowron. "Tacking" marks Robert O'Reilly's last *Star Trek* appearance, allowing him to bring a conclusion to the Klingon Chancellor he introduced in *TNG's* "Reunion" nine years prior. Gowron's new ambition is sudden and feels contrived, and there's really not much more to the story than Worf's internal struggle, but there's something to be said for a Klingon plot that's quick and to the point.

Did you know? Armin Shimerman couldn't participate in this episode because of a commitment to *Buffy the Vampire Slayer*. His, wife, however, appears as Luaran, a Vorta who commands a Jem'Hadar attack ship.

224

"Extreme Measures" (7): F

Bashir and O'Brien lure Sloan to the station in a desperate search for the cure to a disease.

Air date: May 17, 1999
Written by Bradley Thompson & David Weddle
Directed by Steve Posey
TV rating: 4.4

"If you're determined to go on this lunatic mission inside Sloan's head, then somebody with an ounce of sanity has to be with you." —O'Brien

William Sadler, last seen a few episodes before in "Inter Arma Enim Silent Leges," returns to reprise Sloan, with Bashir and O'Brien taking a journey inside the mysterious agent's head, which conveniently takes on the appearance of the station to give the series a cost saving bottle episode. The concept has an early season feel to it and is particularly reminiscent of Season Three's "Distant Voices" but feels out of place in the somewhat serialized nine-episode finale for the series.

The premise itself, built on the idea that Section 31 is behind a disease and knows of a cure, is based on assumptions from Dr. Bashir. Thanks to the writers, however, instead of making an ass out of himself and umption, he turns out to be right. Unfortunately, the "inside Sloan's head" gimmick never develops enough substance to make for serious drama, with too much time spent on mind games and not enough time spent on the development of the story. What the script really needs is more money, allowing Bashir and O'Brien (and/or Odo) to visit the headquarters of Section 31 and seek out information about the disease that could lead Bashir to develop a cure. (In fact, this was the original plan until the producers needed to find a way to save some more money for the final episode of the series.) Instead, the cure becomes a MacGuffin with a simplified "behind door number three" climax. It's a disappointing resolution and a waste of Sloan, who deserves a better final appearance.

Did you know? William Sadler and Ron Perlman (*Star Trek: Nemesis*) were both born on April 13, 1950.

"The Dogs of War" (8): C

As Kira, Damar, and Garak are ambushed on Cardassia, Quark receives a message from the Grand Nagus asking him to be the next leader of the Ferengi Alliance.

Air date: May 24, 1999
Teleplay by Ronald D. Moore & René Echevarria
Story by Peter Allan Fields
Directed by Avery Brooks
TV rating: 3.7

"If you don't mind hiding in a basement, I guess I don't mind having you down here." —Mila

As *DS9's* "final chapter" nears its end, Avery Brooks, following the example of Patrick Stewart before him, directs the penultimate episode of his *Star Trek* series. This one is another smorgasbord of storylines that throws a lot at the viewer, though its various flavors don't always go well together.

The meat of the episode takes place on Cardassia, with Kira, Damar, and Garak trapped on the world now occupied by the Orwellian-like Dominion. It's an interesting juxtaposition for Kira, who formerly was in the same situation on Bajor when it was occupied by Cardassians. But the real story here is about Damar becoming a Cardassian folk hero. It's the same story the show tries with Li Nalas to open the second season, but it works better in "Dogs" because it's developed more organically and Casey Biggs is a better actor than Richard Beymer.

Meanwhile, the Ferengi have their story tied up with a Quark comedy runner that features the final appearances of Grand Nagus Zek, Quark's mom, Brunt, Rom, and Leeta. In fact, Brunt and Weyoun, played by the same actor, finally appear in the same episode together, with the writers/editor even having fun cutting from one character to the other. (Sadly, we dont get a "Brunt meets Weyoun" gag, which would be the icing on the cake.) Not surprising for the Ferengi, they get a sitcom-like plot together, weaving comedy out of confusion. But that's probably a fitting conclusion for them, and Shimerman and the writers make the most of it, with some great moments that include Quark summoning his inner Picard by declaring, "The line has to be drawn here! This far, and no further!"

There are also C, D, and E stories, with virtually every other character getting his or her own moment, with some moments more effective than others. Sisko has a couple of interesting scenes, with Brooks again proving that he knows how to direct himself. But Dax isn't so good repeating her "awkward relationship" storyline from a few episodes ago, even if she's paired up with a new character—Bashir. The diverse storylines all lead to a bit of a disjointed episode. But for one that's set just before the finale, the whole thing is

226

remarkably self-contained until the closing moments. The last scene, serving as a cliffhanger, feels more like the first scene of the next episode.

"Dogs of War" received an Emmy nomination for outstanding make-up.

Did you know? Wallace Shawn appears in seven *DS9* episodes as Grand Nagus Zek. His first two appearances were directed by associate producer David Livingston. His final five appearances were all directed by *Star Trek* actors: René Auberjonois, Alexander Siddig, LeVar Burton, and Avery Brooks.

Did you also know? Over the years, several of *Star Trek's* episode titles have been inspired by the works of William Shakespeare. They include:

- *TOS's* "Dagger of the Mind" (*Macbeth*)
- *TOS's* "By Any Other Name" (*Romeo and Juliet*)
- *TAS's* "How Sharper than a Serpent's Tooth" (*King Lear*)
- *TNG's* "Thine Own Self" (*Hamlet*)
- *DS9's* "Past Prologue" (*The Tempest*)
- *VOY's* "Mortal Coil" (*Hamlet*)
- *DS9's* "The Dogs of War" (*Julius Caesar*)
- *ENT's* "Breaking the Ice" (*Taming of the Shrew*)
- *ENT's* "Sleeping Dogs" (*Henry IV, Part 2*)
- *DSC's* "Vaulting Ambition" (*Macbeth*)
- *DSC's* "What's Past is Prologue" (*The Tempest*)

"What You Leave Behind" (9): B+

The Federation Alliance attempts to defeat the Dominion once and for all. (Series finale)

Air date: May 31, 1999
Written by Ira Steven Behr & Hans Beimler
Directed by Allan Kroeker
TV rating: 5.4

"The Emissary's task is nearing completion." —Sarah

Taking a more leisurely pace than "All Good Things," *DS9*'s two-hour series finale brings the Dominion War to a close while sending the characters off into the sunset in a way that *TOS* doesn't and *TNG*, with its move to feature films, never could. It's a character-based emotional roller coaster filled with action, suspense, laughter, tears, comeuppance, and goodbyes.

To close the book on the series, the episode has to include a record number of guest stars and cover a large number of plot points. But in the sure hands of Allan Kroeker, director of nine *Star Trek* season finales and three *Star Trek* series finales, each beat hits at the right time, giving the war's endgame a satisfying layout and turning the aftermath into an engaging coda. He's helped by previous episodes which carefully position the characters into different facets of the war, allowing the finale to bring us its conclusion from a wide variety of viewpoints, giving us less of a comic book close and more of a realistic representation of victory and defeat than television is known for. There aren't one or two actions that will ultimately decide the lives of billions; there are many events happening simultaneously that shape the conclusion, cutting off options and hemming in the losing side before the leader is finally cornered and forced to accept the checkmate.

And yet it all leaves room for the aftermath to breathe, with the characters embarking on separate paths in a way that leaves no question that this is the end.

Is the episode perfect? Not quite. The pilot indicates that Sisko's mission is to prepare Bajor to join the Federation, but the finale fails to address the issue. Instead, Sisko feels a disturbance in the force and journeys to the cave set to give us a good versus evil fight that seems more like something from *Star Wars* than *Star Trek*, even if it is essentially the same climax as the one in *TOS*'s "Where No Man Has Gone Before." These events bring closure to the characters of Dukat and Winn, a must for the series, but the sequence itself is cartoonish compared to the rest of the episode and gives the series an anticlimactic finish.

To be fair, however, that's a small piece of the puzzle, and what the finale does well, it does very well. There are some thrilling space battles with impressive visual effects that garnered an Emmy nomination. There are death scenes that are all the more dramatic for not being overly so. And there are emotional montages dedicated to the main characters, comprised of footage spanning the seven seasons of the show. There's even the first fully CGI shot of the station, used for a breathtaking final shot.

In the end, the series remains true to what it's always been: the *Star Trek* show that isn't afraid to get some dirt under its fingernails but finds a way, nonetheless, to remain classy.

Did you know? In 2017, Ira Steven Behr reconvened with much of the former cast and crew of *Deep Space Nine* and began work on a documentary film entitled *What We Left Behind – Looking Back at Star Trek: Deep Space Nine*. In 2018, a version of the film premiered before an audience of Trekkers at *Destination Star Trek Birmingham* in the United Kingdom.

The Seventh Season in Review

With few standout episodes and eroding ratings due to increased competition and franchise fatigue, *DS9's* Season Seven is largely forgettable, save for "the final chapter," a nine-part finale tying up most of the loose ends of the series. But as Ira Steven Behr later said, "A lot of things we did were not meant to be that way. The show wasn't geared to be what we kept turning it into. That made it difficult for us because we had to play it as it lays."

As a good illustration of Behr's point, there's the Dax situation. With Terry Farrell leaving the show, a new actress would be needed to keep Nana Visitor from being the only female regular. So writer Hans Beimler, having previously worked with Nicole de Boer on *Beyond Reality* and *TekWar,* arranged for his friend to read for the part. "Before they called me in," de Boer remembers, "I took a drink and it went down the wrong pipe. So they call me in, and I start coughing and turning red and can't breathe. And they're just sitting there looking at me." She lands the part, nonetheless, taking on the thankless task of carrying on Farrell's character.

Meanwhile, with Kira's promotion to Colonel, Nana Visitor gets a new uniform featuring a high-waisted bolero jacket and a new hair color to go along with it after Visitor stopped dyeing her hair.

Behind the scenes, Avery Brooks, Michael Dorn, and René Auberjonois each direct their final episodes, though it's Steve Posey who proves the most prolific in the chair, crossing over from *Hercules: The Legendary Journey* and *Xena: Warrior Princess* to direct his only four *Star Trek* episodes. Meanwhile, Hans Beimler moves from supervising producer to co-executive producer and Bradley Thompson and David Weddle become executive story editors, with all three helping to supervise the staff. And with director of photography Jonathan West frequently absent to help LeVar Burton with a Disney Channel movie, camera operator Kris Krosskove serves as his substitute.

Of course, it's executive producer Ira Steven Behr who has the most to do. In addition to overseeing the show, he works with Beimler to pen seven of the twenty-five episodes for the season. For this task, Behr was given only one specific directive from the studio: don't make the finale about the war! Running two hours, it sort of is, but it's also about much more. Nonetheless, "What You Leave Behind" remains one of *DS9's* most popular episodes, coming in second to "Trials and Tribble-ations" in a poll of favorite *DS9* episodes conducted by *Star Trek's* official fan club. Two other episodes from the final batch, "The Changing Face of Evil" and "Tacking into the Wind" are in the top ten as well.

And so what does the series as a whole, giving us 176 hours of television, leave behind? A product of amazing quality that challenges and rewards its audience while remaining true to itself.

Coming Soon...

The Trekker's Guide to the Janeway Years

Featuring reviews of every episode of *VOY*, the next book in this series is a can't miss! Here's a sample of what's to come.

"Caretaker": A

(Pilot) The newly commissioned starship Voyager and a Maquis raider are flung into the remote Delta Quadrant by a powerful entity known as the Caretaker.

Air date: January 16, 1995
Teleplay by Michael Piller & Jeri Taylor
Story by Rick Berman, Michael Piller & Jeri Taylor
Directed by Winrich Kolbe
TV rating: 13.0

"Captain, if these sensors are working, we're over seventy-thousand light-years from where we were. We're on the other side of the galaxy." —Ensign Kim

Written primarily by the same man who stabilized *TNG's* writing staff and wrote *DS9's* pilot, "Caretaker" skillfully launches *Voyager* with a two-hour romp that simultaneously works well as a beginning and as a standalone story. Like *TNG's* pilot, the story is basically a mystery mixed with a powerful alien, though here the elements are better interwoven and no expense is spared. At $23 million, this is *Star Trek's* most expensive episode of all time, giving the story ample location shooting and visual effects to jumpstart the series and launch a network.

Benefitting from exposition planted in *TNG* and *DS9*, *VOY's* pilot opens with a *Star Wars*-like crawl and then kicks into gear, cutting a quick pace as it moves along to introduce the characters. Surprisingly, the most important of these initially is not the captain, but Tom Paris (Robert Duncan McNeill), who serves as the gateway to the story at large. It's an interesting choice, with Paris being an outcast, but his character arc helps sum up what the show's all about: a new life. *TNG* fans, of course, will remember McNeill as Nicholas Lacarno from "The First Duty," a character with nearly the same backstory as Paris. Naturally, it's easy to wonder why *Star Trek* invents Paris rather than just reusing Lacarno, but the truth is that McNeill's character in "The First Duty" is (appropriately) selfish and arrogant, which is the cause of his trouble. Paris, on the other hand, though similar in demeanor, is more selfless and full of self-doubt. While *VOY* could (and almost did) reuse Lacarno and try to recharacterize him, there's no reason to go to so much trouble because of one *TNG* episode. Instead, having Paris a blank slate allows the show to introduce him to us in a new way and develop him throughout the episode and series without being tethered to the past.

In the meantime, the pilot still offers Kate Mulgrew plenty of opportunities to put her stamp on Captain Janeway, and she uses them to create a character that's vulnerable in private but unquestionably in charge in public. Mulgrew, brought in to replace Geneviève Bujold, gives a performance that's not just extraordinary but extraordinarily important for *Star Trek* and beyond. It might seem sexist today, but after a poor performance by Bujold (who quit the second day), there was some doubt from the executives as to whether a woman could actually front a show they were relying on to launch UPN. Mulgrew, however, owns the part, giving Janeway a Kathryn Hepburn-like quality while proving she's just as good as any leading man.

Meanwhile, with seven other regulars to introduce, some characters get shortchanged. The Doctor, who would go on to be one of the show's breakout stars, gets in a couple funny lines but little more. Seska. who is not a regular but does factor into the first two seasons, doesn't appear at all. But while some have more to do and some less, most of the major characters get a chance to at least outline the basics of their personalities and relationships. (And a visit to Deep Space Nine even gives us a Quark cameo.)

Always remaining a favorite for the cast, crew, and fans alike, the events in "Caretaker" come back into play in several episodes of the series, starting with Season Two's "Projections." Sadly, "Caretaker" is the last *Star Trek* pilot written by Piller, who died of head and neck cancer in 2005. But his work here is superb. In fact it's so good, the show never has to employ an idea planted in the pilot specifically to set up a quick way to get back home if the show's concept were to prove unpopular: a second caretaker. (For the sake of completion, the show cleans up this loose thread in Season Two's "Cold Fire.")

Did you know? The story idea that Tom Paris is unpopular because of a piloting accident that killed a well-liked crewman is similar to something that happened to *Star Trek* creator Gene Roddenberry. One day back in 1943 when Roddenberry was serving as a pilot in World War II, his B-17 didn't pick up enough speed to become airborne, and the brakes wouldn't respond. The plane ended up crashing into a sea of palm stumps, and two respected crewmembers died. Many in Roddenberry's squadron questioned why he didn't perform a ground loop maneuver that might have saved everyone, unaware that there wasn't enough time. Interestingly, the crash prevented Roddenberry from participating in a search for survivors of a Navy PT boat that was destroyed that same morning. Fortunately, that boat's commander, John F. Kennedy, survived nonetheless.

About the Author

When J.W. Braun isn't commanding his starship, he spends his time with his wife in Wisconsin. For more information on his books, visit jwbraun.com. And please, don't hesitate to review this book! Your feedback is appreciated and is an important part of the author/reader relationship.

Made in the USA
Middletown, DE
04 May 2019